P9-DNW-331

PREPARING FOR THE UNITED STATES GOVERNMENT

AP* EXAM

WITH

GOVERNMENT IN AMERICA:
PEOPLE, POLITICS, AND POLICY

EDWARDS/WATTENBERG/LINEBERRY

TEXT PLUS TEST

PEARSON
SERIES
FOR
AP*
SUCCESS

PEARSON

Prentice
Hall

Copyright © 2004 by Pearson Education, Inc.
All rights reserved.

Permission in writing must be obtained from the publisher before any part of this work may be reproduced or transmitted in any form or by any means, electronic or mechanical, including photocopying and recording, or by any information storage or retrieval system.

AP and Advanced Placement Program are registered trademarks of the College Entrance Examination Board, which was not involved in the production of and does not endorse this product.

Printed in the United States of America

10 9 8 7 6 5 4 3 2 1

ISBN 0-536-73159-4

BA 998366

JC

Please visit our web site at *www.pearsoned.com*

PEARSON PPRENTICE HALL
Upper Saddle River, New Jersey 07458
A Pearson Education Company

Part III: *Sample Tests with Answers and Explanations* 205

About Your
Pearson Text Plus Test AP Guide

Pearson Education is the leading publisher of textbooks worldwide. With operations on every continent, we make it our business to understand the changing needs of students at every level, from Kindergarten to college. We think that makes us especially qualified to offer this series of AP test prep books, tied to some of our best-selling textbooks.

Our reasoning is that as you study for your course, you're preparing along the way for the AP test. If you can tie the material in the book directly to the test you're taking, it makes the material that much more relevant, and enables you to focus your time most efficiently. And that's a good thing!

The AP exam is an important milestone in your education. A high score means you're in a better position for college acceptance, and possibly puts you a step ahead with college credits. Our goal is to provide you with the tools you need to excel on the exam . . . the rest is up to you.

Good luck!

Part I

Introduction to the AP U.S. Government & Politics Examination

This section overviews the advanced placement program, introduces the types of questions you will encounter on the exam, and provides helpful test-taking strategies. It also explains the grading procedure used by the College Board. Finally, a correlation chart is provided that shows where key information commonly tested on the exam is covered in *Government in America*. Review this section carefully before trying the sample items in the following parts.

The Advanced Placement Program

This book will help prepare you to take the Advanced Placement (AP) U.S. Government & Politics Exam at the end of the year. To succeed on the exam, you need to follow a plan of curriculum review and practice. This book offers both of these. First, you will review each content area of government and politics that appears on the AP U.S. Government & Politics Exam. Then, for each section, you will complete some practice drills that replicate actual AP exam questions. You will not only receive extra guided study for your coursework, but also you will have the opportunity to apply what you have learned in class to a testing situation. You will become familiar with the types of questions on the AP U.S. Government & Politics Exam and how to approach them. Go through each review section thoroughly and complete all of the accompanying drills. If you have difficulty with particular sections, that's your cue to refer to your textbook for a more detailed review.

For more practice, this book includes two full-length AP U.S. Government & Politics Exams. These will help you practice taking the exam under real-life testing conditions. The more familiar you are with the AP U.S. Government & Politics Exam ahead of time, the more comfortable you'll be on testing day. And the more comfortable you are, the better your chances of achieving a high score.

The AP Program is sponsored by the College Board, a nonprofit organization that oversees college admissions tests. The AP Program offers high school students the opportunity to take advanced college-level courses. According to the College Board, AP courses are intended to offer a curriculum equivalent to that of an introductory college class. If you receive a grade of 3 or higher (5 is the highest possible grade), you may be eligible for college credit. Thousands of colleges and universities grant credit to students who score well on AP exams. If you are taking several AP courses and if you score well on multiple AP exams, you may even be eligible to enter college as a sophomore. Some institutions grant sophomore status to incoming first-year students who have demonstrated mastery of many AP subjects. In addition, the College Board confers a number of AP Scholar Awards on students who score 3 or higher on three or more AP exams. Additional awards are available to students who receive very high grades on four or five AP exams.

The curriculum for each of the thirty-two AP subject areas is designed by a development committee consisting of college professors and high school teachers. The committees revise AP syllabi to bring them up to date with changes in the subject field each year. Every AP course is different. Yours is designed around your textbook, *Government in America: People, Politics, and Policy.* The committee develops guidelines for a test that represents equally and accurately the skill levels of the roughly thirteen thousand AP students across the country. Your score on the AP U.S. Government & Politics Exam reflects your abilities in comparison to other high school students enrolled in the course. Colleges use this information not only to award credit for introductory college classes but also to choose the most suitable applicants.

Why Take an AP Course?

You may be taking one or more AP courses simply because you are thirsty for knowledge. Of course, the fact that colleges look favorably on applicants who have AP courses on their transcripts is another powerful incentive. Because AP classes usually involve rigorous lessons, a great deal of homework, and many tests, they signal to college admissions officers that AP students are willing to work hard to get the most from their education. Because AP course work is more difficult than average high school work, many admissions officers evaluate AP grades on a kind of curve—if you receive a *B* in an AP class, for example, it might carry the same weight as an *A* in a regular high school class.

Your AP U.S. Government & Politics course teaches you many of the skills you will need in college. For example, your teacher may assign research papers and encourage you to use resources beyond your textbook. Some of these resources may be primary sources that permit you to analyze events and issues as a political scientist does. Other class assignments may require you to write longer-than-usual essays on historical subjects. The AP U.S. Government & Politics course will challenge you to gather and consider information in new— and sometimes unfamiliar—ways. Your ability to use these methods and skills will give you a leg up as you enter college.

Taking an AP Examination

If you are interested in taking the AP U.S. Government & Politics Exam at the end of your high school course, check to see if the colleges to which you are applying will give credit in this subject area. Your AP teacher or school guidance counselor can help you determine this and can give you more information on how to sign up for an AP exam. The deadline to sign up and pay the fees for the exam is usually in January, four months before the exam in May.

If your school does not administer the AP U.S. Government & Politics Exam, your teacher or guidance counselor can help you find a nearby school that does. You can visit the College Board's Web site (www. collegeboard.com) for more information. You can also call the College Board directly at (609) 771-7300 if you have any questions about registering for the exam. The cost of the exam frequently changes and can depend on the number of exams taken. However, in 2003 the cost of a single exam was $80. If you cannot afford this fee, you may apply to the College Board for a fee reduction.

When you register, you can arrange to have your score sent automatically to as many as five colleges. In fact, your score can be received at colleges and universities only if it has been sent there directly by the College Board. If you would like your score to be sent to other schools, you must pay an additional fee. You can also cancel your score (you must do so before you find out your score), but either of these requests must be made directly to the College Board by June 15. Your exam grade will be sent to you by mail in early–mid July. If you simply can't wait to find out your score, Educational Testing Service (the organization that develops and scores tests for the College Board) will release your score to you over the phone around July 1 for an additional $15 fee. To get your score by phone after July 1, you can call (609)-771-7300 Monday through Friday. Be ready to provide your AP number or social security number, your birth date, and a credit card number.

AP U.S. Government & Politics: Course Goals

The goal of the AP U.S. Government & Politics course is to provide students with an understanding of the operation of American national government. Specifically, you will develop

- an understanding of the principal themes in U.S. government
- the ability to analyze historical and statistical evidence
- skills to express your knowledge in writing

AP U.S. Government & Politics courses vary somewhat from teacher to teacher and from school to school. Yet the focus of your course should reflect these goals, and the instruction you receive will grow out of these basic principles. The U.S. Government & Politics Development Committee has created a list of major topics and has divided them into the six groups below. These topics will be the focus of your AP course. Many will be revisited in questions on the AP U.S. Government & Politics Exam.

Constitutional Underpinnings of United States Government

- Historical development and adoption of the Constitution
- Separation of Powers
- Checks and balances
- Federalism
- Theories of modern government

Political Beliefs and Behaviors

- Theories of modern government, including elitist, pluralist, and hyperpluralist
- Views that people have about government and their elected officials
- Characteristics and impact of public opinion
- Voting patterns of citizens
- Characteristics of political beliefs and the differences between liberals and conservatives

Political Parties, Interest Groups, and Mass Media

- Characteristics, organization, and history of political parties
- Impact of key elections
- Voting patterns and the effect on the political process
- Laws that affect elections
- Interest groups and political action committees
- Legislation affecting the political process
- The mass media and its effect on politics

Institutions of National Government

▌ Characteristics and power of each institution
▌ Relationships among each institution
▌ Linkage between these institutions and the political process, political parties, interest groups, the media, and public opinion
▌ How public policy is formulated and implemented

Public Policy

▌ The nature of public policy
▌ The creation of public policy
▌ The impact of the three branches of government on public policy
▌ The impact of the bureaucracy on public policy
▌ The relationship between public policy and linkage institutions

Civil Rights and Civil Liberties

▌ The Bill of Rights and how it evolved
▌ The incorporation of the Fourteenth Amendment
▌ Judicial review and key Supreme Court cases
▌ The fight for minority rights

Using class lectures, assignments, and activities, you can immerse yourself in all six themes of AP U.S. Government & Politics. Extensive classroom preparation and your own regular practice and study will be the foundation for your success on the AP U.S. Government & Politics Exam.

Understanding the AP U.S. Government & Politics Examination

The AP U.S. Government & Politics Exam incorporates graphical, cartographic, and statistical materials. This cross-disciplinary approach reflects the methods used today in colleges and universities to present historical subject matter.

The AP U.S. Government & Politics Exam takes two hours and twenty-five minutes. It consists of a multiple-choice section and a free-response section. You can expect to see graphs, charts, and quotations in both sections of the test. You are expected to know the foundations of U.S. government and how and why it has evolved, although the majority of the questions relate to the period from 1960 to the present.

Section I: Multiple-Choice Questions

You will have forty-five minutes to complete the sixty questions in the multiple-choice section of the test. This section accounts for fifty percent of your overall score. Each question has five answer choices, and only one choice is correct. Most of the questions in this section will be fairly straightforward. Some may require interpretation, such as determining cause and effect or drawing a comparison. Others will ask you to analyze data in charts or graphs, or to evaluate a political cartoon or other illustration. The questions tend to appear in order of difficulty, with easier questions appearing first.

Not all multiple-choice questions are the same. The AP U.S. Government & Politics Exam will contain the following types of questions.

Definition or Identification Questions

These questions ask you to recognize something and know what it is. Here is an example.

1. Class action suits
    (A) permit a small number of people to sue on behalf of all other people similarly situated
    (B) are filed by students seeking to force a school district to offer additional sections of perpetually overenrolled courses
    (C) have to do with constitutional issues, thus broadening the standing to sue
    (D) are routinely filed by teachers' groups to prepare the way or strikes
    (E) may be filed only if all of those with standing to sue agree to participate

The answer is *A*. A small group of people who believe, for example, that they have been harmed by a product can sue the manufacturer on behalf of all the people who believe they were harmed. This is the definition of class action.

Cause-and-Effect Questions

This type of question asks which event caused another, or what is the result of something. Here is an example.

2. The increasing speed of technological advance
   (A) has significantly reduced the scope of American government
   (B) helps reduce and accelerate government policymaking
   (C) has helped reduce the cost of health care in the United States
   (D) has dramatically affected health policy, but has had no effect on environmental and energy policy
   (E) has created many new practical and moral problems of the political system

The answer is *E*. You can use the process of elimination. The scope of government has not gotten smaller; policymaking has not become faster; health care costs have risen; if technology has affected health policy, it is unlikely that it has not also affected environmental and energy policies. Answers *A–D* are obviously wrong, leaving *E*.

"Roman Numeral" Questions

Here you are given a question, then several statements, phrases, or words relating to the question. You must decide which of the statements, phrases, or words are correct. It may be one or more than one.

3. Registered voters directly elect which of the following?
   I. The president and vice president
   II. Supreme Court justices
   III. Senators
   IV. The Electoral College
   (A) I only
   (B) IV only
   (C) I and II only
   (D) III and IV only
   (E) II, III, and IV only

The answer is *D*. Registered voters vote for electors who then vote for the president and vice president. This is not *direct* election. So any choice that includes *I* is wrong (*A, C*). Justices of the Supreme Court are appointed by the president and approved by the Senate, so you can also eliminate choice *E*. Voters vote directly for both senators and, as noted above, the Electoral College.

EXCEPT/NOT Questions

In this type of question, four of the answer choices are correct, and you must find the answer that is *wrong*. Be sure to read the question carefully. Here is an example of this type of question.

4. Which of the following is NOT specifically mentioned in the Constitution?
   (A) Protection against double jeopardy
   (B) Right to bear arms
   (C) Freedom of speech
   (D) Right to privacy
   (E) Right to trial by jury

The answer is *D*. Double jeopardy is addressed in the Fifth Amendment. The right to bear arms is mentioned in the Second Amendment. Freedom of speech is protected by the First Amendment. Article III provides for trial by jury. Only the right to privacy is not mentioned in the Constitution.

Supreme Court Decisions

You will be asked to identify, interpret, or compare one or more well-known Supreme Court decisions. Here is an example.

5. *New York Times* v. *Sullivan* addressed
   (A) equal opportunity in the workplace
   (B) libel
   (C) prior restraint
   (D) business monopolies
   (E) obscenity

The answer is *B*. The Court held that statements about public figures are libelous only if made with "reckless disregard for the truth." There is no way to guess here. All the choices are topics the Supreme Court has ruled on, and all might involve a newspaper. You need to remember the significant cases.

Graphic Questions

You can expect to see questions based on graphs, tables, and maps.

DISTRIBUTION OF INCOME AMONG FAMILIES (percentage share by economic level)				
	1970	1980	1990	2000
Lowest fifth	5.5	5.1	4.6	3.6
Second fifth	12.0	11.6	10.8	8.9
Third fifth	17.4	17.5	16.6	14.9
Fourth fifth	23.5	24.3	23.8	23.0
Highest fifth	41.6	41.6	44.3	49.6

6. Which of the following conclusions about income distribution is supported by the table?
   (A) The share of income received by the lowest fifth increased, and the share received by the fourth fifth decreased.
   (B) The share of income received by the second fifth increased, and the share received by the fourth fifth decreased.
   (C) The share of income received by the highest fifth increased, and the share received by the lowest fifth decreased.
   (D) The number of people earning high incomes increased.
   (E) The middle class disappeared.

The numbers clearly show that *C* is the answer. Choice *D* is meant to trick you. The table gives percents. Although the *percent* of families in the highest fifth increased, you know nothing about the actual number of people. Always read the questions and answer choices carefully.

Section II: Free-Response Questions

The second portion of the AP U.S. Government & Politics Exam is an hour-and-forty-minute free-response section consisting of four questions. You must answer all four—none of them is optional (you may, however, have some choice within a question). All four questions count equally, and together they account for fifty percent of your overall score.

Because the free-response questions are open-ended, this is your opportunity to demonstrate your broad understanding of U.S. government and politics. You will be asked to analyze some of the basic concepts that form the foundation of the American political system. Most questions will ask you to characterize relationships among various political institutions, their responsibilities, and the consequences of their actions. Some questions will ask you to analyze both sides of an issue. You will see directives like *analyze, assess, evaluate, examine,* and *discuss.* This means that knowing facts is not enough. You must be able to use facts to construct a thorough and intelligent response.

1. Read and then reread the question to be sure you understand exactly what it is asking. Look for key words like *who, how, what,* and *why.* Also underline directives such as *argue* or *argument, explain,* and *discuss.* It may help to

rephrase the question or to condense it in your own words to be sure you know what is being asked. You can jot notes in the margins.

2. Take a few minutes to brainstorm about the topic. Write down the first things that come to your mind. Then look them over to see which ideas will go well together to serve as examples for your argument and to determine the order in which you will present them. Aim for three pieces of supporting evidence in your response. Three examples are enough to prove your point and still leave you room to develop each one. Too many examples would read more like a list than an essay and could cost you points.

3. After you have decided on your three supporting points, formulate a brief outline. Often you'll find that with a good outline, the essay almost writes itself. Do not go into detail in the outline. It is for your benefit only—the readers will not see it. A few words should be enough to cue you when you're writing. Use the question format as your guide to your outline.

Think about how you want to organize your essay. Some questions are divided into parts, and your body paragraph can logically be organized in that order. Answers to some questions, even if they appear in parts, might be answered better in a more traditional format, with each paragraph addressing a piece of evidence. In that case, your outline should follow this basic format:

Paragraph 1: your position or interpretation of the given information
Paragraph 2: your first piece of evidence and any supporting details
Paragraph 3: your second piece of evidence and any supporting details
Paragraph 4: your third piece of evidence and any supporting details
Paragraph 5: summary of your points and restatement of your
    position

4. Now you're ready to begin writing. Flesh out the ideas you used to construct your outline. Keep in mind that there may be many possible correct answers to the free-response questions. Your answer will be judged on the evidence you use to support your viewpoint and on the way you present this evidence. Of course you should write enough to answer a question thoroughly, but don't write too much. Certainly don't venture beyond the scope of the question. You will not earn extra points, and because each question is scored independently, you will not be able to make up for a question you feel you didn't answer well enough by overcompensating on another question. Keep in mind too that you have one hour and forty minutes to write four questions, or about twenty-five minutes per question. Keep track of the time as you are working.

Many free-response questions on the AP U.S. Government & Politics Exam will ask you to address a single topic in a straightforward way. Here is an example of such a question.

1. The system of checks and balances ensures that no branch of government has unfettered power. Describe—using examples—how each branch has exercised this power over another branch.

In your response to this question, you need to furnish *examples* that help you *describe* how each of the three governmental branches has used the system of checks and balances to wield power.

Some free-response questions are divided into several parts, or subquestions. You might be presented with a list of items, such as specific court cases or interest groups, that you are asked to discuss in your response. These partitioned questions often contain directives like *identify, describe,* and *explain*. Here is an example.

2. Choose two of the following Supreme Court cases.
   - *California Board of Regents* v. *Bakke*
   - *Roe* v. *Wade*
   - *Gideon* v. *Wainwright*
   - *Rust* v. *Sullivan*
   - *Miranda* v. *Arizona*
   - *Korematsu* v. *United States*

For each case you selected, do each of the following.
   a. Explain the position of each side.
   b. Give the Supreme Court's ruling.
   c. Discuss whether the ruling increased or decreased the rights of individuals.

First, you need to recognize (at least two of) the cases. *Bakke* is about affirmative action. *Roe* is about abortion rights. *Gideon* is about an accused person's right to counsel. *Rust* is about abortion counseling. *Miranda* is about a suspect's rights. *Korematsu* is about the internment of Japanese-Americans during World War II.

Then you must know which way the Court ruled. In *Bakke,* the Court said that race can be one factor in college admissions, but colleges could not set quotas. *Roe* legalized abortion. In *Gideon,* the Court ruled that defendants in felony cases have a right to counsel. In *Rust,* the Court held that family-planning clinics that receive government funding may not provide abortion counseling. *Miranda* states that everyone arrested must be informed of his or her legal rights. In *Korematsu,* the Court found the internment of Japanese-Americans constitutional.

Most people would say that *Roe, Gideon,* and *Miranda* expand individual rights. They would say that *Rust* and *Korematsu* limit rights. You could—but probably should not—argue that *Rust* increases the rights of people who are against abortion, or that *Korematsu* increases the rights of the public to be safe during wartime. These are unusual responses to the decisions, and no matter how solid your evidence, you may fail to persuade the reviewer and lose points. *Bakke* is not clear-cut one way or the other, so you shouldn't choose it as a case to examine here.

You must answer all of the subquestions. If possible, answer each subquestion in a separate paragraph. Begin each paragraph with a topic sentence. Try to make your answers flow together, and then draw conclusions. Unless the question specifically asks for your opinion, do not include your personal views. You don't get extra credit for going beyond the scope of a question, and that just wastes your valuable time.

In answering any free-response question, you must focus your response according to the particular directive (or directives) they include. For instance, questions may ask you to *discuss* recent Supreme Court decisions on restraint of trade, to *compare and contrast* the roles of different types of media in American politics, to *explain* the role of political parties, to *identify* influences on members of Congress and to *evaluate* the impact of these influences, to *describe* how the Constitution remedied the weaknesses of the Articles of Confederation, or to *explain* why it is difficult for Congress to pass laws. Again, pay close attention to exactly what the question asks you to do. In explaining the role of political parties, for example, tell why they came into existence and what they do. Do not compare the Democratic and Republican parties—and especially do not mention which party you prefer.

Grading Procedures for the AP U.S. Government & Politics Examination

The raw scores of the exam are converted into the following five-point scale:

5 — Extremely Well Qualified
4 — Well Qualified
3 — Qualified
2 — Possibly Qualified
1 — No Recommendation

Some colleges give undergraduate course credit to students who achieve scores of 3 or better on AP exams. Other colleges require students to achieve scores of 4 or 5. If you're considering using your AP exam score for college credit, check with individual colleges to find out their specific requirements for credit. Below is a breakdown of how the grading of the AP U.S. Government & Politics Exam works.

Section I: Multiple-Choice Questions

The multiple-choice section of the exam is worth fifty percent of your total grade. The raw score of Section I is determined by crediting one point for each correct answer and by deducting one-fourth of one point for each incorrect answer. No points are gained or lost for unanswered questions. If you have no idea what the correct answer is, do not make a wild guess—leave the answer blank. But if you can eliminate two or more of the five choices, you should make an educated guess.

Section II: Free-Response Questions

The free-response section of the exam is worth fifty percent of your total grade. It is graded by a group of AP U.S. Government & Politics instructors and professors known as "faculty consultants." Multiple readers grade each examination booklet, assigning scores to individual essays. (These scores are covered up so that the next reader does not see them.) The raw score for Section II is composed of four separate scores—one for each essay—and then averaged.

Test-Taking Strategies for the AP U.S. Government & Politics Examination

To become comfortable with the both the content and the format of the AP U.S. Government & Politics Exam, begin preparing for the test at least a month in advance. This way, you'll have plenty of time to devote to each of the six main subject areas on the test while practicing your essay-writing skills at the same time. The more relaxed study time you allow yourself, the more prepared you will be and the better you will do on the exam.

Aim to finish the review sections about a week and a half before the exam. Then take the first practice test at the back of this book. Treat the practice test exactly like the real exam. In other words, find a quiet place where you can work without interruption and give yourself only two hours and twenty-five minutes. This allows you to become familiar with the actual testing conditions so that you will be less nervous on testing day.

After you have scored your practice test, take a day just to review your answers. Look at the types of questions you got wrong. Do they fall under the same content area or areas? If so, you should focus further study on those particular areas for the next two days or so. Count the number of questions you skipped. Did they fall near the end of the section? This could mean that you were running out of time. Did you feel rushed? It might be wise, then, to plan ahead of time which kinds of questions you should skip over. For example, if you got every data question right and a lot of questions about Supreme Court cases wrong, plan to skip a few of those judicial questions so that you can answer all of the data questions in the section. You'll need to make sure that you answer the questions you're more likely to know and that you skip the ones that might slow you down.

Now that you know what adjustments to make to your test-taking strategy, give yourself a few days of extra practice with your problem areas and then take the second practice test at least three days before the real exam (don't overwhelm yourself before the real thing!). Again, analyze your performance. Did your adjustments pay off? Is there anything you should do differently? Use your last few days to do any fine-tuning and to relax before the exam.

Below is a brief list of basic tips and strategies to think about *before* you arrive at the exam site.

▮ Try to plan your schedule so that you get *two* very good nights of sleep before exam day. On the day of the exam, make sure that you eat good, nutritious meals. These tips may sound corny or obvious, but your body must be in peak form in order for your brain to perform well.

- Arrive at the exam site thirty minutes before the start time. This saves you additional worry about arriving late.
- It's a good idea to have a photo I.D. with you when you arrive at the exam site. (It is essential if you are taking the exam at a school other than your own.) Carrying a driver's license or a student I.D. card will allow you to prove your identity, if anyone needs such proof.
- Bring at least two pencils for the multiple-choice section, as well as two black or dark blue pens for the free-response section of the exam. Make sure that your pencils are labeled #2 and that they have good erasers. The machine that scores Section I of the exam cannot recognize marks made by other types of pencils. Also, it cannot read a correct answer if a previous answer has not been erased completely.
- It's helpful to have a watch with you at the exam. Most testing rooms will have clocks, and most test administrators will give you periodic reminders of how much time you have remaining. Still, having your own watch makes it easy to keep close track of your own pace. The watch cannot have a calculator or an alarm, however, as these are not permitted in the exam room.
- Do not bring books of any kind, laptop computers, wireless instant-messaging devices, cameras, or portable radios. If you must bring a cellular phone with you, turn it off and give it to the test proctor until you are finished with your exam.

The test administrators are very clear and very serious about what is *not* allowed during the examination. Below is a list of actions to avoid at all costs, since each is grounds for your immediate dismissal from the exam room.
- Do not consult any outside materials during the exam period. Remember, the break is technically part of the exam—you are not free to review any materials at that time either.
- Do not speak during the exam, unless you have a question for the test proctor. Raise your hand to get the proctor's attention.
- When you are told to stop working on a section of the exam, you must stop *immediately*.
- Do not open your exam booklet before the test begins.
- Never tear a page out of your test booklet or try to remove the exam from the test room.
- Do not behave disruptively—even if you're distressed about a difficult test question or because you've run out of time. Stay calm and make no unnecessary noise. Remember, too, the worst-case scenario: If you are displeased with your performance on test day, you can cancel your exam scores.

Section I: Strategies for Multiple-Choice Questions

Having a firm grasp of U.S. government and politics is, of course, the key to your doing well on the AP U.S. Government & Politics Examination. In addition, being well-informed about the exam itself increases your chances of achieving a high score. Below is a list of strategies that you can use to increase your comfort, your confidence, and your chances of excelling on the multiple-choice section of the exam.

▮ Pace yourself and keep track of the remaining time as you complete the multiple-choice section. Remember, you have forty-five minutes to answer all sixty questions. It's important that you don't get stuck on one question for too long.

▮ Make a mark in your test booklet next to any questions you can't answer. Return to them after you reach the end of Section I. Sometimes questions that appear later in the test will refresh your memory of a particular topic, and you will be able to answer one of those earlier questions.

▮ Always read the entire question carefully and underline and define key words or ideas. You might want to circle words such as *NOT* or *EXCEPT* in that type of multiple-choice question.

▮ Read *every* answer choice carefully before you make your final selection.

▮ Use the process of elimination to help you choose the correct answer. Even if you are sure of an answer, cross out the letters of incorrect choices in your test booklet as you eliminate them. This cuts down on distraction and allows you to narrow the remaining choices even further.

▮ If you are able to eliminate two or three answer choices, it is better to make an educated guess at the correct answer than to leave the answer blank.

▮ The multiple-choice section is designed so that many of the easier questions appear at the start of the test. Try to answer easy questions as quickly as you can without sacrificing care and thoroughness. If you are able to rack up many correct answers at the start of the section, you will conserve time (and mental energy) for the more difficult questions toward the end of the test.

▮ Make yourself completely familiar with the instructions for the multiple-choice questions *before* you take the exam. You'll find the instructions in this book. By knowing the instructions cold, you'll save yourself the time of reading them carefully on the day of the test.

Section II: Strategies for Free-Response Questions

Here is a list of strategies that you can use to increase your chance of excelling on the free-response section of the exam.

▮ You have only one hour and forty minutes to outline and write four essays. So you must manage your time carefully.

▮ Be careful not to stray from the focus of the question asked. As you read a question, underline any key words and directives that indicate how you should address the material in your response. Some frequently used directives are listed below, along with descriptions of what you need to do in writing your answer.

  ▪ *analyze:* show relationships between events; explain
  ▪ *compare:* address similarities and differences between two or more things
  ▪ *contrast:* examine to illustrate points of difference
  ▪ *describe:* give a detailed account
  ▪ *discuss:* consider or examine; debate
  ▪ *explain:* clarify; tell the meaning

- *to what extent and in what ways:* tell how much and how
- *assess/evaluate:* give an opinion of; appraise; discuss advantages and disadvantages

▌ As you formulate your answer, always consider whether or not it answers the question directly.

AP Correlation to Government in America: People, Politics, and Policy

The following table is intended for your use as a study device. The left column shows one way to break down into historical eras the time period covered in AP U.S. Government & Politics courses. The two columns to the right include detailed breakdowns of chapters in your textbook where you can learn more about those topics. You may want to use this table throughout the year to review what you've learned. It is also an excellent place to begin your pre-exam review of subjects.

SAMPLE AP COURSE UNITS	CORRELATIONS TO *GOVERNMENT IN AMERICA: PEOPLE, POLITICS, AND POLICY* (10TH EDITION)	CORRELATIONS TO *GOVERNMENT IN AMERICA: PEOPLE, POLITICS, AND POLICY* (11TH EDITION)
Constitutional Underpinnings of United States Government		
The Constitution	**Chapter 2: The Constitution** ■ The Origins of the Constitution ■ The Government That Failed: 1776–1787 ■ Ratifying the Constitution **Chapter 4: Civil Liberties and Public Policy** ■ The Bill of Rights—Then and Now ■ Freedom of Religion ■ Freedom of Expression ■ Defendants' Rights ■ Trial by Jury ■ The Right to Privacy	**Chapter 2: The Constitution** ■ The Origins of the Constitution ■ The Government That Failed: 1776–1787 ■ Ratifying the Constitution **Chapter 4: Civil Liberties and Public Policy** ■ The Bill of Rights—Then and Now ■ Freedom of Religion ■ Freedom of Expression ■ Defendants' Rights ■ Trial by Jury ■ The Right to Privacy
Federalism	**Chapter 3: Federalism** ■ Defining Federalism ■ The Constitutional Basis of Federalism ■ Understanding Federalism	**Chapter 3: Federalism** ■ Defining Federalism ■ The Constitutional Basis of Federalism ■ Understanding Federalism
Separation of Powers	**Chapter 2: The Constitution** ■ The Madisonian Model **Chapter 13: The Presidency** ■ Presidential Leadership of Congress: The Politics of Shared Powers	**Chapter 2: The Constitution** ■ The Madisonian Model **Chapter 13: The Presidency** ■ Presidential Leadership of Congress: The Politics of Shared Powers

Theories of Democratic Government	**Chapter 1: Introducing Government in America** ■ Democracy **Chapter 3: Federalism** ■ Defining Federalism	**Chapter 1: Introducing Government in America** ■ Democracy **Chapter 3: Federalism** ■ Defining Federalism
Civil Rights and Civil Liberties		
Civil Liberties and Judicial Interpretation	**Chapter 4: Civil Liberties and Public Policy** ■ Freedom of Religion ■ Freedom of Expression ■ Defendants' Rights ■ The Right to Privacy ■ Understanding Civil Liberties	**Chapter 4: Civil Liberties and Public Policy** ■ Freedom of Religion ■ Freedom of Expression ■ Defendants' Rights ■ The Right to Privacy ■ Understanding Civil Liberties
Civil Rights and the Fourteenth Amendment	**Chapter 5: Civil Rights and Public Policy** ■ Two Centuries of Struggle ■ Race, the Constitution, and Public Policy ■ Women, the Constitution, and Public Policy ■ Newly Active Groups Under the Civil Rights Umbrella ■ Affirmative Action ■ Understanding Civil Rights and Public Policy	**Chapter 5: Civil Rights and Public Policy** ■ Racial Equality: Two Centuries of Struggle ■ Race, the Constitution, and Public Policy ■ Women, the Constitution, and Public Policy ■ Newly Active Groups Under the Civil Rights Umbrella ■ Affirmative Action ■ Understanding Civil Rights and Public Policy
Political Beliefs and Behaviors		
Citizens' Political Beliefs	**Chapter 6: Public Opinion and Political Action** ■ Measuring Public Opinion and Political Information ■ What Americans Value: Political Ideologies **Chapter 10: Elections and Voting Behavior** ■ How Americans Vote: Explaining Citizens' Decisions **Chapter 13: The Presidency** ■ Power from the People: The Public Presidency	**Chapter 6: Public Opinion and Political Action** ■ Measuring Public Opinion and Political Information ■ What Americans Value: Political Ideologies **Chapter 10: Elections and Voting Behavior** ■ How Americans Vote: Explaining Citizens' Decisions **Chapter 13: The Presidency** ■ Power from the People: The Public Presidency
Processes of Learning About Politics	**Chapter 6: Public Opinion and Political Action** ■ How Americans Learn About Politics: Political Socialization	**Chapter 6: Public Opinion and Political Action** ■ How Americans Learn About Politics: Political Socialization

	Chapter 7: The Mass Media and the Political Agenda	**Chapter 7: The Mass Media and the Political Agenda**
	▪ The News and Public Opinion	▪ The News and Public Opinion
Voting and Participation in Politics	**Chapter 6: Public Opinion and Political Action**	**Chapter 6: Public Opinion and Political Action**
	▪ How Americans Participate in Politics	▪ How Americans Participate in Politics
	▪ Understanding Public Opinion and Political Action	▪ Understanding Public Opinion and Political Action
	Chapter 8: Political Parties	**Chapter 8: Political Parties**
	▪ The Party in the Electorate	▪ The Party in the Electorate
	Chapter 10: Elections and Voting Behavior	**Chapter 10: Elections and Voting Behavior**
	▪ How American Elections Work	▪ How American Elections Work
	▪ Whether To Vote: A Citizen's First Choice	▪ Whether To Vote: A Citizen's First Choice
	▪ Understanding Elections and Voting Behavior	▪ Understanding Elections and Voting Behavior
	Chapter 12: Congress	**Chapter 12: Congress**
	▪ Congressional Elections	▪ Congressional Elections

Political Parties, Interest Groups, and Mass Media

The Mass Media	**Chapter 7: The Mass Media and the Political Agenda**	**Chapter 7: The Mass Media and the Political Agenda**
	▪ The Mass Media Today	▪ The Mass Media Today
	▪ The Development of Media Politics	▪ The Development of Media Politics
	▪ Reporting the News	▪ Reporting the News
	▪ The News and Public Opinion	▪ The News and Public Opinion
	▪ The Media's Agenda-Setting Function	▪ The Media's Agenda-Setting Function
	▪ Understanding the Mass Media	▪ Understanding the Mass Media
	Chapter 13: The Presidency	**Chapter 13: The Presidency**
	▪ The President and the Press	▪ The President and the Press
Political Parties	**Chapter 8: Political Parties**	**Chapter 8: Political Parties**
	▪ The Meaning of Party	▪ The Meaning of Party
	▪ The Party in the Electorate	▪ The Party in the Electorate
	▪ The Party Organizations: From the Grass Roots to Washington	▪ The Party Organizations: From the Grass Roots to Washington
	▪ The Party in Government: Promises and Policy	▪ The Party in Government: Promises and Policy
	▪ Party Eras in American History	▪ Party Eras in American History
	▪ Third Parties: Their Impact on American Politics	▪ Third Parties: Their Impact on American Politics
	▪ Understanding Political Parties	▪ Understanding Political Parties
	Chapter 6: Public Opinion and Political Action	**Chapter 6: Public Opinion and Political Action**
	▪ How Americans Participate in Politics	▪ How Americans Participate in Politics

Campaigning and Elections	**Chapter 9: Nominations and Campaigns**	**Chapter 9: Nominations and Campaigns**
	▪ The Nomination Game	▪ The Nomination Game
	▪ The Campaign Game	▪ The Campaign Game
	▪ Money and Campaigning	▪ Money and Campaigning
	▪ The Impact of Campaigns	▪ The Impact of Campaigns
	▪ Understanding Nominations and Campaigns	▪ Understanding Nominations and Campaigns
	Chapter 10: Elections and Voting Behavior	**Chapter 10: Elections and Voting Behavior**
	▪ How Americans Vote: Explaining Citizens' Decisions	▪ How Americans Vote: Explaining Citizens' Decisions
	▪ The Last Battle: The Electoral College	▪ The Last Battle: The Electoral College
Interest Groups	**Chapter 11: Interest Groups**	**Chapter 11: Interest Groups**
	▪ The Role and Reputation of Interest Groups	▪ The Role and Reputation of Interest Groups
	▪ Theories of Interest Group Politics	▪ Theories of Interest Group Politics
	▪ What Makes an Interest Group Successful?	▪ What Makes an Interest Group Successful?
	▪ The Interest Group Explosion	▪ The Interest Group Explosion
	▪ How Groups Try To Shape Policy	▪ How Groups Try To Shape Policy
	▪ Types of Interest Groups	▪ Types of Interest Groups
	▪ Understanding Interest Groups	▪ Understanding Interest Groups

National Government

Congress	**Chapter 12: Congress**	**Chapter 12: Congress**
	▪ The Representatives and Senators	▪ The Representatives and Senators
	▪ Congressional Elections	▪ Congressional Elections
	▪ How Congress Is Organized To Make Policy	▪ How Congress Is Organized To Make Policy
	▪ The Congressional Process	▪ The Congressional Process
	▪ Understanding Congress	▪ Understanding Congress
The Presidency	**Chapter 9: Nominations and Campaigns**	**Chapter 9: Nominations and Campaigns**
	▪ The Nomination Game	▪ The Nomination Game
	▪ The Campaign Game	▪ The Campaign Game
	Chapter 10: Elections and Voting Behavior	**Chapter 10: Elections and Voting Behavior**
	▪ The Last Battle: The Electoral College	▪ The Last Battle: The Electoral College
	Chapter 13: The Presidency	**Chapter 13: The Presidency**
	▪ The Presidents	▪ The Presidents
	▪ Presidential Powers	▪ Presidential Powers
	▪ Running the Government: The Chief Executive	▪ Running the Government: The Chief Executive
	▪ The President and National Security Policy	▪ The President and National Security Policy

Part II

Topical Review with Sample Questions and Answers and Explanations

This section is keyed to the chapters in *Government in America.* Part II overviews important information in bullet form and provides sample questions for every question type, plus additional review items on core concepts. Use these practice questions to arm yourself thoroughly for all kinds of test items you will encounter on the AP examination. Answers and explanations are provided for each question for your further review.

CHAPTER 1

Introducing Government in America

A **democracy** is a form of government in which policymaking reflects the will of the people. The United States is not a **direct democracy,** however. Instead, the American system is based on **representation**—citizens elect representatives to make political decisions for them. The authors of the Constitution were hesitant to vest too much power in the majority of uneducated Americans at the end of the eighteenth century, so they designed a system that, while democratic in nature, would remove politics from direct public control. Over time, the American political system has evolved into its own form of democracy that draws upon some of the elements of a traditional democracy.

Democracy: Traditional Democratic Theory

▌ **Right to vote:** The public has the right to **vote** for government representatives.
▌ **Opportunities for political participation:** Citizens must have equal opportunities to express their **political views** by such means as voting or joining political groups such as **political parties.**
▌ **Political awareness:** The public should be informed about various political and social issues in order to be able to formulate judgments and make **informed decisions.**
▌ **Influence over the political agenda:** The issues taken up by the government should reflect the needs of the people.
▌ **Citizenship:** All people subject to the laws of a nation must have the opportunity to become citizens and to possess all the **rights of citizenship.**
▌ **Majority rule:** Decisions are made by a vote of the **majority** to reflect the will of the largest percentage of citizens.
▌ **Minority rights:** The American political system protects some rights of the **minority** against the majority. Freedom of speech and of petition, for example, allow the minority to express its opinions despite **majority rule.**

Three Contemporary Theories of American Democracy

Two main competing theories describe contemporary American politics: pluralist theory and elite theory.

Pluralist Theory

▌ The political system is composed of groups representing **competing interests.**
▌ The existences of such groups indicates that the government allows sufficient access to policymaking.

- Interests of the public may be more widely represented in government.
- Power is **decentralized** so that no one body or group has too much influence over policymaking.

Elite and Class Theory

- Government favors only a narrow percentage of the public, primarily the **wealthy.** Wealth is directly proportional to political influence.
- There may be many political groups, but the distribution of government resources among them is not necessarily equal. The more wealth and influence a group has, the more it benefits from the government.
- Groups do not have equal access to policymaking or equal power.
- **Big business** plays a prominent role in politics because corporations that have money also have power.

Hyperpluralism

Political theorists have developed a third concept of American politics, called **hyperpluralism.** According to hyperpluralism, the proliferation of political groups has weakened the government. With so many interests vying for political influence, power is decentralized, and ultimately policies become muddled and therefore less effective.

For Additional Review

After reviewing the relevant pages of your textbook, make a chart that shows the important characteristics of the pluralist theory, the elite and class theory, and hyperpluralism.

Multiple-Choice Questions

1. Which of the following is the best indication of pluralism in American politics?
   (A) The American Association of Retired Persons has the largest membership of any interest group.
   (B) Third parties often endorse candidates for office, but rarely do they win elections.
   (C) The federal bureaucracy is expanding as more and more citizens are hired for federal jobs.
   (D) More than 20,000 interest groups lobby Congress each year.
   (E) Citizens are able to vote in local, state, and national elections.

2. All of the following are characteristics of a traditional democracy EXCEPT
   (A) an informed electorate
   (B) a bill of rights
   (C) public participation
   (D) equal access to government institutions
   (E) national elections

3. According to elite theorists, which of the following statements describe the American political system?
   I. Political action committees translate the financial power of large corporations into political influence.
   II. Interest groups fairly shape the public agenda by representing the interests of all Americans.
   III. The wealthiest 1 percent of the public are in some way responsible for most policy-making.
   IV. Policymaking relies heavily on compromise, because interest groups receive equal access to the policy arena.
   (A) I only
   (B) II only
   (C) I and III only
   (D) II and IV only
   (E) I, II, and IV only

4. The United States is not a direct democracy because
   (A) the population has increased too rapidly in the last 100 years
   (B) the authors of the Constitution did not trust the public to make informed decisions
   (C) the Constitution prohibits direct representation
   (D) the separation of powers would not work in a direct democracy
   (E) a direct democracy would not fairly represent all Americans

5. Which of the following concepts best demonstrates the theory of democracy?
   (A) The rights of the accused
   (B) Separation of powers
   (C) Majority rule
   (D) Bicameralism
   (E) Big business

6. Approximately 56 percent of interest groups do favors for government officials as a means of lobbying. This is an example of
   (A) elite theory
   (B) hyperpluralism
   (C) decentralization
   (D) pluralist theory
   (E) representative democracy

7. A citizen who disapproves of proposed legislation can do all of the following EXCEPT
   (A) call or write a letter to his or her senator
   (B) vote for a different candidate in the next election
   (C) join a political interest group
   (D) vote against the legislation
   (E) participate in a protest

8. According to pluralists, a wealthy interest group would
   (A) have more access to policymakers
   (B) compete with other interest groups for an equal share of influence
   (C) buy all of the votes on a piece of legislation
   (D) manipulate public opinion to influence Congress
   (E) have no influence on the policy agenda

9. Which of the following is the best example of a right of the minority?
   (A) Protection against double jeopardy
   (B) Equal access to public education
   (C) The ability to become a civil employee
   (D) The practice of one person, one vote
   (E) Freedom to circulate pamphlets

10. Hyperpluralists differ from pluralists in their belief that
   (A) the representation of too many interests is detrimental to policymaking
   (B) only the wealthiest lobbyists are heard in Congress
   (C) power should be centralized in one branch of government
   (D) competition among groups leads to compromise and, hence, stronger policy
   (E) political groups get their funds exclusively from big business

Free-Response Question

"We hold these truths to be self-evident, that all men are created equal, that they are endowed by their Creator with certain unalienable Rights, that among these are Life, Liberty and the Pursuit of Happiness.—That to secure these rights, Governments are instituted among Men, deriving their just powers from the consent of the governed,—That whenever any Form of Government becomes destructive of these ends, it is the Right of the People to alter or to abolish it . . ."

How does this passage from the Declaration of Independence foreshadow the political system later set forth in the Constitution? In your response, cite TWO examples of traditional democratic theory.

ANSWERS AND EXPLANATIONS

Multiple-Choice Questions

▌ **1. (D) is correct.** Pluralist theory holds that numerous groups participate in politics to represent a wider variety of public concerns. Interest groups are usually a good example of pluralism in American politics. The fact that there are thousands of them would indicate, according to pluralists, that these groups are speaking on behalf of many different public needs. The political agenda would therefore be determined by the people.

▌ **2. (B) is correct.** Although a bill of rights often reinforces a democracy, it is not necessarily indicative of a democracy. For example, the structure delineated by the Constitution establishes the United States as a democracy. The Bill of Rights does protect the freedoms guaranteed under this democratic form of government, but it does not itself establish a form of government in which the people control the agenda through participation and representation.

▌ **3. (C) is correct.** Elite theorists believe that the government is mainly controlled by an elite and wealthy minority, most of whom are involved in big business. Statement I is therefore correct, because political action committees are one method by which the elite influence politics during elections. Statement III mentions the wealthy, so there's a good chance this statement is in keeping with elite theory. Only Choice *C* lists statement III as well as statement I.

▌ **4. (B) is correct.** The authors of the Constitution were an elite group of well-educated, mostly wealthy men. They distrusted the majority of citizens who were less educated. Therefore they designed a system of government that would remove power from the majority. Instead of creating a direct democracy in which each citizen is able to vote directly for legislation, the authors established a representative democracy in which citizens vote for representatives who then make political decisions for them.

▌ **5. (C) is correct.** A democracy is founded on the needs and wants of the people. All people may not have the same needs, but the closest representation of the whole populace is the majority. Therefore, in a democracy, decisions are made by majority rule.

▌ **6. (A) is correct.** Elite theorists believe that government responds to the will of the most influential interest groups rather than to the will of the people. They also distrust the lobbying techniques of interest groups because they believe that whoever spends the most money gains the most access to the political agenda.

▌ **7. (D) is correct.** Because the United States is a representative democracy, citizens cannot vote directly on a piece of legislation. They must elect a representative who makes decisions on their behalf. The First Amendment also grants citizens the right to protest or speak out against the government. Citizens may do this by contacting their representative directly, by joining a political group, or by participating in a protest.

▌ **8. (B) is correct.** Pluralists believe that all groups have access to policymaking, thereby representing a wide range of public needs. Elite theorists, not pluralists, believe that there is a connection between wealth and influence. A pluralist would expect all interest groups, regardless of their financial resources, to vie for influence. If a group fails to influence policy on one issue, it might still succeed on another. Competition among groups ultimately balances out inequities among them.

▌ **9. (E) is correct.** Circulating pamphlets is an exercise of one's freedom of speech. This freedom protects the minority from tyranny of the majority by allowing the minority to voice its concerns. Even if the minority cannot generate enough votes to shape legislation, it has the freedom to mobilize public support, thereby reinforcing its own power.

▌ **10. (A) is correct.** Hyperpluralists agree with pluralists in asserting that a number of groups represent the interests of the public in the political arena, but they contend that so many groups are essentially glutting the whole policymaking system. Representatives who are eager to appease as many groups as possible end up producing conflicting or diluted policies.

This passage from the Declaration of Independence essentially states that the new United States would be founded on the principles of democracy. Unlike the monarchy from which the new nation was separating itself, a democracy allows for a government based on the needs and demands of the people. The Constitution effectively established such a democracy by creating a system of representation and guaranteeing the rights of the people.

A representative democracy is based on the principle that a government's legitimacy is derived from the consent of the people. The Constitution established a bicameral legislature in which representatives would be elected by the people to make policies in their behalf. It also gave all men (and eventually all people) the right to vote. In many countries, this "right" depended on whether or not a person owned property, but in the new United States, each man would be granted one vote. As prescribed by democratic theory, such a system of government would be derived from each man's equal vote and would make policies based on the needs of the constituents who elected each representative.

The Constitution also protects the "certain unalienable rights" mentioned in the Declaration of Independence. According to traditional democratic theory, all people are guaranteed the rights of citizenship. This includes the right to vote and the right to the privileges of a government, such as police protection. The Constitution and the Bill of Rights especially maintain these rights for all citizens. For example, all people are allowed the freedom to express their views, regardless of their income, race, or religion. All citizens have the protection of a military, and all citizens are allowed to have a trial by jury.

The Declaration of Independence calls for a democratic form of government, and the Constitution, after the failure of the Articles of Confederation, established such a government. Even after two centuries of growth and change, the American political system is still deeply rooted in the principles of democratic theory.

This essay effectively draws connections among the Declaration of Independence, the Constitution, and democratic theory. The opening paragraph makes the connections and clearly identifies the two examples to be discussed in the body of the essay. The student displays a solid understanding of the principles underlying the form of American government set forth in the Constitution. The student also successfully uses two examples of democratic theory as points to illustrate how the Constitution translates the theory of democracy into practice.

CHAPTER 2

The Constitution

The foundation of the American political system rests on the **Constitution,** a document originally consisting of just seven articles that laid out the basic structure of the government. It established the United States as a **federal republic** composed of three branches: the **legislative, executive,** and **judicial.** Over time, the Constitution has been amended to account for the growth of the nation and changes to the political system.

The Origins of the Constitution

- Declaration of Independence (1776)
    - Lists grievances against the king of England
    - Justifies revolution
- The idea of **natural rights**
    - Philosophy of John Locke
    - Rights that are derived from people's basic moral sense supersede the authority of a government.
    - **Consent of the governed:** A government is legitimate only if the people approve of it.
    - **Limited government:** Because natural rights are superior to a government, governments should have limited power.
    - Government should protect people's property.
- American Revolution ends in 1783

The Articles of Confederation

- Establish the first government of the United States (enacted in 1781)
- Designed to preserve the independence of the states
- A national government without any centralized power proves to be ineffectual.

National Government Under the Articles of Confederation

- **Unicameral** national legislature
- No executive or judicial institutions
- Most power rests with state legislatures.
- No power to tax
- No regulation of foreign or interstate trade
- No national currency
- No national defense

Weaknesses of the Articles

▌ Without the power to **collect taxes,** the national government had few financial resources with which to repay its war debts.

▌ The development of a national economy was inhibited also by the government's inability to establish and **regulate trade.**

▌ The Articles **prevented the formation of a unified nation** out of a collection of states with different political, economic, and social concerns.

▌ **Shays' Rebellion** was not easily quelled, because the government had no power to raise a militia. The incident provided the final proof that the Articles were not a sufficient plan of government.

Making a Constitution: The Philadelphia Convention

Many issues were hotly debated during the writing of the **Constitution.** In effect, the framers faced the momentous task of defining the nature of government. They did, however, agree on some basic principles:

▪ The government should check the **self-interest** of the people yet protect their **individual liberties** and advance **natural rights** such as equality.

▪ **Factions** should not be allowed to create political conflict and thereby undermine the government.

▪ No one faction should have the opportunity to prevail upon the others.

The Agenda in Philadelphia

Two plans were proposed to ensure **equal representation** of the people in the legislature: the New Jersey Plan and the Virginia Plan.

▌ **New Jersey Plan:** Each state should be allowed the same number of representatives in the national Congress. Under this plan, all states, regardless of size or population, would have an equal voice in policymaking.

▌ **Virginia Plan:** Representation in the national Congress should be determined by the **population** of each state. Thus, larger states such as Virginia and Pennsylvania would have a greater number of representatives than less populous states such as New Jersey and Georgia.

▌ **The Connecticut Compromise,** or Great Compromise, established a **bicameral legislature.** The **Senate** would include two representatives from each state as per the New Jersey Plan, and representation in the **House** would be determined by the population of each state.

▌ The **Three-Fifths Compromise** mandated that only three-fifths of slaves be counted in determining state representation (this was repealed by the **Fourteenth Amendment** in 1868).

The authors ensured the protection of other individual rights in the Constitution:

▪ The **writ of habeas corpus** cannot be suspended.

▪ **Bills of attainder,** which punish people without a trial, cannot be passed.

▪ **Ex post facto laws,** which are retroactive criminal laws, are prohibited.

- **Religious qualifications** cannot be used as a prerequisite for public office.
- All citizens are entitled to a **trial by jury** in a criminal case.

The Madisonian Model

- James Madison warned that both the **majority** (poorer and less-educated Americans) and **minority** (the wealthy elite) **factions** could pose a threat to the stability of a government.
- To protect government from the will of the majority, the president (and, until the Seventeenth Amendment in 1913, senators as well) would be chosen by the **Electoral College,** not directly by the people.
- Madison proposed that the national government be divided into three branches: the **executive, legislative,** and **judicial.** Each branch would have its own powers and responsibilities.
- A system of **checks and balances** would ensure that no branch could become more powerful than the others. The majority or the minority might be able to take control of any one branch but not necessarily the whole political system.
- Establishing a **federal** system of government allowed power to be shared between the national and state levels of government.

Checks and Balances

Legislative Branch

- House and Senate can veto a bill of the other house.
- Approves presidential nominations for judges and other officials
- Can impeach the president
- Controls the budget
- Can pass laws over a president's veto with a two-thirds majority

Executive Branch

- Can veto bills passed by Congress
- Nominates judges and other government officials

Judicial Branch

- Can declare laws passed by Congress to be unconstitutional
- Can declare acts of the president to be unconstitutional
- Note that the Constitution did not grant to the courts the power to check the other branches. The Supreme Court did not assert its authority to declare laws **unconstitutional** until the case of *Marbury* v. *Madison* in 1803.

Ratifying the Constitution

The approval of at least nine states was needed to ratify the Constitution, and it did not come easily.

Anti-Federalists

- Feared that the Constitution **favored an elite minority**
- Believed that the Constitution failed to protect too many **individual freedoms**
- Believed that a strong central government would limit the power of the states

■ Published scathing articles and political cartoons denouncing the Constitution as a tool of the aristocracy

Federalists

■ Published a series of articles called the **Federalist Papers** to defend the Constitution
■ Asserted that the Constitution would benefit the growing middle class of tradesmen as well as the wealthy plantation owners
■ Promised to add a **bill of rights** to guarantee individual liberties
■ The Constitution was ratified in 1787, largely because the authors promised to add a bill of rights.
■ It established the United States as a **federal republic** in which power would be divided among levels of government.
■ It created a **representative** form of democracy rather than a direct democracy.
■ The Constitution is considered a **"living document"** because it can be amended as the United States grows and changes. Over the years, it has become **more democratic** than the authors intended.

For Additional Review

Make a chart comparing and contrasting the Articles of Confederation and the Constitution. How did they organize government differently? In what ways did the Constitution amend the failures of the Articles?

Multiple-Choice Questions

1. Which of the following institutions was specifically outlined in the Constitution?
   (A) Federal Reserve System
   (B) Cabinet
   (C) Federal district courts
   (D) Electoral College
   (E) Department of State

2. The Seventeenth Amendment changed the nature of senatorial elections by
   (A) prohibiting PACs from contributing to senatorial campaigns
   (B) establishing a group of electors from each state to nominate senators
   (C) permitting senatorial debates to be aired on television
   (D) scheduling them to be held every two years
   (E) allowing senators to be elected directly by the public

3. Which of the following statements accurately describe the system of checks and balances?
   I. The system of checks and balances prevents the rule of the majority, because one institution cannot gain more power than the others.
   II. The power to veto bills allows the president to check Congress.
   III. The system of checks and balances grew out of a long political tradition but is not defined by the Constitution.
   IV. Congress checks the power of the judicial branch by nominating justices.
   (A) I only
   (B) III only
   (C) I and II only
   (D) III and IV only
   (E) I, II, and III only

4. All of the following are guaranteed under the Fifth Amendment EXCEPT
   (A) due process of law
   (B) a person cannot be tried twice for the same crime
   (C) the accused cannot be made to serve as witness against himself or herself
   (D) property may not be taken without due process of law and fair compensation
   (E) bail cannot be denied

5. Which of the following concepts of government introduced in the Articles of Confederation was maintained in the Constitution?
   (A) Exclusionary rule
   (B) Limited government
   (C) Checks and balances
   (D) State supremacy
   (E) Direct democracy

6. The Bill of Rights was added to the Constitution to
   (A) clarify the Supreme Court's power of judicial review
   (B) ensure equal voting rights
   (C) protect individual rights
   (D) define the powers reserved for the federal and state governments
   (E) prevent the supremacy of one faction of government over another

7. Which of the following statements are true about freedom of speech as guaranteed by the Constitution?
   I. Political protests first require the submission of a formal application to the federal government.
   II. In cases where national security may be compromised, the government has the authority to censor the news media.
   III. The possession of obscene material is protected under the First Amendment.
   IV. An amendment would be required to prevent the practice of flag burning.
   (A) I only
   (B) IV only
   (C) I and II only
   (D) II and IV only
   (E) I, II, and III only

8. Anti-Federalists argued against adoption of the Constitution for all of the following reasons EXCEPT
   (A) it failed to centralize power
   (B) it responded to the needs of the minority, not the majority
   (C) it placed too many restrictions on the states
   (D) it neglected individual rights
   (E) it favored property owners

9. The Constitution established a system of equal representation by creating
   (A) a system of federal courts
   (B) a bicameral legislature
   (C) the Electoral College
   (D) three branches of government
   (E) the Bill of Rights

10. In which of the following ways does the
    Constitution protect the rights of individuals?
    (A) It gives Congress the power to impeach
        the president.
    (B) It invests the president with the powers
        of commander in chief.
    (C) It prevents Congress from passing bills
        of attainder.
    (D) It allows states to collect taxes.
    (E) It divides government into the national
        and state levels.

Free-Response Question

The Constitution has been amended over time to reflect changes in the American political system. No issue has received more attention among these amendments than that of voting rights. Discuss three amendments that had an impact on voting rights. For each of your examples, explain the following:

- What circumstances brought about the need for changing the Constitution?
- How did each amendment affect the scope of American politics?

ANSWERS AND EXPLANATIONS

Multiple-Choice Questions

▌ **1. (D) is correct.** All but one of the answer choices evolved out of interpretations of the Constitution. Bear in mind that the Constitution is really only a blueprint for government—it lays out only the basic structure and powers of the three branches and defines the powers of the federal and state governments. Most governmental bodies have resulted from particular needs neither specified nor denied in the Constitution. However, the authors of the Constitution did create the Electoral College to choose the president as a means of keeping government out of the hands of the poor and uneducated majority.

▌ **2. (E) is correct.** The Seventeenth Amendment allows voters to directly elect their own senators. Previously, as stated in Article I of the Constitution, senators had been chosen by a body of electors. This was another way the framers attempted to distance government from the populace.

▌ **3. (C) is correct.** Madison devised the system of checks and balances primarily to prevent any one branch, if it came under the control of the majority, from dominating the whole government. The system is clearly defined in the first three articles of the Constitution; it is not merely a part of the unwritten body of tradition that has evolved.

▌ **4. (E) is correct.** According to the Fifth Amendment, all citizens are guaranteed the due process of law. The Fifth Amendment also protects the accused from double jeopardy, or being tried twice for the same crime, and from self-incrimination. While the Eighth Amendment does grant the opportunity for bail, which is considered a due process right, in cases where the accused is likely to flee, bail may be denied by a court of law.

▌ **5. (B) is correct.** The authors of the Articles of Confederation were so determined to minimize the power of the federal government that ultimately they created one that was not politically or economically viable. The challenge they faced in writing the Constitution was to create a more centralized government without risking giving it too much power. The concept of limited government is therefore the correct answer.

▌ **6. (C) is correct.** Recall the debate surrounding the ratification of the Constitution: Anti-Federalists feared that it favored the elite over the majority, whose individual freedoms were not sufficiently addressed. The promise of a bill of rights was necessary to win over those states that hesitated to vote for adoption of the Constitution. Think also about what rights are guaranteed by the first ten amendments: free speech, freedom of religion, freedom to petition, protection against unlawful searches and seizures, and the right to a trial by jury. All of these address personal liberty and assert the basic natural rights of citizens.

▌ **7. (D) is correct.** In order to uphold national security, the government can in fact censor the media. A notable example of this practice is the media coverage of the Gulf War. Statement II is therefore correct. Statement IV is also correct. Flag burning has been a controversial issue since the Vietnam War; there is strong opposition to this form of expression, but as a means of free speech, it is protected under the First Amendment.

▌ **8. (A) is correct.** Anti-Federalists feared that the Constitution would give the national government too much power. They felt that the states should retain as much authority as possible to allow a greater public voice in politics. A centralized government could too easily become the tool of the elite planters of the early United States.

▌ **9. (B) is correct.** The formation of a bicameral legislature settled the debate over equal representation. Seats in the House would be distributed according to the population of each state, and membership in the Senate would be divided equally among the states regardless of size or population.

▌ **10. (C) is correct.** The Constitution prohibits Congress from infringing on individual rights by passing bills of attainder. Every citizen is entitled to the right of due process by law—no one may be found guilty without first being tried. This idea of justice forms the cornerstone of the American judiciary system.

Free-Response Question

These amendments would serve as appropriate examples for this question:
- **Fifteenth Amendment (1870):** extended voting rights to freed slaves (male) after the Civil War
- **Seventeenth Amendment (1913):** abolished the system of using state electors to choose senators, allowing the election of senators directly by the constituency

- **Nineteenth Amendment (1920):** gave women the right to vote
- **Twenty-third Amendment (1961):** granted the residents of Washington, D.C., the right to vote
- **Twenty-fourth Amendment (1964):** prohibited states from using poll taxes or literacy tests to prevent the poor from voting
- **Twenty-sixth Amendment (1971):** changed the voting age from 21 to 18

The Constitution, though it was intended to establish a democracy in the United States, granted voting rights only to free males. While this was not uncommon at the end of the eighteenth century, today such a limited percentage of voters would not make the United States a true representative democracy. Over time, however, amendments such as the 15th, 19th, and 24th have been added to the Constitution to extend voting rights to all Americans.

The call for each amendment arose when the lack of voting privileges for a subset of the American population became too apparent to ignore. The 15th Amendment was ratified in 1870. The Civil War ended slavery in the South, but it would take government intervention to ensure that newly freed slaves would be treated as citizens. Southern states held out against the 14th Amendment, which extended citizenship to freed slaves, so it became necessary to add a new amendment that would specifically allow these disenfranchised Americans to vote. For the first time, African Americans were able to hold public office. The 15th Amendment was not wholly successful, but it did act as an enormous first step toward righting the wrongs of slavery.

It took 100 years and another amendment for the 15th Amendment to be fully realized. Because elections fall under the jurisdiction of state governments, southern states sidestepped the 15th Amendment by imposing poll taxes or requiring literacy tests of voters. Most freed slaves were poor and uneducated, so these measures prevented them from voting. Finally, the civil rights movement of the 1960s brought to light such injustices. The 24th Amendment was passed to prohibit southern states from using these methods to prevent African Americans from voting. Today people of all races are able to vote.

Finally, American women too were denied the right to vote for more than a century. Only after World War I had forced women out of the home and into the workplace, where they took on the roles and responsibilities of men, was the women's rights movement taken seriously. Finally, in 1920, the 19th Amendment extended the vote to them. Since then, not only have women been able to serve as senators, representatives, mayors, and governors, but also women's issues have found a place in the political arena. Politicians, in order to win the votes of half the electorate, now address such issues as abortion, family leave, and equal opportunity in the workplace. The 19th

Amendment, therefore, both doubled the number of eligible voters and changed the political landscape of the United States.

As the United States has grown and expanded, so has the need to ensure an inclusive political system that responds to the needs and demands of *all* Americans. Without these three amendments, policymaking would be controlled by a small, elite percentage of the population, and the United States would be more like an oligarchy than a democracy. Furthermore, these amendments show that the Constitution is a living, adaptable document that is both stable enough to maintain democracy over the centuries and flexible enough to allow the changes that come with such radical expansions of the electorate.

This response correctly identifies and explains three amendments that affected voting rights in the United States. The student discusses the factors that brought about the need for each amendment and what each one mandated. Moreover, the student displays a grasp of American politics by discussing the impact of each amendment on the political agenda and on the premise of equal representation as practiced in the United States.

CHAPTER 3

Federalism

In a **federal system,** government is divided between the national and state levels. Each level of government has its own powers and responsibilities, but often their spheres overlap. This bi-level form of government, while not unique to the United States, is fairly uncommon.

Defining Federalism

- **Federal government:** Government is **divided into more than one level.** Different bodies share power over the same group of people. Every citizen of the United States must obey both federal laws and the laws of his or her state. Citizens may also vote for their representatives in both state and federal elections. Germany, Canada, and India also have federal systems.
- **Unitary government:** Only **one central government** has authority over a nation. There are no levels of government that share power. Japan, France, and Great Britain all operate under unitary governments. Most countries today have either a federal or a unitary form of government.
- **Confederation:** an association of states with some authority delegated to a national government. The states in such a system retain most of the power, but the national government is authorized to carry out some functions, such as diplomatic relations. Although rare today, many of the former Soviet republics have formed the Confederation of Soviet Republics.

Decentralized Government

A federal system of government decentralizes power.
- **Opportunities for political participation** at all levels: Citizens can run for numerous government positions or take part in campaigns.
- **Public involvement:** Citizens can elect local, state, and federal representatives.
- **Access:** A greater number of interests can be represented across levels, ensuring that the government will be more responsive to public concerns.
- **Decisions** can be made at lower levels, thereby allowing the federal government to concentrate more fully on fewer issues.
- **Parties** also function at **two levels:** The loss of an election does not pose as serious a setback, and it is less likely that one party will dominate the whole political system.

Decentralized Policy

- Policymaking is **shared between levels.** Often states act as innovators by trying out new laws before they are adopted nationally.

- Policies can be made separately. For example, family and other social issues are usually addressed by state laws.
- Policies may be discussed at both levels. For example, issues of the economy, environment, and equality are addressed by both federal and state laws.
- Debate often arises over which level of government should have the authority on an issue. A major consequence of this is the development of the court system, for it is a court's ruling that determines whether a state or federal law is constitutional.

Powers Reserved for the Federal Government	Powers Reserved for State Governments	Powers Shared by the Federal and State Governments
Coin money	Create local level of government	Make and enforce laws
Regulate the economy and foreign and interstate commerce	Regulate intrastate commerce	Collect taxes
Declare war	Hold elections	Maintain courts
Manage national military	Ratify amendments	Allocate money for
Direct foreign relations	Conduct social policymaking	public needs

The Constitutional Basis of Federalism

Supremacy Clause

- Located in Article VI.
- Asserts the authority of the national government over the states: The Constitution, national laws, and treaties made by the national government should be held as the supreme law of the United States.
- In cases of discrepancy, federal laws usually supercede state laws.

Tenth Amendment

- Located in the Bill of Rights
- Grants all powers not specifically reserved for the national government to the states
- Often cited in arguments in favor of states' rights

McCulloch *v.* Maryland

- 1819 Supreme Court case in which the states battled the formation of a national bank
- The court, under Chief Justice John Marshall, ruled against the states, thereby reinforcing the supremacy of the national government.

Elastic Clause

- Also called the *necessary and proper clause*
- Located in Article I, Section 8 of the Constitution
- Gives Congress the authority to pass any laws necessary to carry out its duties as enumerated in the Constitution

- The elastic clause, as interpreted in *McCulloch* v. *Maryland,* allows Congress to act on implied powers that are not specifically defined in the Constitution.

Full Faith and Credit Clause

- Located in Article IV, Section 1
- Requires each state to formally recognize the documents and judgments handed down by courts in other states
- Helps coalesce the state laws under a national umbrella

Extradition

- Located in Article IV, Section 2
- Allows for the return (**extradition**) of fugitive criminals arrested in one state to the state in which the crime was committed for prosecution

Privileges and Immunities Clause

- Located in Article IV, Section 2
- Also helps unify the states by assuring that all citizens are treated equally when they travel from state to state

Intergovernmental Relations Today

- **Dual federalism:** Each level of government has distinct responsibilities that do not overlap.
- **Cooperative federalism:** Levels of government share responsibilities.
  - Shared costs: To receive federal aid, states must pay for part of a program.
  - Federal guidelines: To receive funding, state programs must follow federal rules and regulations.
  - Shared administration: Though programs must adhere to basic federal guidelines, they are administered according to the state's directives.
- **Fiscal federalism:** the system of distributing federal money to state governments
  - About a quarter of states' fiscal spending is derived from federal aid.
  - Money is distributed through **categorical grants** and **block grants.**

For Additional Review

To understand more fully the idea of fiscal federalism, brainstorm a list of some services that your state provides. Then do Internet research to see how those programs receive funding.

Multiple-Choice Questions

1. All of the following are concurrent powers of the federal and state governments EXCEPT the
   (A) imposition of export tariffs
   (B) collection of taxes
   (C) management of the court system
   (D) construction of roads
   (E) authority to borrow money

2. In *United States* v. *Darby,* the Supreme Court ruled that the Tenth Amendment
   (A) violates the supremacy clause in Article VI
   (B) cannot be interpreted to assert state supremacy over the national government
   (C) can bestow unlimited implied powers to state governments
   (D) cannot deny states the power to regulate interstate commerce
   (E) authorizes the federal government to impose restrictions on state governments

3. The elastic clause gives Congress the authority to
   (A) overrule the president's veto
   (B) pass laws necessary to carry out its assigned powers
   (C) form an unlimited number of committees and subcommittees
   (D) check the power of the Supreme Court by approving the president's nominees for justices
   (E) regulate money and control the budget

4. Which of the following statements is true of a federal system of government?
   (A) Power is concentrated in a central government that oversees policymaking and the enforcement of laws.
   (B) Power is shared among state governments in such a way that all states must recognize and respect the laws of other states.
   (C) Power is divided among levels of government so that more than one level has authority over a body of people.
   (D) Power is relegated primarily to local governments.
   (E) Power is vested mostly in state governments.

NUMBER OF GOVERNMENTAL UNITS BY TYPE: 1952 TO 2002										
Type of Government	1952¹	1962	1967	1972	1977	1982	1987	1992	1997	2002
Total Units	116,807	91,237	81,299	78,269	79,913	81,831	83,.237	85,006	87,504	87,900
U.S. government	1	1	1	1	1	1	1	1	1	1
State government	50	50	50	50	50	50	50	50	50	50
Local governments	116,756	91,186	81,248	78,218	79,862	81,780	83,186	84,995	87,453	87,849
County	3,052	3,043	3,049	3,044	3,042	3,041	3,042	3,043	3,043	3,034
Municipal	16,807	18,000	18,048	18,517	18,862	19,076	19,200	19,279	19,372	19,431
Township and town	17,202	17,142	17,105	16,991	16,822	16,734	16,691	16,656	16,629	16,506
School district	67,355	34,678	21,782	15,781	15,174	14,851	14,721	14,422	13,726	13,522
Special district	12,340	18,323	21,264	23,885	25,962	28,078	29,532	31,555	34,683	35,356

¹Adjusted to include units in Alaska and Hawaii which adopted statehood in 1959.

SOURCE: U.S. Census Bureau, *2002 Census of Governments, Governmental Units in 2002*, series GC02-1(P).

5. Which of the following conclusions may be drawn from the data in the table?
   (A) The number of school districts dropped dramatically before 1967 and then leveled off.
   (B) The most significant changes in local governments occurred between 1967 and 1972.
   (C) The number of township and town governments has decreased because the number of municipal governments has risen.
   (D) The number of county governments has not changed significantly because changes to county lines were prohibited in 1952.
   (E) The increasing number of local governments may be attributed to the growing number of municipal and special district governments.

6. The full faith and credit clause would require all of the following EXCEPT
   (A) that a marriage performed in Las Vegas be valid in other states
   (B) that a driver's license serve as identification when a person travels across state lines
   (C) that a divorced parent pay child support even if his or her children reside in another state
   (D) that a birth certificate issued by any state can be used to open a bank account
   (E) that something against the law in one state is against the law in all other states

7. To receive federal funding, state programs usually must
   (A) comply with some federal regulations
   (B) hire federal employees to oversee the program
   (C) be approved by the Supreme Court
   (D) return a percentage of the funds as profit
   (E) apply to the Department of the Treasury

8. A resident of New Mexico is robbed while he is visiting relatives in Texas and calls the local police, who later find the culprit. This is an example of
   (A) the Tenth Amendment
   (B) the supremacy clause
   (C) the rights of the accused
   (D) the privileges and immunities clause
   (E) dual federalism

9. Which of the following statements accurately describe public participation in a federal system?

    I. Multilevel elections allow voters more influence over government bodies.

    II. Concerned citizens may join both state and national political groups to try to influence policymaking.

    III. People are more likely to participate in state-level politics because state governments are more responsive.

    IV. Political parties offer voters more choice among candidates.

(A) I only

(B) III only

(C) I and II only

(D) I, II and III only

(E) II, III, and IV only

10. When it is unclear whether an issue falls under the jurisdiction of the federal or a state government,

(A) the president decides and issues an exec utive order

(B) a federal court rules on the matter

(C) Congress votes to determine who has the authority

(D) the state legislatures must decide whether to overrule the federal government

(E) the federal and state governments must share authority

Free-Response Question

The responsibility of providing public education falls largely under the domain of the states. However, most school districts receive federal aid and are answerable to certain federal regulations. Moreover, given the deterioration of public education in many districts, debate has arisen over how much the federal government should become involved in public education. Using your knowledge of American politics, discuss how this issue exemplifies both the benefits and the disadvantages of a federal system of government.

ANSWERS AND EXPLANATIONS

Multiple-Choice Questions

▌ **1. (A) is correct.** The federal government has sole jurisdiction over foreign relations, both political and economic. States, therefore, do not have the power to regulate export tariffs. Otherwise each state would be dealing independently with foreign nations, thereby inhibiting a the formation of a national economy.

▌ **2. (B) is correct.** The Tenth Amendment reserves all powers not specifically relegated to the federal government or denied in the Constitution to the states. This does not mean that state governments have unlimited powers, however. In fact, the Supreme Court ruled that, even though the Tenth Amendment bestows a fair amount of freedom to the states, it should not be too heavily interpreted in favor of the states. This 1941 case confirmed federal supremacy.

▌ **3. (B) is correct.** This clause in Article I of the Constitution gives Congress the authority to "make all laws which shall be necessary and proper for carrying into execution the foregoing Powers, and all other Powers vested by [the]

Constitution." In other words, it gives Congress implied powers beyond those specifically listed in the Constitution. The elastic clause allows flexibility for the federal government to change and adapt over time.

▌ **4. (C) is correct.** This question simply asks you to identify the basic premise of federalism, which is that the government is divided into levels that share jurisdiction over the same body of people. In the United States, government is divided into local, state, and national levels.

▌ **5. (E) is correct.** Over the time span shown in the table, the number of municipal governments has risen from 16,807 to 19,431. The number of special district governments has risen dramatically from 12,340 to 35,356. Together, these two categories contribute to the total number of municipal governments. Because they both have increased to a greater extent than other types of municipal government have decreased, the number of municipal governments has risen overall.

▌ **6. (E) is correct.** The full faith and credit clause requires that any official document issued by one state be recognized in all other states. These include driver's licenses, birth and death certificates, and marriage licenses. States pass many of their own laws—speed limits, for example—that do not automatically apply elsewhere.

▌ **7. (A) is correct.** Federal aid packages often come with strings attached. One of the most common requirements is that the state must follow specific federal regulations in order to receive the money. If a state program practices discrimination in hiring, for example, the federal government can withhold funding for that program.

▌ **8. (D) is correct.** The privileges and immunities clause gives residents of any state equal protection under the law, no matter what state they happen to be in. This clause serves to unite the states by extending equal national citizenship regardless of state lines.

▌ **9. (C) is correct.** In a federal system, the electorate chooses local, state, and national representatives. This gives them a greater degree of control over government at each level. Similarly, a government divided into levels offers more points of access for political groups; a citizen concerned about gun control can join either a state or a national advocate group, or both. State governments are not necessarily more responsive, and, while political parties do offer more choice, they are not exclusive to a federal system—many unitary governments have multiparty systems.

▌ **10. (B) is correct.** It is the role of the courts to settle disputes between the federal and state levels of government. A court, through its interpretation of the Constitution, determines whether a particular issue falls under the scope of the federal or state level of government. This is one reason why the court system has grown more extensive over the course of American history.

Free-Response Question

Both the federal government and state governments bear the responsibility of providing free public education for all children in the United States. The federal government offers funding but requires certain regulations to be met, and the state is responsible for spending the money in ways that best suit its schools. This issue exemplifies some of the advantages and disadvantages of the current system of cooperative federalism in the United States.

Public education benefits from the combined resources of two levels of government. Federal aid not only contributes to state funding but also compensates for differences in available resources among states. A state with very little public money of its own still is able to spend a comparable amount per student as other states. Similarly, by attaching certain strings to its aid packages, such as prohibiting discrimination in the hiring of teachers, federal involvement encourages uniformity of and equal access to education across states. Lastly, when state and local governments oversee the day-to-day operation of schools, they not only have the ability to tailor the system to their own particular circumstances, but they also free up the time and resources of the federal government. By working together, the federal and state governments ideally would provide the optimal public education system.

However, the involvement of two sets of government bodies in public education can be a disadvantage. States alone might be better equipped to handle the circumstances surrounding their own public school districts. For example, they would be able to determine how busing should be handled, or how much reduced-price lunches should cost. However, in order to receive necessary funding, the schools would still have to adhere to federal regulations that might not work well for them. Moreover, with two different governments claiming authority, conflicting policies could arise. Then time and money might be wasted on resolving differences between the state and federal policies. Federalism in public education, therefore, might at times do more harm than good.

This question asks not for an argument but for an analysis of both sides of an issue. Moreover, the issue is not whether the federal government should become heavily involved in public education but rather the strengths and weaknesses of federalism itself. The student therefore correctly identifies and explains three advantages and three disadvantages of the federal system. The student also helps the reader by "sign-posting" each new argument with linking words such as moreover, similarly, *etc.*

CHAPTER 4

Civil Liberties and Public Policy

Civil liberties are the individual freedoms guaranteed in the Bill of Rights. They are primarily concerned with protecting citizens from too much government control. While these freedoms are specifically addressed in the first ten amendments, however, they are not always clearly defined, especially in light of today's social, political, and technological circumstances. Because civil liberties are rarely absolute and often conflict with other societal values, the courts must continually define and interpret the meaning and practice of these freedoms.

The Bill of Rights—Then and Now

- The Bill of Rights protects freedoms at a national level, but these freedoms were not necessarily guaranteed in some state constitutions.
- In the case of *Barron* v. *Baltimore* (1833), the Supreme Court ruled that states could not be forced to uphold the Bill of Rights if it conflicted with their state constitution.
- In *Gitlow* v. *New York* (1925), the Court reversed its earlier decision, citing the **Fourteenth Amendment** as reason to enforce states' protection of the civil liberties listed in the **First Amendment.**
- *Gitlow* v. *New York* began a tradition called the **incorporation doctrine,** by which the Supreme Court has gradually ensured the protection of most freedoms listed in the Bill of Rights from state infringement.

Freedom of Religion

Establishment clause: in the First Amendment, prohibiting Congress from making laws establishing any religion in conjunction with the government

- Some critics interpret the clause loosely: The government should not favor one religion over another in its policies. Others, including Thomas Jefferson, argue that the establishment clause endorses the **separation of church and state.**
- The establishment clause is at the center of the debate over prayer in school and over federal funding to private religious schools.
- *Lemon* v. *Kurtzman* (1971): the Supreme Court allowed federal funding of parochial schools, provided that the money neither advances nor inhibits religious teaching, but instead is used for administrative purposes.
- *Engel* v. *Vitale* (1962) and *School District of Abington Township, Pennsylvania* v. *Schempp* (1963): Forbid the practice of prayer in school as a violation of the establishment clause and a breaching of the separation of church and state.

- Federal funds may be used to construct school buildings and to provide administrative and academic supplies, but not to endorse religious teaching.
- Student religious groups cannot be denied access to school buildings for the purpose of meeting or worship.

  Free exercise clause: a First Amendment right that guarantees the freedom to practice or not practice any religion
- The Court has upheld that the government cannot infringe on people's beliefs, but it can regulate religious behavior to some degree.
- State laws can ban religious practices that conflict with other laws, but they cannot forbid religious worship itself.

Freedom of Expression
Speech

- Courts grapple with the definition of "speech." Political protests and picketing are protected by the First Amendment, but **libel,** pornography, and fraud are not.
- The Constitution forbids **prior restraint,** or government censorship of the press. This policy was strengthened by the case of ***Near* v. *Minnesota*** (1931), in which the Court found in favor of the press.
- Prior restraint is granted in situations where **national security** might be compromised.
- As decided in ***Schenck* v. *United States*** (1919), freedom of speech may be curtailed when it threatens **public order.**

The Press

- Freedom of the press can interfere with the **right to a fair trial,** but the press does have a right to report on any criminal proceeding, and all trials must be open to the public.
- ***Roth* v. *United States*** (1957): The Court asserted that obscenity is not protected under the First Amendment. However, the definition of "obscenity" continues to be a point of controversy.
- Cases of libel are usually difficult to win because the person libeled must prove that the insults were intentionally malicious, as mandated in ***New York Times* v. *Sullivan*** (1964).
- Acts of symbolic speech, such as protesting and flag burning (***Texas* v. *Johnson,*** 1989), are protected under the First Amendment.
- **Commercial speech,** such as advertising, is more closely regulated by the **Federal Trade Commission.**
- Commercial speech on radio and television is regulated by the **Federal Communications Commission.** The broadcast media have significantly less freedom than do print media.

Assembly

- **Freedom of assembly** includes the right to protest, picket, or hold a demonstration.
- The right to establish groups of people with similar political interests, from political parties to the Ku Klux Klan, is protected under the First Amendment.

Defendants' Rights

As with free speech, the courts must continually interpret the vague language of the Constitution in order to apply it to today's issues and events.

- **Searches and seizures:** The **Fourth Amendment** protects citizens from **unreasonable searches and seizures.**
  - Police investigators cannot search private property without a **search warrant** issued by a court unless there is reason to believe that the evidence will disappear or be destroyed or removed in the meantime.
  - The police cannot arrest someone unless there is **probable cause** to believe that he or she is guilty.
  - The **exclusionary rule** prevents prosecutors from using evidence acquired through unreasonable search and seizure.
  - The case of *Mapp* **v.** *Ohio* (1961) extended the exclusionary rule to state as well as federal cases.
- **Self-incrimination:** The **Fifth Amendment** protects people from being forced to supply evidence against themselves.
  - Because a person is innocent until proven guilty, the prosecution is responsible for proving a defendant's guilt.
  - *Miranda* **v.** *Arizona* (1966): Established that suspects must be informed of their constitutional rights before they are questioned by the police.
- **Right to counsel:** The **Sixth Amendment** guarantees that all accused persons tried in a federal court have the right to be represented by an attorney.
  - *Gideon* **v.** *Wainwright* (1963): Extends this privilege to cases tried in state courts as well.
  - Most cases are settled by **plea bargaining** between lawyers instead of by a trial.
  - The Sixth Amendment requires a trial by a jury of twelve people in federal cases; in state cases this number may be fewer, and a conviction does not require a unanimous vote.
- **Cruel and unusual punishment** is prohibited by the **Eighth Amendment,** though the term is not clearly defined in the Bill of Rights.
  - In *Gregg* **v.** *Georgia* (1976) and *McCleskey* **v.** *Kemp* (1987), the Supreme Court confirmed that the death penalty does not violate the Bill of Rights —that is, it is not considered "cruel and unusual."
  - Debate over the death penalty continues as DNA tests sometimes prove the innocence of inmates on death row.
- **Right to privacy** is not specifically guaranteed by the Bill of Rights, but the Supreme Court has interpreted the first ten amendments to imply this right.

- **_Roe_ v. _Wade_** (1973) asserted the right to privacy and allowed abortions during the first trimester.
- **_Webster_ v. _Reproductive Health Services_** (1989): The Supreme Court upheld a Missouri law that prevented the use of state funds for abortion clinics and that prohibited state employees from performing abortions.
- The Supreme Court, while allowing abortions, has increasingly permitted regulation of them.
- Medical technology also causes debate over the right to privacy in cases of surrogate parenthood and physician-assisted suicide.

For Additional Review

Make a three-column table. In the first column, write all of the civil liberties discussed in this chapter. In the second column, list all Supreme Court cases that have addressed each liberty, including the date, the chief justice, and brief synopsis of the case. In the third column, list the corresponding amendment or any previous court cases on which the Supreme Court based its decisions about each civil liberty.

Multiple-Choice Questions

1. In which of the following cases did the Supreme Court enforce the use of the exclusionary rule in state trials?
   (A) _Near_ v. _Minnesota_
   (B) _Miranda_ v. _Arizona_
   (C) _Miller_ v. _California_
   (D) _Mapp_ v. _Ohio_
   (E) _Gregg_ v. _Georgia_

2. _Roth_ v. _United States_ and _Texas_ v. _Johnson_ are Supreme Court cases that address the
   (A) Sixth Amendment rights of defendants
   (B) definition of obscenity
   (C) right of free speech
   (D) definition of probable cause
   (E) right to privacy

3. Which of the following statements accurately describe the exercise of religious freedom in public schools and universities?
   I. Prayer in school was found unconstitutional by the Supreme Court because it violates the First Amendment.
   II. Administrators must allow religious groups to meet on school property as a form of extracurricular activity.
   III. Federal funding may be used by religious schools to construct buildings and acquire educational supplies.
   IV. States can forbid religious worship when it violates the laws of their state constitution.
   V. The separation of church and state is clearly stated in the elastic clause of the Constitution.
   (A) I and IV only
   (B) II and V only
   (C) I, II, and III only
   (D) II, III, and IV only
   (E) III, IV, and V only

4. All of the following are protected under the right of free speech EXCEPT
   (A) picketing
   (B) libel
   (C) flag burning
   (D) political demonstrations
   (E) criticizing government officials

5. Approximately 90 percent of criminal cases in the United States
   (A) are cases in which the defendant's rights have been abused by law enforcement officials
   (B) are appealed to the Supreme Court
   (C) involve First Amendment rights
   (D) are closed to the public during the trial
   (E) are resolved by plea bargaining and do not go to trial

6. The Supreme Court has regularly cited the Fourteenth Amendment in order to
   (A) extend the protection of the Bill of Rights to defendants in state trials
   (B) assert its power of judicial review
   (C) prevent the executive branch from infringing on civil liberties
   (D) enforce the use of search warrants in criminal investigations
   (E) impose limitations on the exercise of defendants' rights

7. In which of the following cases did the Supreme Court rule that the death penalty is not a form of cruel and unusual punishment?
   (A) *Gregg* v. *Georgia*
   (B) *Gideon* v. *Wainwright*
   (C) *Barron* v. *Baltimore*
   (D) *Engel* v. *Vitale*
   (E) *Gitlow* v. *New York*

8. Which of the following generalizations about the Supreme Court's stance on abortion is true?
   (A) The Supreme Court ruled in *Roe* v. *Wade* that under no circumstances can a woman have an abortion.
   (B) The Supreme Court is usually conservative and therefore favors the right to life in all situations unless the mother's health is at risk.
   (C) The Supreme Court has always been distinctly pro-choice and has struck down state laws that attempted to interfere with the performing of abortions.
   (D) The Supreme Court permitted the right to an abortion in *Roe* v. *Wade*, but it has since enforced greater regulation of abortions.
   (E) The Supreme Court has consistently upheld a woman's right to an abortion, even in if she is in her third trimester or if she is a minor.

9. All of the following concepts underlie the protection of civil liberties by the court system EXCEPT
   (A) all Americans have the right to a fair trial
   (B) a person is innocent until proven guilty
   (C) increasingly, state as well as federal courts must uphold the Bill of Rights
   (D) courts must rule in favor of a person who claims that his or her rights have been violated
   (E) the Constitution forbids the government from infringing on personal freedoms

10. The right to assemble extends to groups in all of the following situations EXCEPT
    (A) a hate group such as the Ku Klux Klan holding a rally
    (B) right-to-life advocates attempting to prevent access to abortion clinics
    (C) students holding an antiwar demonstration on a university campus
    (D) a religious group holding a public prayer meeting
    (E) a labor union starting a picket line

Free-Response Question

The Supreme Court is responsible for interpreting the law in order to protect the civil liberties of Americans.

Select one of the following Supreme Court cases.

- *Miranda* v. *Arizona*
- *School District of Abington Township, Pennsylvania* v. *Schempp*
- *Roe* v. *Wade*
- *Texas* v. *Johnson*

For the case you selected, do the following.

a. Identify the two parties in the case and the issue it addressed.

b. Discuss the Court's ruling. What did it decide, and how did it make its decision?

c. Assess the impact of the case on future court decisions, policymaking, or citizens' rights in the United States.

ANSWERS AND EXPLANATIONS

Multiple-Choice Questions

1. (D) is correct. In *Mapp* v. *Ohio,* the Supreme Court extended the protection of the Fourteenth Amendment to defendants in state trials. Specifically, as in federal cases, state courts must adhere to the exclusionary rule: Prosecutors cannot use evidence acquired through unreasonable search and seizure to convict a person.

2. (C) is correct. In *Roth,* the Court ruled that obscenity is not protected under the Constitution as a form of free speech. However, in *Texas* v. *Johnson,* it decided that flag burning is protected as an act of symbolic speech. These two cases clarify the First Amendment right of free speech.

3. (C) is correct. In both *Engel* v. *Vitale* and *School District of Abington Township, Pennsylvania* v. *Schempp,* the Supreme Court ruled that prayer in schools violates the separation of church and state and is therefore unconstitutional. It did, however, find that student religious groups should have the same right to assemble as any other extracurricular group and, in *Lemon* v. *Kurtzman,* that parochial schools may receive federal funding as long as they use it for educational rather than religious purposes.

■ **4. (B) is correct.** Only libel is not protected by the First Amendment, because it represents an intentional misconstruing of the truth. However, libel is difficult to prove in court because the prosecutor must present evidence of malicious intent. Furthermore, the negative attention generated by a libel suit often dissuades public officials from pursuing claims.

■ **5. (E) is correct.** Most cases are resolved through plea bargaining. The prosecutor and the defendant's attorney work out a deal in which the defendant receives a lighter sentence for pleading guilty to a lesser charge. This saves the court and attorneys considerable time and money, since, as a result of frequent plea bargaining, only 10 percent of all cases actually go to trial.

■ **6. (A) is correct.** Throughout the twentieth century, the Supreme Court has increasingly extended the protection of the Bill of Rights to defendants in state trials. It has done so by citing the Fourteenth Amendment, which asserts that "no State shall make or enforce any laws which shall abridge the privileges or immunities of the citizens of the United States." Previously, state courts had asserted their right to act independently of federal courts and their rulings.

■ **7. (A) is correct.** In the 1976 case of *Gregg* v. *Georgia,* the Supreme Court allowed capital punishment, citing it as "an extreme sanction, suitable to the most extreme of crimes." This case set the precedent for excluding the death penalty from the definition of cruel and unusual punishment.

■ **8. (D) is correct.** In *Roe* v. *Wade,* the Supreme Court allowed abortion in the first trimester—and allowed it in the second trimester with some state regulation. However, the Court has become increasingly conservative in its opinion and has upheld several state laws that limit abortion.

■ **9. (D) is correct.** Courts are by no means required always to find in favor of the claimant. They must evaluate each case in a constitutional context, and often courts find that the person's rights have in fact *not* been violated. *Gregg* v. *Georgia* and *McCleskey* v. *Kemp* are two examples of cases in which the Court did not rule in favor of the claimant.

■ **10. (B) is correct.** The right to assemble clearly is protected by the First Amendment; even a hate group may convene as long as it is not endorsing or performing any crime against an individual. Right-to-life advocates who attempt to block access to an abortion clinic are, however, violating the right of women to enter the clinic. This was decided by the Supreme Court in 1994 and was then endorsed by Congress, which passed the Freedom of Access to Clinic Entrances Act.

Free-Response Question

The case of *School District of Abington Township, Pennsylvania* v. *Schempp* had a significant impact on the issue of religion in public schools. It called into question the First Amendment freedom of religion and ultimately reinforced the separation of church and state.

In 1963, this case came before the Warren court, now remembered for its liberal position and advancement of civil rights. Parents of high school students in Abington Township brought a suit over a state law that required public schools to include reading of the Bible as part of the curriculum. Participation in the reading was a mandatory part of academics, not an optional extracurricular activity. The parents claimed that the law violated the First Amendment freedom to practice any religion, or none. A state court agreed, but the school district appealed the case to the Supreme Court.

The Supreme Court found the state law to be unconstitutional. Not only did it infringe upon the freedom of students who practiced a religion other than Christianity (or none), but also it violated the establishment clause of the First Amendment. The establishment clause says that no state can make a law either endorsing or restricting religious practice. In other words, it implies the separation of church and state. Because public education is administered by the government, the law requiring Bible readings in school crossed the line between church and state. Pennsylvania was forced to revoke its law.

This case sparked a debate that continues today. Many schools, particularly in southern states, endorse prayer in school. Students feel that the ruling violates their freedom to practice their religion. Some administrators see prayer in school as an important way to strengthen America's deteriorating "moral fabric." The court has been consistent, however. In the 1971 case of *Lemon* v. *Kurtzman,* it determined that religious schools could have access to funding, but only if they used the money for nonreligious purposes. In other words, as long as a school receives federal funding, it cannot advance any one religion over another. No one has yet successfully challenged the decision in *School District of Abington Township, Pennsylvania* v. *Schempp.* According to the Court, prayer in school ultimately is not a question of religious freedom but of the separation of church and state.

This is an example of an essay that is nicely organized in the a, b, c paragraph format. The student displays a thorough understanding both of the case chosen and of the issue that makes that case relevant to the concept of civil liberty in the United States. The essay sufficiently addresses each of the three parts of the question. Moreover, the student defines key terms, such as establishment clause, *and includes such details as the character of the Warren court.*

CHAPTER 5

Civil Rights and Public Policy

The Constitution secures equal treatment under the law for all citizens. Civil rights guarantee that people are not discriminated against by the government or by other individuals on account of their race, religion, gender, or age. Such rights were not inherent in the Constitution, however. Many legal and political battles have been fought to extend civil rights to all groups of people in the United States.

The Constitution and Inequality

- The original Constitution did not mention equality, and only white males were allowed privileges such as voting rights.
- The **Fourteenth Amendment** first clarified the concept of equality by ensuring that all citizens must receive **"equal protection of the laws."**
- The Supreme Court's modern interpretation of equality has brought civil rights to the forefront of the political agenda.

Race, the Constitution, and Public Policy

- *Dred Scott* v. *Sanford* (1857) upheld the constitutionality of slavery and forbade Congress from banning it in new states.
- The **Thirteenth Amendment** (1865) outlawed slavery after the Civil War.
- The **Fourteenth Amendment** (1868) extended rights of citizenship to former slaves. With the Fifteenth Amendment guaranteeing the ability to vote, many African Americans were elected to government posts.
- In the 1876 election, Rutherford B. Hayes promised to withdraw federal supervision of southern states in exchange for their votes. Civil rights advances came to a halt and Jim Crow laws took effect.
- *Plessy* v. *Ferguson* (1896): The Supreme Court officially recognized a policy of "separate but equal" facilities, thereby endorsing the practice of segregation.

The Era of Civil Rights

- *Brown* v. *Board of Education* (1954) overturned the *Plessy* decision—asserting that segregation is unconstitutional—and ordered the desegregation of public schools.
- Several more court decisions were required to enforce the *Brown* decision. Congress also passed the **Civil Rights Act** (1964), bringing the cause of civil

rights to the legislative as well as the judicial agenda. The Civil Rights Act accomplished the following measures.

- Outlawed racial discrimination in public places
- Prohibited discrimination in employment
- Withheld government funding from any school or institution that prac ticed discrimination
- Established the Equal Employment Opportunity Commission to monitor job discrimination
- Granted the Justice Department power to enforce civil rights laws by suing institutions still practicing segregation

■ *Swann* v. *Charlotte-Mecklenberg County Schools* (1971): The Supreme Court allowed busing to be used as a means to balance racial percentages in schools. This policy later met with opposition when it caused impractical school districting. In *Shaw* v. *Reno* (1993) and *Miller* v. *Johnson* (1995), the Court denounced such redistricting.

■ Other minority groups, including Native Americans, Hispanic Americans, and Asian Americans, have benefited from advances made in the civil rights movement. This legislation applies to all races and has encouraged many minority groups to speak out for their rights.

Getting and Using the Right to Vote

■ The **Fifteenth Amendment** (1870) granted African Americans the right to vote. Southern states circumvented the law by instituting **literacy tests,** which most ex-slaves could not pass, and **poll taxes.**

■ Southern states cited a **grandfather clause** to exempt from literacy tests illiterate whites whose grandfathers had been allowed to vote before 1860. This practice was found unconstitutional in *Guinn* v. *United States* (1915).

■ *Smith* v. *Allwright* (1944): The Supreme Court outlawed the use of **white primaries** to exclude African Americans from the election process.

■ The **Twenty-Fourth Amendment** (1964) outlawed the use of poll taxes to prevent poor people from voting.

■ Congress passed the **Voting Rights Act** in 1965 to prevent states from using any methods to disenfranchise voters. The law provided for enforcement by allowing federal registrars to oversee elections.

Women, the Constitution, and Public Policy

■ Women were excluded also from the rights of equality implied in the Constitution. The women's rights movement grew out of abolitionism in the 1840s, when female activists encountered discrimination among male activists.

■ The **Nineteenth Amendment** (1920) granted women the right to vote.

■ The **Equal Rights Amendment** (1923) was intended to enforce full equality for women, who still were discriminated against in such areas as employment. It was passed by Congress in 1972 but was never ratified by the necessary three-fourths of state legislatures.

■ *Reed* v. *Reed* (1971): For the first time, the Supreme Court found a law unconstitutional based on arbitrary gender bias. Since then, it has struck down laws that discriminate against both women and men.

▮ Civil rights legislation barring discrimination in the workplace applies to women as well as to other minority groups, and it includes employment opportunities, equal pay, and pregnancy leave.

▮ The Supreme Court has not yet ruled on the issue of **comparable worth,** which insists that women be paid the same as men for jobs that require the same skills.

▮ Women are allowed to serve in all branches of the military but cannot engage in ground combat.

Newly Active Groups under the Civil Rights Umbrella

▮ People over the age of 65 are now the largest group of Americans. Discrimination laws prevent employers and universities from rejecting applicants because of their age. Congress also revoked the policy of mandatory retirement.

▮ The **Americans with Disabilities Act of 1990** protects disabled Americans against job discrimination and requires employers to provide "reasonable accommodations."

▮ **Gay rights** are protected by some laws but are hardly advanced by the Supreme Court. The **"don't ask, don't tell"** policy introduced by Clinton into the military bypasses restrictions on homosexuality by preventing labeling. The **right to privacy** also factors into debates over gay rights.

Affirmative Action

▮ **Affirmative action** is a policy that attempts to prevent discrimination by forcing employers and universities to hire a certain percentage of minority groups or to give them compensatory preferential treatment.

▮ *Regents of the University of California* v. *Bakke* (1978): A white student sued the university for admitting a less-qualified minority student so that the university could fulfill its enrollment quota. The Court ruled that race could be used as one factor by which to choose applicants, but that enrollment quotas were unconstitutional.

▮ *Adarand Constructors v. Pena* (1995): The Court ruled against affirmative action because—even if the intent is to advance the opportunities of minorities—it still classifies people by race and is therefore unconstitutional. In recent years the court has made decisions about affirmative action on a case-by-case basis, rather than assuming a single position.

For Additional Review

Debate continues over the policy of affirmative action. Make a chart listing arguments on each side of the issue.

Multiple-Choice Questions

1. The Civil Rights Act did all of the following EXCEPT
   (A) create the Equal Employment Opportunity Commission
   (B) deny federal funding to businesses and schools that practiced discrimination
   (C) prevent discrimination in state voting procedures
   (D) prohibit discrimination in hotels, in restaurants, and on public transportation
   (E) outlaw job discrimination

2. Which of the following cases initiated the controversy over busing as a means to overcome desegregation?
   (A) *School District of Abington Township, Pennsylvania v. Schempp*
   (B) *Guinn v. United States*
   (C) *Regents of the University of California v. Bakke*
   (D) *Shaw v. Reno*
   (E) *Swann v. Charlotte-Mecklenberg County Schools*

3. Which of the following generalizations accurately describe the advancement of civil rights in the twentieth century?
   I. The Fifteenth Amendment served as the foundation upon which the Supreme Court based many of its decisions regarding civil rights.
   II. By pursuing the cause of civil rights, the government has maintained the constitutional premise of limited government.
   III. The Supreme Court typically finds laws that rely on an *inherently suspect* classification of race to be unconstitutional.
   IV. The concept of equality poses a threat to liberty when the majority rule imposes on minority rights.
   (A) II only
   (B) IV only
   (C) I and II only
   (D) III and IV only
   (E) I, III, and IV only

4. The Equal Rights Amendment has not become a part of the Constitution because
   (A) it was not ratified by enough states
   (B) the Senate voted against it after the House had passed it
   (C) the women's rights movement has focused primarily on preserving protectionist laws
   (D) the Supreme Court found it unconstitutional
   (E) feminists decried it for neglecting to take a firm position on women's rights

5. Critics of affirmative action claim that it
   (A) violates the First Amendment freedom of speech
   (B) fails to sufficiently compensate minorities for past discrimination
   (C) encourages reverse discrimination
   (D) excuses the federal government from having to enforce civil rights
   (E) favors certain minority groups over other minority groups

6. Which of the following statements accurately describes the relationship between *Plessy* v. *Ferguson* and *Brown* v. *Board of Education*?
   (A) *Plessy* reinforced the advancement of civil rights begun by the Supreme Court in *Brown*.
   (B) The Supreme Court overturned its decision in *Plessy* with its *Brown* ruling.
   (C) Both *Plessy* and *Brown* extended voting rights to disenfranchised African Americans in the South.
   (D) Both *Plessy* and *Brown* made desegregation in public schools compulsory.
   (E) The Supreme Court used *Plessy* as a precedent upon which to base its *Brown* decision.

7. All of the following are major consequences of the civil rights movement EXCEPT
(A) women gained the right to vote
(B) it led to other groups, such as gays, seeking civil rights protections
(C) African Americans now hold thousands of government posts
(D) other minority groups began to assert their rights
(E) affirmative action became a common deterrent to job discrimination

8. There was no constitutional basis for an argument in favor of civil rights until after the Civil War because
(A) the Bill of Rights applied only to white males
(B) Supreme Court justices were predominantly from southern states
(C) inequalities of the law did not become apparent until the abolition of slavery
(D) the Constitution did not explicitly mention equality until the Fourteenth Amendment was passed
(E) the Constitution prevented the government from interfering with people's individual liberties

9. In which of the following cases did the Supreme Court first declare gender bias unconstitutional?
(A) *Faragher* v. *City of Boca Raton*
(B) *Reed* v. *Reed*
(C) *Stanton* v. *Stanton*
(D) *Craig* v. *Boren*
(E) *Dothard* v. *Rawlinson*

10. All of the following were methods used by southern states to prevent African Americans from voting EXCEPT
(A) tests about the Constitution
(B) white primaries
(C) literacy tests
(D) poll taxes
(E) the grandfather clause

Free-Response Question

Many civil rights causes have been advanced in the past 50 years. Select ONE minority group and answer all of the following questions.

a. What gains have been made by the minority group you selected, and how did the group achieve its goals?
b. Has the group been wholly successful? Defend your position.
c. How have the advances of the group you selected had an impact on American government and politics?

ANSWERS AND EXPLANATIONS

Multiple-Choice Questions

▌ **1. (C) is correct.** The Twenty-Fourth Amendment and the Voting Rights Act prohibited discrimination in voting, but the Civil Rights Act did not. It did, however, enforce voting rights by authorizing federal officials to oversee state elections and by granting the Justice Department authority to prosecute states for any violation of election laws.

▌ **2. (E) is correct.** In *Swann* v. *Charlotte-Mecklenberg County Schools,* the Supreme Court ruled that busing could be used as an effective means of integrating public schools. Redistricting became impractical, however, when lines were drawn solely for the purpose of desegregation through busing. The Court later backed down in cases such as *Shaw* v. *Reno.*

▌ **3. (D) is correct.** The Supreme Court considers arbitrary classification based on race to be *inherently suspect.* In such cases, it must be proved that the classification is necessary for the purposes of the law. It is also true that equality, which is based in part on the principle of majority rule, can pose a threat to the individual liberties of the minority when the majority seeks to use its power to deny the rights of others. Only statements III and IV are correct. The Fourteenth Amendment is regularly cited in civil rights cases, and the scope of the government has actually expanded as it has begun to enforce civil rights.

▌ **4. (A) is correct.** The Equal Rights Amendment was introduced in Congress in 1923 and finally passed both houses in 1972. It was submitted to the states for ratification within a ten-year period but fell short of the necessary three-fourths approval. Critics judge the amendment to be too radical, but it has received a good deal of public support.

▌ **5. (C) is correct.** Some critics of affirmative action see it as a mechanism of reverse discrimination. One such example is the case of *Regents of the University of California* v. *Bakke,* in which the Supreme Court found the university's quotas for enrolling minorities unconstitutional. Allan Bakke was denied enrollment in favor of a minority applicant in order to fulfill the university's quota.

▌ **6. (B) is correct.** In *Plessy* v. *Ferguson,* the Supreme Court judged segregation to be constitutional, as long as races were allowed facilities of equal quality. More than 50 years later, the Warren court struck down segregation in its *Brown* ruling, declaring that "the doctrine of 'separate but equal' has no place" in public education. The *Brown* ruling, therefore, overturned the Court's earlier ruling in *Plessy.*

▌ **7. (A) is correct.** The civil rights movement did significantly inspire the modern women's rights movement. The fight for civil rights encouraged women to seek an end to protectionist laws that relegated their place in society to the home. However, women gained the right to vote by the Nineteenth Amendment in 1920, before the civil rights movement of the 1950s and 1960s.

▌ **8. (D) is correct.** Nowhere does the Constitution endorse equality for all citizens, and because the Supreme Court makes its decisions by interpreting the Constitution, it would have had little on which to rule in favor of a constitutional guarantee of civil rights. Only when the Fourteenth Amendment was ratified could the court officially endorse civil rights by guaranteeing all people "equal protection of the laws."

▌ **9. (B) is correct.** The Supreme Court first ruled against gender discrimination in the case of *Reed* v. *Reed.* It struck down an Idaho law that stated that judges in parental cases must always find in favor of males. The court ruled that gender cannot be used as the sole qualification for determining the winner of a case.

■ **10. (E) is correct.** The grandfather clause was not a measure used to prevent African Americans from voting. It was rather a method of allowing poor, uneducated whites to bypass all such measures so that they could still vote even if they could not pay the tax or pass a literacy test. The grandfather clause granted the right to vote to all people whose grandfathers had been able to vote before 1860. The clause thus exempted all white men while denying the vote to all descendents of slaves.

Free-Response Question

Even though women actually outnumber men in the United States, they are considered a minority group because they were denied equal rights under the law until only recently. After more than a century of political activism, women are by degrees achieving the privileges afforded them by their civil rights.

Women began to organize themselves after participating in the abolitionist movement of the 1840s and '50s, when they became aware of the irony of fighting for equality for others while they themselves were still subjects in a male-dominated society. Throughout the Industrial Revolution, women formed unions, picketed, and lobbied Congress for the right to vote. This was finally granted with the ratification of the Nineteenth Amendment in 1920. After a few decades, women became more independent—they joined the workforce in large numbers and broke away from their traditional role in the home. They demanded laws to protect them from job discrimination and sexual harassment in the workplace. Congress granted them such protection under the Civil Rights Act of 1964. The case of *Reed* v. *Reed* also brought gender discrimination onto the judicial agenda in 1971. The Supreme Court ruled that arbitrary bias against women because of their gender was unconstitutional.

Since then, women have achieved many other victories, such as access to equal public education, equal retirement benefits, pregnancy leave, and greater control over family property. However, women still lag behind men in many ways. Their wages are often lower than those of men for jobs of the same skill level. Furthermore, women hold comparably few positions of power. For example, Congress is still composed primarily of white males. The military is also predominantly male, and while women can be promoted to higher positions, they cannot fight in ground combat. Finally, social customs inhibit true equality for women.

Women's rights and civil rights in general have greatly expanded the scope of the federal government. The government now has significantly more power over employers and businesses, because it can regulate to some degree who is hired, fired, and promoted. Women's rights also force the federal government to take on more social issues, such as the right to privacy and the family. Women's rights have also changed the nature of politics because the political agenda now includes traditionally women's issues such as abortion and birth control. Women's rights have therefore had a major impact on American politics, and yet, like most other minorities, women still have many battles to fight before reaching true equality.

This essay addresses each part of the question. The student selects one minority group and offers specific examples of how that group has advanced its rights. The student also provides four good examples in the third paragraph to back up the argument that the women's rights movement has not yet been wholly successful. Finally, the student demonstrates how American politics have been affected by the women's rights movement.

CHAPTER 6

Public Opinion and Political Action

More than two centuries of immigration to the United States has created an incredibly **diverse population** of Americans. Numerous social and economic factors therefore contribute to a varied forum of **public opinion.** However, despite their differences, Americans overall share a common **political culture** based on democracy and federalism. Today, public opinion can be a powerful tool, especially during elections. Increasingly, politicians, pundits, and even voters are paying close attention to what polls tell them is the public's opinion.

The American People

▌ The Constitution requires that a **census** be taken every ten years. The census collects demographic data about the population of the United States. This information is used to

- distribute money to federal and state programs,
- **reapportion** seats in the House to each state,
- determine each state's number of electors in the Electoral College,
- redraw state and federal congressional districts,
- allocate funds for public services such as schools, roads, and public transportation.

▌ According to recent census data, the percentage of minorities is increasing while the percentage of Caucasians is decreasing. This could lead to a **minority majority** in the next few decades. Also, for the first time, Hispanic Americans outnumbered African Americans.

▌ **Reapportionment** in the last two decades has given more seats to the increasingly populated states **California, Florida,** and **Texas,** whereas states in the Northeast have lost seats.

▌ **Senior citizens** make up the largest population group by age. This gives them significant political influence. It will also put a serious strain on the Social Security system in the next few decades.

How Americans Learn About Politics: Political Socialization

Americans learn about politics and form their political beliefs through the process of **political socialization.** There are several different means through which people informally acquire political information.

- **The family:** Families have a significant degree of influence, especially over younger members. Most people identify with the same party that their parents do.
- **The mass media:** Most Americans, especially children and teenagers, watch a significant amount of **television.** Political information is often disseminated through TV. Younger people are much less likely to watch the news than are adults, however, and as a result, the political knowledge of young people today is significantly lower than that of young people a few decades ago.
- **School:** Schools educate children in American values such as democracy and capitalism, both through academics and through practices such as reciting the Pledge of Allegiance. A good education also tends to produce more politically active and aware citizens.

Measuring Public Opinion and Political Information

Polls are the most common means of assessing public opinion.
- A **random sample,** or group that statistically represents the whole population of the United States, is asked to fill out a questionnaire or answer some questions over the phone.
- The wording of a question is critical, and ambiguously worded questions can affect the accuracy of a poll.
- Some critics argue that polls allow politicians to be influenced easily by shifts in public opinion and that polls receive more media attention than do candidates' political platforms during elections. Others assert that, by advancing the public's political agenda to poll-sensitive politicians, polls advance the principles of democracy.
- Recent polls indicate that Americans have little political knowledge and little faith that the government is acting on their behalf.

What Americans Value: Political Ideologies

In recent years, more Americans have considered themselves **conservative** than **moderate** or **liberal.**
- **Conservative ideology:** Favors limited government and freedom of the private sector.
  - More likely to support military spending, free markets, prayer in school, and reduced taxes.
  - Opposes abortion, affirmative action, and government spending on social programs.
- **Liberal ideology:** Favors an active central government with social and economic responsibilities.
  - Favors a more equal distribution of wealth, more government regulation of big business, more government spending on social programs, and abortion.
  - Opposes increases in defense spending and military actions, prayer in school, tax breaks for the wealthy.
- Women and minorities tend to be more liberal. The **gender gap** is the pattern

that predicts that women are more likely to vote for a Democratic candidate, however, this was less prevalent in the 2002 elections.

▌ Traditionally, people of higher socioeconomic classes tend to be conservative. This trend is declining, however.

▌ Conservative groups tend to have more resources and therefore more political power.

▌ Ronald Reagan was one of the most conservative presidents of the twentieth century. Bill Clinton shifted the Democratic party and government back to a more centrist position.

How Americans Participate in Politics

Americans express their political views and try to influence policy by voting, petitioning, participating in protests, or corresponding with their representatives.

▌ **Voter turnout** has been declining over the last few decades, though it is still the most common way people participate in politics. **Young people** are the group **least likely to vote.**

▌ **Campaign contributions** to candidates as a form of political participation are on the rise.

▌ **Protest** and **civil disobedience** have a long tradition in American history. Protests against globalization and war continue to be a means of political expression today.

▌ People of high socioeconomic status are much more likely to participate in politics, though African Americans and Hispanic Americans are becoming more active.

For Additional Review

Brainstorm a list of topics in the news. Then write down what you think the conservative and the liberal opinion of each issue would be. If you are not sure, do some library or Internet research to find out.

Multiple-Choice Questions

1. Reapportionment of seats in the House of Representatives occurs
   (A) every four years after a presidential election
   (B) when the minority party wins a majority in the House
   (C) after every four congressional election cycles
   (D) every ten years as a result of the census report
   (E) when the president requests it through an executive order

2. Which of the following factors has a significant influence over the accuracy of a political poll?
   (A) The wording of the questions
   (B) The number of people in the sample
   (C) The age of the people in the sample
   (D) The number of questions asked
   (E) The geographic distribution of the people in the sample

3. All of the following influence the way citizens form their political beliefs EXCEPT
   (A) schooling
   (B) the family
   (C) religion
   (D) the mass media
   (E) state of residence

4. One reason that minority groups are more likely to favor liberal policies is that they
   (A) have highly developed political knowledge
   (B) typically pay more in federal income taxes
   (C) have benefited from federal social programs in the past
   (D) have a greater distrust of government
   (E) usually belong to a high socioeconomic class

5. Senior citizens are the most politically active age group of Americans for which of the following reasons?
   I. They have had more experiences from which to form their political beliefs and reinforce their ideology.
   II. They have more disposable income with which they can influence politicians through campaign contributions.
   III. They are the largest age group, and therefore they form a majority.
   IV. Enrollment programs such as Social Security require recipients to vote.
   (A) I only
   (B) III only
   (C) I and III only
   (D) II and IV only
   (E) II, III, and IV only

6. Conservatives are likely to endorse all of the following EXCEPT
   (A) the right to life
   (B) tax cuts
   (C) deregulation of the economic sector
   (D) welfare programs
   (E) defense spending

7. Politicians usually pay attention to public opinion as reported in polls in order to
   (A) decide whether to change party affiliation
   (B) shape their platform for the next election
   (C) form coalitions in Congress
   (D) know if they should run for reelection
   (E) solicit campaign contributions

8. According to the prediction of the gender gap, women are more likely to
   (A) vote for a Democratic candidate
   (B) support military spending
   (C) vote for an Independent candidate
   (D) disapprove of increased social spending
   (E) vote for a Republican candidate

9. Which of the following would occur if a minority majority developed in the electorate?
   (A) Hispanic Americans would outnumber African Americans.
   (B) Female conservatives would outnumber male conservatives.
   (C) Asian Americans would outnumber Hispanic Americans.
   (D) Voters under the age of 30 would outnumber senior citizens.
   (E) The minority population would outnumber the Caucasian population.

10. Young Americans are the least politically active group for all of the following reasons EXCEPT
    (A) they have little political experience
    (B) they are not likely to watch the news or read newspapers
    (C) they have been taught to distrust the government
    (D) they have not developed a sense of what they need from government
    (E) they have not witnessed the impact of governmental policies

Free-Response Question

Political scientists have coined the phrase "the graying of America" to describe a specific shift in demographics. To what does this phrase refer, and how might this phenomenon have an impact on politics?

ANSWERS AND EXPLANATIONS

Multiple-Choice Questions

1. **(D) is correct.** The apportionment of seats in the House is based on the population of each state. The Constitution specifically requires that a national census be taken every ten years. The results of the census then determine the number of seats each state receives. If a state gains or loses seats, new congressional district lines must be drawn. State legislatures are responsible for this process, and majority parties have in the past attempted to create districts that are more likely to carry a vote for their candidates. This practice, now considered unconstitutional, is called gerrymandering.

2. **(A) is correct.** The method of random sampling ensures that the sample, regardless of size, statistically represents the opinions of the majority of Americans. However, the wording of the questions does have a significant psychological impact on the responses gathered in the sample. Two polls that ask the same question in different ways can have noticeably different results.

3. **(E) is correct.** People learn about government and form their beliefs primarily through their family, what they are taught in school, and what they see and hear on television. Factors such as a religious upbringing can also influence a person's political ideology. However, a person's home state has little direct bearing on his or her political beliefs.

4. **(C) is correct.** Liberal policies typically endorse social programs and enforce civil rights for minority groups. Generally, minority groups tend to view the government as being on their side and therefore favor a central government with a wide social and economic scope.

5. **(C) is correct.** Senior citizens have had much time to develop and refine their political beliefs and to increase their political knowledge. This makes them more likely to participate in politics. Because they are the largest age group of Americans, they are also more likely to win the attention of people who are seeking election.

6. **(D) is correct.** Conservatives are less likely to endorse any programs that widen the scope of the government. They are especially suspicious of government interference in social issues. Conservatives therefore generally do not favor welfare programs.

7. **(B) is correct.** Poll results allow politicians to get a sense of what issues are important to the public. From this, politicians can best shape their political agenda so as to maximize their chance of reelection. For example, if a politician sees that people overwhelmingly favor a certain program, he or she will probably endorse that program in his or her campaign platform.

8. (A) is correct. The gender gap predicts that women are more likely to vote for a Democratic candidate than a Republican. Bill Clinton was the first president to be elected by a majority of women over men. The gender gap is a significant predictor because women outnumber men in the United States.

9. (E) is correct. A minority majority means that more than half the population of the United States would be nonwhite. Hispanic Americans have become the largest minority group, recently surpassing African Americans. If the percentages continue to change at the same rate, the United States will reach a minority majority sometime in the middle of the twenty-first century.

10. (C) is correct. Young people do not vote primarily because they have not had enough experience to develop political awareness and form their beliefs about government. In school, students are taught the virtues of a federal government, not distrust of it.

Free-Response Question

The term "the graying of America" refers to the increasing number of senior citizens in the electorate. This phenomenon has occurred in part because people are living longer as a result of medical technology, but also because families had more children when this generation was born than families do today. Ultimately, the rise in this section of the population is having a profound effect on the political landscape.

There are several reasons why senior citizens are becoming such a powerful group. The fact that they are now the majority age group gives them significant political power. In a democracy, the majority rule determines the policy agenda. Therefore, issues that concern senior citizens, such as health care and rights for people with disabilities, are more likely to receive the attention of politicians. If senior citizens make up the majority of a politician's constituency, it is his or her responsibility to pursue their needs in Congress. Moreover, a politician is more likely to favor the majority in order to be reelected with the help of that group. Second, senior citizens are a powerful group because they are very active. They are generally the most informed and experienced group, and therefore vote in much greater numbers than people of other age groups. Again, this gives them significant political power. Senior citizens are also more likely to join interest groups such as the AARP (American Association of Retired Persons) and to contact their representatives than other citizens are.

Their willingness to participate in politics gives senior citizens distinct advantages—they can influence priorities in the policy agenda. For example, under their watchful eye, the Social Security program continues to receive the support of Congress, thereby guaranteeing that this generation and the baby-boom generation will receive their payments even at the risk of draining the system for future generations. Health care and prescription drug policy also continue to attract the attention of policymakers. However, while the needs of this one part of the electorate are met, the concerns of others are neglected. For example, senior citizens are less likely to vote in favor of local spending on education, thus leaving parents of school-age children frustrated and unable to influence policy. Other social issues, such as welfare might also be neglected at the expense of the unemployed or of poor, single-parent families. The graying of America, while beneficial to senior citizens who might otherwise be powerless to vocalize their needs, ultimately threatens to upset the balance of policymaking in favor of a specific majority of Americans.

This essay not only fully defines the concept of "the graying of America" but also insightfully addresses both the positive and negative consequences of this trend. Moreover, the student draws connections to and defines such terms as democracy and majority rule, and includes pertinent details such as Social Security and the AARP. The student understands the scope of the issue addressed by the question and applies that knowledge to the current political landscape.

CHAPTER 7

The Mass Media and the Political Agenda

The **mass media,** including **newspapers, radio, television,** and the **Internet,** have had a profound impact on politics. In today's media-savvy world, politicians are highly visible to the public. This has both positive and negative consequences for policymakers, campaigns, and the public's trust in government.

The Development of Media Politics

Politics and the mass media go hand in hand. However, whereas once they worked together to communicate with the public, today they often oppose each other.

- **Press conferences** are a common means by which presidents convey their goals and opinions to the public. However, they are a recent phenomenon begun by Franklin Roosevelt in the 1930s. FDR was also the first president to address the electorate directly through the radio.
- Traditionally, the press favored politicians and limited coverage to conveying the facts of an event rather than interpreting them.
- The Watergate scandal and the Vietnam War changed the government's relationship with the press, as the press became more suspicious about political motives.
- Today the media engage in **investigative journalism,** often with the intent of revealing political **scandals.** This has shifted their political coverage away from straightforward reporting of the facts and has made it significantly more **negative** than it used to be.

The Print Media

- Only a few newspaper chains own all of the newspapers in the United States, as well as radio and television stations. These major corporations have significant control over information conveyed in the media.
- Newspaper readers tend to be politically informed, active citizens, but newspaper circulation has been declining since the advent of television.

The Broadcast Media

- Now most Americans, especially young people, get their information from the **broadcast media.**
- Television shifts the public's focus from a politician's achievements and political views to his or her **appearance** and performance in front of the cameras.

■ Cable television encourages **narrowcasting,** which allows viewers to select what information they do and do not want to see. Critics fear that this will lead to an even less informed electorate that can selectively avoid politics.

Reporting the News

Newscasting is a business geared toward achieving high ratings. This can have detrimental consequences for both the political agenda addressed in the news and for the political knowledge of Americans.

■ Profits largely determine what is considered news, and sensational, unusual, or negative events usually receive more attention than more positive or everyday policymaking does. This leads the public to believe that most of politics is scandalous and to distrust political leaders.

■ Journalists usually have regular **beats** such as the White House, the Senate, or the Pentagon. Most of their information comes directly from press secretaries at these institutions. This has significant advantages for politicians, who can control how much information is reported to the public.

■ News reporting, especially through the broadcast media, has very little depth of content. Information is reported in **sound bytes,** which gloss over the complexity of issues and focus the public's attention on politicians rather than on their policies. This contributes further to Americans' lack of political knowledge.

■ Sound bytes allow politicians to craft political personas without having to directly address an issue. They don't have to say much when a typical sound byte is only seven seconds long.

■ **Bias** is not apparent so much in the way news is presented, but it is a factor in determining what news is reported and what news isn't. Dramatic stories of violence or conflict are more likely to draw an audience, so they are more likely to be featured in the news.

The News, Public Opinion, and the Media's Agenda-Setting Function

■ The mass media have an enormous influence over the **public agenda.** By selecting what issues to focus on, news organizations define which are the most pressing political topics and thereby determine the political priorities of the public. By selectively assigning importance to certain issues, the media essentially tell Americans what to think about.

■ Politicians, interest groups, and protestors use the media to their advantage by staging dramatic **media events** to draw attention to themselves and their message.

■ The media have shifted attention to individual politicians and away from government as a whole. The biggest consequence of this is the increasing amount of attention paid to the president, which as a result enhances his power.

■ The media perform a watchdog function by forcing the government to be answerable to the public. However, they strongly discourage Americans from thinking critically about politics.

■ At the same time, because the news is based on ratings, its content reflects what citizens want to see and read—and they seem to express little interest in politics.

For Additional Review

Over a period of a few days, watch the news and critique it. How much attention is given to different kinds of issues? Do you detect any bias? For each news segment, think about what is not said, or which angles might be overlooked.

Multiple-Choice Questions

1. Which of the following is a significant political consequence of the trend toward investigative journalism?
   (A) The job requirements for becoming a journalist are now more stringent.
   (B) Public attention is focused more on scandal than on political issues.
   (C) Americans are better informed than they were in the decades before television.
   (D) The public now gets most of its information from television news sources.
   (E) Americans are now more likely to think critically about political issues.

2. Who is most likely to receive attention in the media?
   (A) The secretary of defense
   (B) The speaker of the House
   (C) The Senate majority leader
   (D) The president
   (E) The chief justice of the Supreme Court

3. The majority of journalists label themselves
   (A) liberal
   (B) politically apathetic
   (C) independent
   (D) conservative
   (E) radical

4. During a presidential campaign, the media focuses its attention primarily on
   (A) each candidate's position on foreign policy issues
   (B) the candidates' previous political experience
   (C) the issues most important to the electorate
   (D) the party platform of each candidate
   (E) the daily campaign activities of the two candidates

5. Which of the following statements are true about the media's agenda-setting function?
   I. Media outlets choose which stories to cover based on which ones are likely to receive high ratings.
   II. By focusing on stories that attract public attention, the media can force politicians to confront issues that they might not have otherwise addressed.
   III. The media have become less influential over the political agenda in the past few decades.
   IV. The Federal Communications Commission is primarily responsible for determining the content of the news.
   V. The government has a significant amount of influence over the political agenda presented in the media because most news is gathered from official sources.
   (A) I and II only
   (B) IV and V only
   (C) I, II, and V only
   (D) II, III, and IV only
   (E) I, IV, and V only

6. What is one foreseeable political consequence of narrowcasting?
   (A) The print media will appeal to a greater percentage of the public.
   (B) Politicians will have more freedom to act according to their own agenda, because they will be able to avoid the public eye.
   (C) Journalists will be forced to concentrate more on political issues than on politicians.
   (D) The gap between the political elite and the politically uninformed majority will increase.
   (E) The public will have less access to political information.

STORIES CITIZENS HAVE TUNED IN AND STORIES THEY HAVE TUNED OUT

The Pew Research Center for the People and the Press asked Americans how closely they have followed major news stories. The percentage in each case is the proportion who reported following the story "very closely."

The explosion of the space shuttle *Challenger*	80%
San Francisco earthquake	73%
Los Angeles riots	70%
Rescue of baby Jessica McClure from a well	69%
Crash of TWA 800	69%
Littleton, Colo., school shootings	68%
Iraq's invasion of Kuwait	66%
Hurricane Andrew	66%
Summer 2000 increases in gasoline prices	58%
Explosion during Atlanta Olympics	57%
Supreme Court decision on flag burning	51%
Opening of the Berlin Wall	50%
Arrest of O. J. Simpson	48%
Nuclear accident at Chernobyl	46%
Attack on ice skater Nancy Kerrigan	45%
Whether Elian Gonzalez should return to Cuba	39%
2000 presidential election outcome	38%
Iran-Contra hearings	33%
Impeachment trial of President Clinton in the Senate	31%
Congressional debate about NAFTA	21%
2000 New Hampshire primary	18%
Election of Ariel Sharon in Israel in 2001	9%
Debate about expanding NATO into Eastern Europe	6%

SOURCE: The Pew Research Center for the People and the Press.

7. Which of the following conclusions can you draw from this table?
   (A) Americans don't care about events that happen in other parts of the world.
   (B) People are most interested in disasters and human-interest stories.
   (C) People pay more attention to news today than they did 25 years ago.
   (D) People rely on television rather than newspapers for their news.
   (E) The influence of the news media is declining.

8. A journalist who regularly reports on predictions about the stock market would probably be on which of the following beats?
   (A) White House
   (B) Senate Appropriations Committee
   (C) Department of the Interior
   (D) Congress
   (E) Federal Reserve Board

9. All of the following have resulted from the growing profusion of sound bytes in news reporting EXCEPT
   (A) the news media have had to narrow their scope of coverage because they have only a limited amount of material to broadcast
   (B) the news media have increased their influence over the public agenda by selecting what material to feature in sound bytes
   (C) the complexity of most issues is not fully understood by the electorate, who might as a result be misled about government actions
   (D) the public tends to judge candidates by their appearance as much as, if not more than, the candidates' stand on foreign and domestic issues
   (E) politicians do not have to explain their views in much detail because most of their speeches go unreported to the public

10. If a political candidate wanted to deliver her message to the most politically informed Americans in the electorate, through which medium would he or she be most likely to reach them?
    (A) Television
    (B) Radio
    (C) Mass mailings
    (D) Newspapers
    (E) Internet

Free-Response Question

The mass media have a profound influence over what political information is conveyed to the American public. Since most people learn about politics through the news on television, their political knowledge is limited to whatever stories the media outlet chooses to report. At the same time, however, the content of the news is largely determined by ratings. The heads of media organizations contend that they are merely delivering the type of stories that Americans are most interested in. Who, then, is responsible for the decline in the quality of news reporting?

    a. Discuss TWO characteristics of news coverage today that indicate a decline in quality.

    b. Choose ONE side of this argument and defend your position.

ANSWERS AND EXPLANATIONS

Multiple-Choice Questions

▌ **1. (B) is correct.** Investigative journalism often seeks to root out political scandal. Scandals are more likely to achieve higher ratings than, say, an in-depth analysis of an issue. Scandals therefore receive more air time and, consequently, greater public attention.

▌ **2. (D) is correct.** The president is the most likely politician to be featured in the media. This is because, visually, it is easier to focus on one person than on the 535 members of Congress. As a result, presidents have been able to gain significant political power through public opinion.

▌ **3. (A) is correct.** Most journalists identify themselves as liberals. Studies show, however, that most news pieces contain little bias. Bias is not apparent in the presentation of the news, but it can play a role in defining what is considered news and what is not.

▌ **4. (E) is correct.** The media concentrate surprisingly little on important campaign issues and the ideological differences of the candidates, in part because these are difficult to show on television. It is much easier to report on campaigning activities such as public appearances and hand shaking.

▌ **5. (C) is correct.** Media outlets are businesses that need to make a profit, so they are apt to run sensational stories to attract viewers. Investigative journalism is popular because it produces such stories, but at the same time it forces politicians to confront issues by focusing the public's attention on them. Still, the government retains significant control over what is reported in the news since most journalists gather their information directly from official government sources.

▌ **6. (D) is correct.** People who choose to watch news stations like CNN and C-SPAN will have direct access to congressional proceedings and in-depth political analysis. They will gain more political knowledge than was ever available to the public before. However, the majority of Americans will choose to watch other specialized stations instead and will become even less politically knowledgeable.

■ **7. (B) is correct.** Of the 12 stories that at least 50 percent of Americans followed closely, 9 were about disasters or crises. Choice A is intended to mislead you. Americans are more interested in topics close to home, but they are not uninterested in foreign events.

■ **8. (E) is correct.** Journalists typically stick to one beat and become familiar with that policy area. A journalist covering the stock market would most likely get his or her information from the spokespeople for the Federal Reserve Board, which helps regulate the economy through the stock market.

■ **9. (A) is correct.** Sound bytes have little bearing on how much news material is broadcast by the media. The medium of television, moreover, has actually allowed media outlets to widen their scope—today TV crews can be sent everywhere from Capitol Hill to Vietnam to the Middle East.

■ **10. (D) is correct.** Studies have shown that newspaper readers possess the most political knowledge and usually are the more active members of the electorate. The print media generally analyze issues in greater depth than do the other media, which instead tend to rely on sound bytes and other visual information.

Free-Response Question

In comparison to the news reporting of Walter Cronkite's day, today's coverage is much poorer in quality. It lacks depth and focuses too much on the negative aspects of politics and world events. This is primarily the fault of the media outlets that are responsible for choosing stories and presenting them. Ultimately, the news media should be held accountable for the quality of their products.

Two characteristics account for poorer media coverage today. The advent of television has shifted the public's focus toward appearance and spectacle, and away from the content of important issues. As a result, voters are as likely to judge presidential candidates by their appearance as by their opinions. One well-known example of this is the Nixon-Kennedy presidential debate of 1960, in which Kennedy looked "presidential" in front of the cameras while Nixon came across as haggard. Viewers judged that Kennedy won the debate, but radio listeners who did not see the candidates asserted that Nixon won. Furthermore, to be televised, the news now has to be visible. This means that scandals and dramatic (often violent) events receive coverage, whereas day-to-day operations of the government do not. It is much easier to win over viewers by showing them the rescue of baby Jessica or the police chase of O. J. Simpson than to present the day's vote in Congress or an expert's analysis of the current recession. Consequently, media coverage also lacks depth. Short sound bytes don't effectively convey the complexity of issues or allow candidates to express their opinions thoroughly. In short, there is much less information in the news today. As a result, Americans are generally uninformed about politics and world events.

Because the media are a business, they tailor the news to whatever will generate the most profit. It is true that the public is more likely to tune in to dramatic events, but at the same time, if they were not afforded the opportunity by the media, they wouldn't. News organizations should set the bar higher and concentrate more on the quality of their output; then Americans would have no choice but to accept this too as their news, probably without even noticing the improvement. The role of the media is to communicate and to inform the public, but by concentrating on scandal, they actually present a misleading picture of politics. Ultimately, by presenting news that skims the surface of issues, the news media prevent Americans from becoming well informed and from making politically sound judgments, and therefore ultimately deter them from being politically aware and active citizens.

The student discusses these key items: scandals, the effects of television, sound bytes, and Americans' lack of political knowledge. Moreover, the student provides illustrative supporting information, such as the Nixon-Kennedy debate and the O. J. Simpson and baby Jessica incidents. Last, the student presents a convincing argument by clearly articulating a single point of view and backing it up with several pieces of evidence.

CHAPTER 8

Political Parties

Political parties are the main vehicles for nominating candidates and running campaigns. They serve as **linkage institutions** that help bring the concerns of the electorate to the political arena through elections. Political parties also unite groups of politicians and the electorate by offering an ideological framework with which people can choose to identify themselves. The United States has for the most part always had a **two-party system.**

The Meaning of Party

The two main political parties in the United States are the **Democratic Party** and the **Republican Party.** Democrats tend to be more liberal than Republicans, but both parties, in order to achieve a majority, usually remain fairly moderate. Political parties carry out the following tasks.

- **Choosing candidates:** Originally parties internally nominated their candidates to run in an election. Today, the public can choose candidates in primary elections.
- **Running campaigns:** Parties organize political campaigns and try to convince voters to elect their candidate. Today, by directly communicating with the public through television, candidates can operate more independently from their parties.
- **Providing a political identity:** Each party has an image. This offers the public a familiar ideology or platform with which they can choose to identify themselves and identify politicians.
- **Endorsing specific policies:** Politicians of a party often support each other, because typically they agree on a general party platform.
- **Coordinating policymaking:** Through party identification, politicians in different branches of government are able to work together or support each other.

The Party in the Electorate

- Many voters cast their ballots on the basis of **party identification.** For instance, people who consider themselves Democrats usually vote for Democratic candidates.
- Party identification is declining, however. As of 2000, the majority of voters considered themselves **Independent** rather than Democratic or Republican.
- **Ticket splitting,** or voting for members of different parties for different offices in an election, is also on the rise. This practice leads to a divided party government—the president may be of a different party from the majority party in Congress, for example.

The Party Organizations: From the Grass Roots to Washington

▌ Unlike the more formal parties of other countries, American political parties are fairly decentralized, with city, state, and national administrative bodies.

▌ Until the 1930s, local parties had tremendous influence over city governments. These often corrupt **party machines** maintained their power by using the **patronage system** to reward loyal members with important positions in the government. Today local parties have declined, while county-level organizations have increased their election activities.

▌ Holding elections is one important task performed by the states, each of which has its own unique party organization. Each state's parties go about the election process differently, such as by choosing which type of primary to hold.

　▪ **Closed primary:** Only people who have already registered with the party are allowed to vote in the primary.

　▪ **Open primary:** Voters can choose on Election Day which party's primary they would like to participate in.

　▪ **Blanket primary:** Candidates from both parties are listed on the primary ballot, so voters can choose different parties' candidates for different offices.

▌ State parties are becoming more formally organized, but most presidential campaigning is still conducted through the candidate's personal campaign organization.

▌ The national party organization, or **national committee,** writes the official party platform and holds the national convention through which a presidential and vice presidential candidate are nominated. The national committee maintains the party organization during nonelection years.

The Party in Government: Promises and Policy

▌ Parties help members of Congress form **coalitions** that support a particular policy objective.

▌ However, presidents do not need to rely on party support as much as they used to because they can gain the favor of the public directly through television.

Party Eras in American History

Most democratic nations have multiparty systems that allow many interests to be represented. The United States, however, has always had a two-party system. Political scientists divide American history into **party eras** in which one party dominated politics for a significant period of time. Party eras change when a **critical election** reveals new issues and a failure of the traditional coalitions. This usually causes **party realignment,** when the party redefines itself and attracts a new coalition of voters.

▌ The First Party System: 1796–1824

　▪ Alexander Hamilton's short-lived Federalist Party was the first political party.

　▪ **Jefferson's Democratic-Republicans** maintained control of the White House.

- The Democrats and the Whigs: 1828–1856
  - **Andrew Jackson** appealed to the masses rather than to the elite, and he formed a new coalition and, ultimately, the Democratic Party.
  - The opposition party was the **Whig Party,** though it had little political success.
- The Two Republican Eras: 1860–1928
  - The Republican Party formed out of a coalition of **antislavery** groups and nominated Lincoln as its first presidential candidate.
  - The election of 1896 began another strongly Republican era during which industrialization and capitalism were advanced.
- The **New Deal** Coalition: 1932–1964
  - Franklin Roosevelt brought the Democratic Party back into favor by starting scores of federal programs to combat the **Great Depression.**
  - The new Democratic coalition brought together the poor, southerners, African Americans, city dwellers, Catholics, and Jews.
  - Kennedy's **New Frontier** and Johnson's **Great Society** and **War on Poverty** continued the democratic New Deal tradition.
- The Era of Divided Party Government: 1968–Present
  - Johnson's poor handling of the **Vietnam War** paved the way for the election of Republican Richard Nixon.
  - Nixon was the first president to be of a different party from the majority in Congress (which has usually remained Democratic). This has since happened several times, and may continue as voters become more independent. Political scientists call this phenomenon **party dealignment.**
  - A divided government makes policymaking difficult and leads to gridlock when the president and Congress do not agree.

Third Parties: Their Impact on American Politics

Third parties occasionally arise to challenge the two major parties, but they rarely gain enough support to put a candidate in office.
  - Some parties form around a specific cause.
  - Some are splinter parties formed from smaller factions of the two major parties.
  - Some form around a specific individual.
- Though they rarely win, third-party candidates do force particular issues onto the political agenda and allow Americans to express their discontent with the two major parties.
- They may also shift the votes of the electorate. Many political scientists think George W. Bush won the 2000 election because Green Party candidate Ralph Nader took votes away from Democrat Al Gore.
- Criticisms of the two-party system:
  - There is little choice for voters because the two parties keep to the middle of the road.

- There is less opportunity for political change.
- It is so decentralized that it fails to translate campaign promises into policy because politicians do not have to vote with the party line.

For Additional Review

Look at the list of United States presidents in the appendix at the back of your book. When did the presidency change hands between parties? What significant social and economic factors might have played a role in that transition? Note also the occurrences of third-party nominees. Select one third party that is unfamiliar to you and learn more about it in an encyclopedia or other reference book.

Multiple-Choice Questions

1. The influence of political parties has been declining for all of the following reasons EXCEPT
   (A) candidates can share their views directly with the electorate through television
   (B) voters can nominate party candidates in primary elections
   (C) candidates largely fund their own campaigns or hire campaign firms
   (D) the government has failed to enforce party membership among the electorate
   (E) the electorate is becoming increasingly independent from party affiliation

2. A two-party system differs from a multiparty system in that it
   (A) encourages moderation in policymaking and discourages change
   (B) offers voters no choice among ideologies
   (C) usually includes a liberal and a conservative party
   (D) relies on popular elections to change the party in power
   (E) allows parties to choose their own leaders in the legislature

3. Which of the following statements are generally true of third parties?
   I. Having a third-party president in the White House would threaten the political standing of the United States in the eyes of other nations.
   II. Third parties expand the political agenda by forcing the candidates of the two major parties to address the issues that it introduces into a campaign.
   III. Third parties rarely gain enough support in the electorate in part because they tend to focus on narrow issues and have extreme views.
   IV. Any success that a third party achieves in an election is a measure of public discontent with the major political parties and their platforms.
   (A) I only
   (B) III only
   (C) II and III only
   (D) I and IV only
   (E) II, III, and IV only

4. Political parties play an important role in democracy because they
   (A) give voters radically different choices of policy initiatives
   (B) offer politicians a distinct political identity
   (C) connect the public with policymaking institutions
   (D) contribute to a centralized federal government
   (E) influence policy in each of the three branches of government

5. Which of the following has led to ticket-splitting in recent elections?
   (A) Party dealignment
   (B) Blanket primaries
   (C) Party realignment
   (D) Patronage system
   (E) Closed primaries

6. The process through which parties nominate their candidate for the presidency is called
   (A) a critical election
   (B) a national convention
   (C) an open primary
   (D) a closed primary
   (E) a national committee

7. Policy gridlock is most likely to occur when
   (A) a party wins a significant majority of the seats in Congress
   (B) there is a third-party candidate in the presidential election
   (C) a political party forms a coalition around a specific policy
   (D) the president is of a different party from the majority party in Congress
   (E) the same party wins the majority in both houses of Congress

8. Local party organizations have little power because
   (A) party machines no longer control large cities
   (B) they must turn most of their resources over to state organizations
   (C) most voters are not able to participate in politics at the local level
   (D) the Constitution limits the scope of their activities
   (E) campaign finance reforms have prevented them from fundraising

9. Which of the following statements accurately describe critical elections?
   I. Critical elections tend to occur only after significant political or social events.
   II. After a critical election, the minority party usually collapses and a new party forms.
   III. A critical election ensures that the majority party will maintain its position of power.
   IV. Critical elections usually signal the beginning of a new political era.
   (A) II only
   (B) IV only
   (C) I and IV only
   (D) II and III only
   (E) I, II, and IV only

10. All of the following were political consequences of the Great Depression EXCEPT
   (A) the Democratic Party forged a new coalition
   (B) the New Deal greatly expanded the scope of federal activities
   (C) it defined the Democratic Party that exists today
   (D) it began a new party era of Democratic control of the federal government
   (E) it initiated the current trend of divided government

PARTY IDENTIFICATION IN THE UNITED STATES, 1952–2000			
Year	Democrats %	Independents %	Republicans %
1952	48.6	23.3	28.1
1956	45.3	24.4	30.3
1960	46.4	23.4	30.2
1964	52.2	23.0	24.8
1968	46.0	29.5	24.5
1972	41.0	35.2	23.8
1976	40.2	36.8	23.0
1980	41.7	35.3	23.0
1984	37.7	34.8	27.6
1988	35.7	36.3	28.0
1992	35.8	38.7	25.5
1996	39.3	32.9	27.8
2000	34.8	41.0	24.2

SOURCE: 1952–2000 National Election Studies conducted by the University of Michigan, Center for Political Studies.

Using the data in the table above and your knowledge of U.S. government and politics, answer the following questions.

a. Identify ONE trend in the party identification of the electorate and give TWO reasons for the change.

b. What are TWO factors that influence a voter's party identification?

ANSWERS AND EXPLANATIONS

Multiple-Choice Questions

1. **(D) is correct.** Political parties are losing influence primarily because both candidates and voters can act more independently today. Candidates can run their own campaigns and interact directly with the electorate through television. Because voters can see and listen to candidates on television, they do not need to rely on party images or party identity to decide how to vote. However, party membership in the United States is not regulated by the government.

2. **(A) is correct.** With only two parties offering policy alternatives, there is little opportunity or incentive for political change. Each party, in order to draw in a majority of the electorate, stays toward the middle of the road and maintains the status quo. If it were to move too far left or right, or to take a risk in introducing a radically new policy, it would probably lose the support of some voters.

3. **(E) is correct.** Third parties are always at a disadvantage in campaigns because they must work harder to be visible in the media and to convey their message, which is probably unfamiliar to the public. In order to do this, they need a great deal of money, which they usually do not have at their disposal to the degree that Democrats and Republicans do. However, they bring new

issues into the political arena, and they offer an alternative to voters who are displeased with the two major parties.

▌ **4. (C) is correct.** Political parties are important to democracy because they link the American people with their government. Voters, members of Congress, and even a president of the same party all share at least a basic ideology. By electing the candidate of their preferred party, voters are able to advance their own ideology in the political arena.

▌ **5. (B) is correct.** In a blanket primary, candidates of all the parties are listed together on the ballot. Voters can choose a Democrat for one office and a Republican for another. This is called ticket splitting. In recent years, many states have adopted blanket primaries instead of other kinds of primaries in which voters can choose only from among nominees of the same party.

▌ **6. (B) is correct.** A party's national committee officially nominates its candidate for the presidency at a national convention. It is attended by party delegates from all 50 states. Today, the outcome of national conventions is known ahead of time because the delegates from each state have been elected with known presidential preferences.

▌ **7. (D) is correct.** Gridlock occurs when politicians have a difficult time agreeing on policies. A Republican president, for example, might be more inclined to veto the policy proposals of a Democratic Congress. This has become an issue in recent decades—it has more often been the case that the president is of a different party from the majority party in Congress.

▌ **8. (A) is correct.** Local parties were once incredibly powerful in large cities such as New York and Chicago, where bosses used the patronage system to reward people who supported the party. Today such activity is illegal, and local parties have declined significantly.

▌ **9. (C) is correct.** Critical elections are significant because they usher in a new majority party that is likely to stay in power for several presidential terms. Such changes tend to occur in conjunction with important events, such as the Civil War and the Great Depression.

▌ **10. (E) is correct.** The Great Depression began a new era of Democratic control over the government. The party united large groups of otherwise diverse people who were all affected by unemployment during the depression in a new Democratic coalition. The New Deal, the pet project of the popular FDR, initiated countless new federal programs to combat the Depression and kept Democrats in power for nearly 40 years.

Free-Response Question

The table clearly demonstrates the trend toward independence among the electorate. The number of voters considering themselves Independent has nearly doubled in the past fifty years. At the same time, the number of Democrats has decreased significantly while the number of Republicans has not changed much. One reason for this is that many of the new Independents either were or would have been more likely at one time to call themselves Democrats. In fact, the new Independents represent most social groups that were once a part of the Democratic coalition, such as southerners, Catholics, Jews, and people of lower income. Furthermore, according to the table, independence has been rising since 1968. This was about the time that the baby boom generation came of voting age, and statistically, young people are the most likely to identify themselves as Independents. Moreover, the voting age was lowered to 18 in the 1970s, which may have brought even more Independents into the electorate.

Another reason for the shift away from the Democratic Party toward independence is that fewer people identify themselves with parties in general today. Local parties, which once held sway over major cities, have declined in prominence, so people are less connected to the two major parties. Moreover, television now allows candidates to reach the public directly. Candidates no longer need to rely heavily on parties to carry their message and support their campaigns. At the same time, viewers who have more direct exposure to the candidates are better able to judge them without having to rely as heavily on party labels to understand the candidates' positions on important issues. Party identification, or a voter's predisposition to vote for a certain party, is therefore declining.

Party identification does still influence many voters, however. One factor is often simply the voter's parents' voting preference. Because families play a major role in political socialization, most people are inclined to hold similar political views to those of their parents, and therefore to vote accordingly. Also, as people gain political knowledge and experience through life, they are less likely to change their opinion of the political parties; once a person considers himself a Republican, for example, he is more inclined to vote for Republican candidates on the assumption that the candidate probably shares his political ideology. Interestingly though, since the United States is a two-party system, even those people who consider themselves Independents will presumably have to choose either the Democratic or the Republican candidate on Election Day and may have to rely on their party identification to do so.

This student correctly identifies one trend apparent in the table—the rise in self-proclaimed independence among the electorate—then provides two reasons for the change: 1) the shift away from the Democratic Party, especially among youths; and 2) the decline in party identification. The student also clearly defines the concept of party identification and provides two factors that influence a voter's party identification: 1) his or her family's preferences; and 2) his or her political experiences and habits.

CHAPTER 9

Nominations and Campaigns

To run for a political office, a person must first receive a party's official **nomination.** Then, with the party's endorsement and assistance, the candidate must **campaign** to win the support of voters. These two processes require a great deal of money and media exposure. Presidential campaigning has become a major part of the political process in the United States.

The Nomination Game

▌ Politicians begin their bid for a presidential nomination more than a year in advance of the election. In most other countries, campaigns are limited to only a few months.

▌ Most candidates have previously held a government post, such as representative, senator, governor, or military general.

Presidential Primaries

Each state selects delegates to send to the Democratic and the Republican **national conventions.**

▌ A few states still use traditional **caucuses** to choose delegates.

▌ Most states now use **primaries.** Voters can nominate a presidential candidate directly, or else they can choose delegates who have pledged to vote for that candidate.

▌ Each state decides how to divide its delegates' votes. Some give all votes to the candidate who won the primary, whereas others divide the votes based on some form of proportional representation.

▌ The rise of primaries has allowed the electorate to take control of the election process away from political parties.

▌ The primary system has raised numerous criticisms:
1. The early caucuses and primaries receive far too much media attention, which can distort campaigns.
    ▪ This places too much attention on the outcome of early caucuses and primaries—notably in **Iowa** and **New Hampshire,** two states that are not very representative the country as a whole.
    ▪ Candidates who do not score early victories are likely to be dismissed by the media and the public and to be unable to raise funds to continue campaigning.
    ▪ States, in order to cast influential votes, try to hold their primaries

early, before other states. This practice, called **frontloading,** has made the campaign process longer.

2. The lengthy campaign and rigors of the primary season discourage capable politicians who already hold full-time offices from running.
3. It requires and encourages an exorbitant amount of spending in campaigns.
4. Primaries are unrepresentative of the electorate because few people vote in them, and those who do are typically older and more wealthy than the majority of Americans.
5. It allows the media, which focus on winners and dismiss losers so early in the running, too much influence in shaping campaigns.

National Conventions

The delegates selected in each state's primary attend the **national convention,** where they cast their votes for their presidential candidate.

- The parties, especially the Democrats, have made efforts to **reform** delegate selection in order to ensure a more equal representation at the convention, particularly after the **1968 Democratic National Convention** in Chicago, when violence erupted both out on the streets and inside the convention center.
- Some convention seats are reserved for **superdelegates,** party leaders and politicians who automatically earn a vote at the convention.
- The outcome of conventions today is usually predetermined by previous primary results, so conventions today are **media events.**
- At a national convention
    - delegates support their candidate, but they no longer hold debates;
    - the party presents its official **party platform** for the next four years;
    - the candidate formally accepts the party's nomination;
    - the vice president is chosen, usually based on the presidential nominee's preference for a running mate.

The Campaign Game

The two presidential candidates then embark on a **national campaign** to win the votes of different socioeconomic groups in different regions of the country. Campaigns today are run fairly independently by each candidate.

- Modern campaign techniques include
    - **television advertising;**
    - televised **public appearances;**
    - **direct mail** campaigns;
    - an official **Web site** to advance the candidate's platform.
- The media closely follow campaigns. Coverage focuses on the candidates' daily activities, **campaign strategies,** and poll results.
    - Studies show that voters learn more about the candidates' positions on important issues from their advertisements than from the news.
    - Critics fear that campaigns have become centered around candidates' images rather than their political beliefs.
- In order to coordinate a campaign, a candidate must hire a campaign team

that serves both to organize his or her daily activities and to conduct **public relations.** This adds significantly to the enormous cost of a campaign.

Money and Campaigning

Candidates rely on television to communicate directly with the electorate, and air time often translates into votes. Therefore, the necessity of television has made American campaigns extremely expensive.

▌ Politicians spend as much time fund-raising as doing their jobs.

▌ In 1974, Congress passed the **Federal Election Campaign Act** to control campaign costs and donations.

  ▪ Established the **Federal Election Commission** to enforce campaign laws

  ▪ Initiated public financing of elections—taxpayers can choose to donate $3 to a federal campaign fund that is divided among all candidates by checking a box on their income tax form

  ▪ Set a limit for spending in each election by those who accept public funds

  ▪ Required candidates to **report all campaign contributions and how the money was spent**

  ▪ Individual campaign contributions were limited to $1,000.

▌ **Soft money** is one loophole through which businesses and wealthy individuals can make unlimited contributions.

  ▪ Soft money is intended for a party's general use and is therefore not a donation to a specific candidate, but it can be channeled into presidential campaigns. The **McCain-Feingold Bill** proposes to limit soft money, as contributors are often rewarded by the candidate once he or she is in office. Although it has passed in Congress, it faces free speech challenges in the courts.

▌ **Political action committees (PACs)** are another method, established by the 1974 act, through which interest groups try to influence policy through campaign contributions.

  ▪ To contribute to a campaign, an interest group must channel money through a PAC, which must be registered with the FEC so that it can be monitored.

  ▪ There is **no limit** to the amount PACs can spend.

  ▪ PACs can act independently of the candidate and his or her campaign team, such as by running an advertisement without the candidate's approval

  ▪ Candidates rely on PACs to help finance costly campaigns, and PACs allow business interests to assert themselves in the political arena.

  ▪ PACs play a greater role in congressional elections than in presidential elections, which are partially funded by the public.

  ▪ Created to provide unions and other groups the opportunity to contribute, PACs have been organized and used by businesses to affect elections.

▌ Despite the massive amount of money spent on campaigns and the media's constant focus on them, campaigns rarely convert voters away from their predisposed party identification.

For Additional Review

Some critics say that in the United States, the campaign never stops. Look on the Web for presidential hopefuls. Also read about the financial statistics of the 2000 election at www.fec.gov. This information could be very helpful on a free-response question on the AP U.S. Government & Politics Exam.

Multiple-Choice Questions

1. The Federal Election Campaign Act established all of the following EXCEPT
   (A) a fund for public donations to presidential campaigns
   (B) rules for the disclosure of all campaign financing and spending information
   (C) a limit of $1,000 for personal contributions to congressional candidates
   (D) restrictions on the amount of soft money a party can receive for campaigning
   (E) the Federal Election Commission to regulate campaign financing

THE BIG-SPENDING PACS		
	Amount Contributed	Percentage Given to Republicans
Business		
Microsoft	$3,942,435	53
Goldman Sachs Group	3,546,432	32
AT&T	3,510,391	62
National Association of Retailers	3,298,100	58
Association of Trial Lawyers	2,951,500	12
United Parcel Service	2,919,584	74
Philip Morris	2,830,985	80
Labor		
American Federation of State/ County/Municipal Employees	6,500,889	1
Service Employees International Union	4,724,664	4
Communication Workers of America	3,687,614	1
International Brotherhood of Electrical Workers	3,369,840	3
United Food and Commercial Workers Union	3,242,057	1
Ideological/Single-Issue		
National Rifle Association	2,884,127	92
Emily's List	1,979,829	0

SOURCE: Center for Responsive Politics.

2. Which of the following conclusions may be drawn from the data in the table above?
   (A) Labor groups overwhelmingly contributed to Democratic or Independent campaigns.
   (B) Single-issue groups divided their contributions equally between the two parties.
   (C) Overall, Republicans received more campaign donations than Democrats did.
   (D) The National Rifle Association made the biggest donation to the Republican Party.
   (E) All of the business groups listed supported Republicans, whereas all of the labor groups listed supported Democrats.

3. The news media influence the outcome of a presidential election by
   (A) focusing more on the campaign competition than on campaign issues
   (B) making rushed judgments about the contest early in the primaries
   (C) endorsing the political views of one candidate in particular
   (D) devoting too much coverage to the candidates' public appearances
   (E) allotting more air time to one candidate than another

4. All of the following are criticisms raised against the primary system EXCEPT
   (A) this process of selecting delegates is unfair because it prevents equal representation of minority groups at the national conventions
   (B) too much weight is placed on the early primaries, especially because states like Iowa are not representative of the American electorate
   (C) it has extended the length of the campaign process to an impractical and unmanageable degree
   (D) it prevents many qualified politicians from running, because fund-raising for and participating in primaries distracts them from their current office
   (E) it allows the media too much power in shaping presidential campaigns

5. Which of the following is true concerning the use of PACs in political campaigns?
   (A) The Constitution requires businesses to finance campaigns.
   (B) Businesses can channel only a limited amount of funds through a PAC.
   (C) The president officially established them in a 1974 executive order.
   (D) PACs must be registered with and monitored by the FEC.
   (E) The Supreme Court found campaign finance reform laws unconstitutional.

6. In addition to officially nominating a party's candidate for the presidency, national conventions perform which of the following tasks?
   (A) Select new party leaders
   (B) Present fund-raising strategies
   (C) Announce the party's platform
   (D) Elect delegates to the next convention
   (E) Organize new party coalitions in Congress

7. Primary elections are not very representative of the electorate's preferences because
   (A) they occur in only a few states
   (B) voters in primary elections are usually less politically knowledgeable than the majority
   (C) only college graduates are allowed to vote in them
   (D) they take place early, before voters have a chance to learn about the candidates
   (E) voters in primary elections are usually older and more affluent than the majority

8. Which of the following factors contributes most to the cost of a presidential campaign?
   (A) Direct mail campaigns
   (B) Television advertising
   (C) Hiring a campaign coordinator
   (D) Soliciting donations via the Internet
   (E) Printing posters and campaign paraphernalia

9. Presidential campaigns in the United States differ most from campaigns in other countries in which of the following ways?
(A) American campaigns cost candidates less in personal contributions.
(B) Candidates in other countries are not allowed to appear on television.
(C) Campaigns in the United States are geared toward a general election.
(D) American campaigns are much longer than other campaigns.
(E) Candidates in the United States are officially endorsed by political parties.

10. All of the following are techniques employed in a modern campaign EXCEPT
(A) direct mail
(B) Web sites
(C) television advertising
(D) public appearances
(E) newspaper articles

Free-Response Question

The United States holds some of the longest and most expensive political campaigns in the world. In order to finance their campaigns, candidates rely heavily on contributions from businesses and wealthy individuals. Does the current campaign system interfere with the practice of democracy in America? Defend your position.

ANSWERS AND EXPLANATIONS

Multiple-Choice Questions

▌ **1. (C) is correct.** There are currently no restrictions to soft money donations. This is one of the major concerns of proponents of campaign reform. In the 2000 election, both parties acquired about $200 million in soft money. Critics argue that, in return for soft money contributions, politicians are likely to serve in the interests of those businesses once they are in office.

▌ **2. (A) is correct.** The only conclusion that may be drawn strictly from the information given is that the labor groups listed did contribute significantly to non-Republican candidates. This is confirmed by the fact that only a small percentage of their large donations went to Republicans. The rest must have gone to other candidates.

▌ **3. (B) is correct.** The media play a major role in political campaigns. However, critics argue that they go beyond reporting and intrude upon the election process when they make early judgments about the primary races. By playing up a contender's losses in one or two states, they unfairly brand that person an unlikely winner. As a result, that person has a more difficult time raising money and succeeding in other primaries.

▌ **4. (A) is correct.** On the contrary, the Democratic Party has taken significant measures to ensure that delegates to the convention are representative of all groups in the party coalition. The Republican Party was forced to comply with the new requirements as well and also allows for greater representation among delegates.

■ **5. (D) is correct.** In order for a business to make contributions through a PAC, it must register the PAC with the Federal Election Commission. The PAC then must report on all of its activities and spending so that the FEC can closely monitor it to ensure that it is not making illegal contributions directly to candidates.

■ **6. (C) is correct.** National committees meet and write the party's official platform for the next four years. The platform is then presented at the national convention, on the day before the party officially nominates its presidential and vice presidential candidates.

■ **7. (E) is correct.** Voter turnout at primary elections is significantly lower than voter turnout for the general election. Moreover, those who do vote in primary elections are usually older and wealthier than the majority of Americans. This can distort the results of primary elections in many states.

■ **8. (B) is correct.** Television time is enormously expensive, but it is also crucial to a campaign. Candidates rely on television as the medium through which they can reach the greatest number of people. Because the news media actually focus very little on the candidates' platforms, the only way for candidates to convey their political beliefs to the public is through paid advertising that airs frequently throughout the long campaign.

■ **9. (D) is correct.** The United States often receives criticism for its long campaign season. In most European countries, for example, campaigns last only a few months. As a result, European campaigns are also less expensive than American campaigns.

■ **10. (E) is correct.** Only a relatively small percentage of the electorate reads newspapers, so this is not the best way for candidates to reach the public. Television, though expensive, is the best tool at their disposal. Direct mail is also effective because it allows candidates to target people with certain characteristics or interests, and the Web is both inexpensive and useful because it is interactive—people can even make campaign donations through the candidate's Web site.

Free-Response Question

Today's political campaigns are long, drawn-out media extravaganzas that cost millions of dollars. In order to reach voters, candidates must spend large sums of money on television advertising, travel, and a professional campaign staff. The difficulties of financing such an event and the ways these difficulties are overcome ultimately infringe on the practice of democracy.

In order to run for office, a candidate must have hundreds of thousands of dollars at his or her disposal. This money is necessary to buy a candidate exposure—it allows the candidate to convey his or her political beliefs to the public through television and even just to maintain a constant presence in the minds of the public. The more money you can spend, the more visible you will be, and ultimately the more successful you'll be in the race. Any candidates who cannot afford to spend such large sums on campaigning are instantly at a disadvantage. Some qualified people interested in running are not able to due to the impossibility of acquiring such funds. In a true democracy, anyone with political knowledge and experience should be able to run for office. However, very few Americans can, thus putting wealthy people and incumbents at a distinct advantage. Furthermore, third-party candidates who represent the middle and lower classes or who have innovative new ideas are not able to spread their message and compete against wealthier politicians. The cost of campaigns therefore limits political participation and discourages the introduction of innovative policies from different sectors of the electorate.

Expensive campaigns also act as a deterrent to democracy because they often allow businesses to gain a foothold in the political arena. Candidates are able to finance their campaigns only with the help of soft money and PACs. Soft money is all the donations to a party for its general use, most of which goes indirectly to campaigning, and PACs are funding vehicles established by businesses to channel money into campaigns. Candidates, then, receive a great deal of campaign support indirectly from businesses, to which they are somewhat beholden when they reach office. Campaigns therefore allow business interests to play a role in the election process. Rather than being elected by the will of the people and taking office with their needs in mind, politicians shape the political agenda around the needs of those businesses which helped them get to Capitol Hill.

By enacting campaign finance reforms that limit soft money and PAC donations, campaigns might become more democratic. Moreover, if all candidates were guaranteed the same amount of money with which to run their campaigns, and free, equal air time, as is done in many other countries, all people who wanted to run for office would have a fair chance, and businesses would not be able to influence politics so easily.

This essay presents a concise argument with clear, supporting details. The student argues that campaigns impede democracy because 1) they prevent many people from running and lesser-known candidates from promoting their messages; and 2) they are funded largely by businesses that expect their interests, rather than those of the people, to be addressed in politics. The student also defines key terms such as soft money *and* PACs. *Overall, he or she demonstrates a good understanding of how campaigns are run and judged that situation against the traditional theory of democracy.*

CHAPTER 10

Elections and Voting Behavior

Elections are the process through which power in government changes hands. Such a change is possible because elections bestow **legitimacy** both on the process and the incoming officials, who have been chosen to lead by the majority of the people. According to the theory of democracy, elections give voters a voice in policymaking because they allow people to choose the candidate who is most likely to act in their interests or according to their political beliefs. For this to work in practice, however, candidates must represent distinct stands on the issues.

Whether to Vote: A Citizen's First Choice

Suffrage has been expanded several times throughout American history. Although the Constitution left the issue up to the states, generally only white, male property owners had the right to vote. Today, **all Americans over the age of 21** can vote in elections.

- The **Fifteenth Amendment** granted suffrage to African Americans.
- The **Nineteenth Amendment** extended voting privileges to women.
- The **Twenty-sixth Amendment** set the minimum voting age at 18.

Although more people are able to vote, fewer people are exercising this right. Only 51 percent of eligible voters cast ballots in the 2000 election. Some of their reasons for not voting:

- They believe that one vote in more than 100 million makes little difference.
- They are unable to take off work to vote on a Tuesday. Reformers have suggested moving Election Day to a Saturday.
- **Voter registration** is difficult or inconvenient in most states. Procedures have been made easier, especially with the **Motor Voter Act,** but turnout has still decreased.
- There is little ideological difference between the two parties' candidates.

Some reasons people are more likely to vote:

- They perceive a significant ideological difference between the two parties' candidates.
- They have a sense of **political efficacy**—if they believe their vote will make a difference.
- They want to perform their **civic duty** in a democracy.

Who Votes?

- People with a college education
- Older people, especially senior citizens
- Hispanic Americans and African Americans are less likely to vote, but those with higher levels of education vote in greater percentages than educated Caucasians.
- More women than men have voted in recent elections.
- Union members
- People who are married

  Politicians who rely on these voters to be elected are more likely to address their concerns in the policy arena.
- Studies show that if turnout increased among groups with low rates, Democrats would probably receive more votes.
- Reforms are unlikely because Republicans do not want to lose this advantage

How Americans Vote: Explaining Citizens' Decisions

1. People vote according to their **party identification.**
   - A candidate of their chosen party probably shares their political beliefs.
   - They do not have to decide on or become informed about every issue.
   - This trend is declining as parties have lost some significance in the political process.
2. Voters evaluate what they know and see of the **candidates' personalities** to make a decision.
   - A candidate's appearance may play an unconscious role in voter decision making.
   - People tend to value integrity, competence, and reliability in a candidate.
   - Voters with a college education are more likely to base their decision on a candidate's personality. They make inferences about the candidate's performance.
3. People vote for candidates who share their **policy preferences.**
   - Voters must have firm policy convictions.
   - They must be familiar with each candidate's policy preferences.
   - They must be able to discern differences among candidates' stands on issues.
   - A person may also **vote retrospectively** by choosing a candidate who vows to continue policies helpful to him or her, or by choosing the opposition candidate who promises to change the policy.
   - Candidates may avoid taking a clear stand on a controversial issue, **making policy** voting difficult.
   - This method requires a lot of effort on the part of voters.

The Last Battle: The Electoral College

In the United States, the president is not chosen directly by the people in a popular election. The **Electoral College** casts the final vote. This institution was created by the writers of the Constitution to keep the presidency at a distance from the masses. It was intended to allow only the elite to choose the president.

- Each state's number of electors is equal to its total number of representatives and senators. Electors are chosen by the state party organizations.
- Almost all states are **winner take all:** The candidate who receives the highest popular vote in the state gets all of that state's electoral votes.
- Electors convene in December and mail their votes to the president of the Senate (the vice president), who officially announces the majority winner at the opening of the congressional session in January.
- If no candidate receives a majority of electoral votes, the members of the House of Representatives vote.

This system has received an enormous amount of criticism.

- It gives an unfair advantage to states with larger populations. Because they have a greater number of electoral votes at stake, large states and their policy concerns receive more attention from presidential candidates.
- A candidate may need to win in only a few large states to win the election. This neglects the less populous states.
- Because most large states also have large cities, the system is biased in favor of urban voters.
- It is possible to win the popular vote but lose the election because of the electoral votes. This happened to Al Gore, who won the popular vote in 2000.

For Additional Review

The 2000 presidential election was an extraordinary political event for many reasons. Not only was it one of the few elections in American history in which a candidate won the popular vote but lost the electoral vote, it was also the first presidency to be determined ultimately by the Supreme Court. Read more about the controversies of this election at www.supremecourtus.gov/florida.html
http://www.c-span.org/campaign2000/Florida/ussupcourt.asp

Multiple-Choice Questions

1. The electoral votes of most states are allocated by which of the following methods?
   (A) Each party's candidate receives electoral votes based on his or her percentage of the state's popular vote.
   (B) Each elector chooses the candidate whom he or she feels is best suited to represent the needs of the state.
   (C) The winner of the popular election in the state receives 75 percent of the state's electoral votes and the loser receives 25 percent.
   (D) All of the state's electors cast their votes for whichever candidate won the state's popular vote.
   (E) The loser in the popular election receives one electoral vote and the winner receives the rest of the state's electoral votes.

2. Which of the following groups usually has the highest voter turnout in a presidential election?
   (A) Women
   (B) People aged 25–44
   (C) Members of minority groups
   (D) Union members
   (E) Adults with a college education

3. All of the following conditions should be met in order for a person to vote according to his or her policy preferences EXCEPT
   (A) the person must be familiar with each candidate's political beliefs
   (B) the person must have developed a pattern of policy voting over several elections
   (C) the person must be politically knowledgeable and have decided his or her own position on political issues
   (D) the person must decide which policies he or she would like to see continue or change
   (E) the person must be able to determine political differences among the candidates in order to make an informed decision

4. Suffrage has been granted to many groups in the United States in which of the following ways?
   (A) By amendments to the Constitution
   (B) By rulings of the Supreme Court
   (C) By presidential executive orders
   (D) By a majority vote in the Senate
   (E) By a two-thirds vote in the House

Questions 5 and 6 refer to the map below.

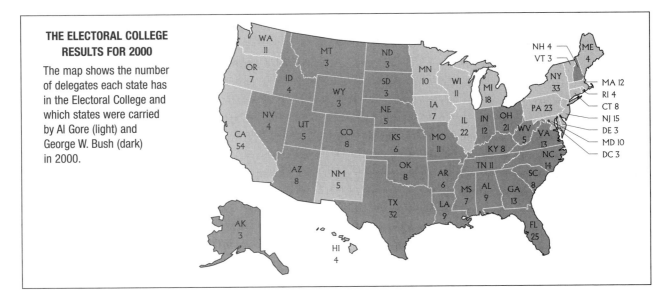

THE ELECTORAL COLLEGE RESULTS FOR 2000

The map shows the number of delegates each state has in the Electoral College and which states were carried by Al Gore (light) and George W. Bush (dark) in 2000.

5. In the 2000 election, Texas had among the lowest statewide voter turnout in the country, at 43 percent. Based on this information and the information in the map above, which of the following conclusions may be drawn?
   (A) People in the Midwestern states had an unfair advantage over people in Texas because states in the Midwest had higher voter turnout rates than Texas did.
   (B) If there had been a higher turnout in Texas, the state's electoral votes would have gone to the Democratic candidate.
   (C) The votes of those people who did vote in Texas were unfairly weighted in comparison to the votes in smaller states where voter turnout was high.
   (D) Texas would have received more electoral votes if its voter turnout had been higher.
   (E) The electoral votes in Texas were given to the Republican candidate because he received 43 percent of the popular vote.

6. All of the following statements about the information in the map above are accurate EXCEPT
   (A) states on the West Coast and in the Northeast are more liberal than states in the Midwest
   (B) most Republican states had fewer electoral votes
   (C) California, Texas, and New York are the states with the highest populations
   (D) many states have more than twice the number of electoral votes of other states
   (E) landlocked states have an unfair electoral advantage over coastal states

7. About what percentage of the electorate voted in the last few presidential campaigns?
   (A) 20 percent
   (B) 35 percent
   (C) 50 percent
   (D) 65 percent
   (E) 80 percent

8. One of the most important personal characteristics on which voters base their decision is a presidential candidate's
(A) competence
(B) age
(C) charisma
(D) appearance
(E) oratory skills

9. The Motor Voter Act was intended to
(A) expand suffrage to minorities
(B) lower the voting age
(C) redistribute states' electoral votes
(D) increase voter registration
(E) raise the voting age

10. Candidates hinder voters from making their decision most by
(A) appearing in more than one presidential debate
(B) being ambiguous about their positions on important issues
(C) focusing their attention more on some states than others
(D) failing to draw attention to their previous political experience
(E) introducing new policy issues into the campaign

Free-Response Question

PATTERNS IN VOTING BEHAVIOR: 2000			
	Gore	Bush	Nader
Protestant	47	50	2
Catholic	48	49	2
Jewish	90	10	0
White	44	53	3
African American	89	8	2
Hispanic	57	34	9
Male	44	51	4
Female	54	42	3
18–34	50	43	6
35–64	49	48	2
65+	52	46	1
Lowest income third	63	34	2
Middle income third	48	47	4
Upper income third	46	50	4
Union	58	36	6
Not union member	48	48	3

SOURCE: 2000 National Election Survey.

NOTE: The survey slightly overrepresents Gore voters, giving him a margin in the national popular vote of 3.7%, as compared to the actual margin of 0.5%.

The table above shows how different groups in the United States voted in the 2000 election. The percentages are determined by the number of people in each group who voted, *not* the total number of people in that group. Select ONE of the presidential candidates.

a. Using your knowledge of American politics, discuss the voting behavior of different groups in relation to the candidate you selected.

b. Describe what impact the behavior of different groups had on the outcome of the election.

Multiple-Choice Questions

▌ **1. (D) is correct.** It has become an unwritten practice that states award their electoral votes in a "winner-take-all" system. Whichever candidate wins the popular vote in the state receives all of that state's electoral votes. One criticism of the electoral system is that this gives larger states an unfair advantage because they have more electors than smaller states.

▌ **2. (E) is correct.** Americans with a college education are the most likely group to vote in a presidential election. This is true across other groups; for example, minorities with a college degree are also more likely to vote than those without.

▌ **3. (B) is correct.** While many people who vote according to policy preferences probably have developed certain voting habits over the course of several elections, this is not necessarily a requirement for choosing candidates in this manner. Well-informed young people could also vote according to those policies on which they agree with a particular candidate.

▌ **4. (A) is correct.** The Constitution clearly delineates election procedures and voting requirements. Therefore, it was necessary to amend the Constitution in order to change voting rights. Minority groups and women have obtained the right to vote through the Fifteenth and Nineteenth amendments respectively.

▌ **5. (C) is correct.** Because Texas has a large population, it is one of the states with the most electoral votes. However, less than half of the population voted, so the votes of those Texans who did counted more in the whole election. A smaller state with high voter turnout might have had about the same number of popular votes as Texas, but the small state may have had only 6 to 10 electoral votes, while Texas had 32.

▌ **6. (E) is correct.** In fact, the opposite is true—coastal states have an advantage because they usually have higher populations than landlocked states. This gives the coastal states more electoral votes, which may seem fair, but as a result, candidates might make more promises to help coastal states in order to win their electoral votes.

▌ **7. (C) is correct.** Only about half of Americans voted in the 2000 election. This number generally has been declining since the 1960s. Even expanded suffrage and easier voter registration procedures have not encouraged more people to vote. In fact, the United States has a much lower turnout rate than many other countries worldwide.

▌ **8. (A) is correct.** Voters value what they judge to be a candidate's competence. This includes the candidate's political experience and past successes. If the candidate has succeeded previously in introducing or passing policies, he or she is likely to do so again. Voters see this as proof of the candidate's abilities as a politician.

▌ **9. (D) is correct.** The Motor Voter Act allows people to register to vote when they get or renew a driver's license. This increases voter registration by making it easier for people to register. However, while more people have registered, voter turnout has not been significantly affected by the Motor Voter Act.

10. (B) is correct. In order for voters to make an informed decision, they must be able to distinguish the platforms of the candidates. If a candidate fails to take a clear stand on an important issue, voters cannot gauge his or her intentions once in office and might be less likely to choose that candidate.

Free-Response Question

The election of 2000 was one of the few cases in American history in which the winner of the popular vote lost the election because of the distribution of electoral votes. Not only did Al Gore receive more votes from Americans than Bush did, but, as the table indicates, the votes Gore won were also representative of more social and economic groups in the United States.

Gore won the majority in a greater number of groups than Bush, who as president therefore represents fewer groups of Americans. An overwhelming number of Jewish people, African Americans, and people of low income voted for Gore. As has become typical of Democratic candidates, he also won the majority of union members and women. In many ways these voting patterns are not unusual for Democrats. The gender gap, for example, predicts that women are more likely to vote for the Democratic candidate. What is more surprising, perhaps, is that Gore was preferred by people in all age groups. In contrast, the majorities that Bush did win among groups of the electorate were by a much slimmer margin than most of the majorities won by Gore. Ultimately, if Gore had won the election, he would have more effectively represented the diverse body of Americans with a greater degree of legitimacy.

However, Gore was faced with two major disadvantages. Although the table shows that he was preferred by more groups of Americans, it does not indicate voter turnout among these groups. For example, Gore was selected by an impressive 89% of African American voters, but only about half of all African Americans actually voted. Overall this does not add up to as many votes as it might appear in the table. Similarly, Bush won the group of upper income voters by only 4%, but this group votes in much higher numbers than people of lower income. Bush therefore probably received a significant number of votes from this group. Second, Gore may have lost liberal voters to Ralph Nader, who ran as the Green Party's candidate. Nader attracted the votes of people who are more educated and politically knowledgeable, and of young voters, who are the most likely group to vote for an Independent candidate. Had these people voted for Gore, they might have closed the very small margin in Florida so that he would have won its electoral votes and, therefore, the presidency.

This essay clearly and correctly enunciates the information in the table as it relates to one of the presidential candidates. The student gives many specific examples, both from the table and from his or her knowledge of politics, displaying a good understanding of the voting behavior of Americans. The student also earns points for touching on such key concepts as the gender gap and the electoral system.

CHAPTER 11

Interest Groups

One of the most pronounced political trends in the last few decades is the rise of **interest groups.** Today there are more than 20,000 of these private organizations in Washington and in state capitals. Interest groups represent bodies of people with shared interests and lobby legislators on their behalf. In this sense, they are a natural part of a democracy. However, Americans tend to view them with skepticism because, most often, the language of influence is money.

The Role and Reputation of Interest Groups

▌ Interest groups may pursue any kind of policy, in all levels and branches of government. They differ from political parties in several ways.

  ▪ They pursue their agenda through the **political process,** whereas parties advance their agendas through elections.
  ▪ Interest groups specialize in one or two policy areas, whereas parties focus on only general policies in order to win a majority.
  ▪ Many people criticize interest groups for encouraging a policymaking system based on money.
  ▪ Interest groups donate heavily to campaigns through PACs to "buy" votes.
  ▪ The more money an interest group has, the more it is able to influence policy.
  ▪ Proponents of interest groups argue that they are effective **linkage institutions.**
  ▪ They represent the interests of the public in the policy arena.
  ▪ Because they are carefully monitored and regulated, the methods of interest groups are much more honest than those employed by people and groups in the past.

Theories of Interest Group Politics

1. **Pluralist theory:** Interest groups are important to democracy because they allow people to organize themselves in order to change policies.

▌ Because hundreds of interest groups must compete for influence, no one group will dominate the others.

▌ Groups put up a fair fight; they do not engage in illegal activities to surpass other groups.

▌ Groups are equal in power because they have different resources at their disposal.

2. **Elite theory:** There may be hundreds of interest groups, but only a select few have any real power.

- The interests of only a handful of elites, usually businesspeople, are almost always favored over other interests.
- The policy battles that smaller interests do win are usually minor.
- Power rests mostly with large multinational corporations.
- The system of elite control is maintained by a well-established structure of interlocking policy players.

3. Hyperpluralist theory or **interest group liberalism**
- **Subgovernments,** or **iron triangles,** form around specific policy areas.
- These are composed of an **interest group,** a **federal agency,** and any **legislative committees or subcommittees** that handle the policy area.
- By avoiding having to choose between policy initiatives, the government creates conflicting policies that waste time and money.
- Groups have too much political influence because they usually get what they want.
- Competing subgovernments only add to the confusion.

What Makes an Interest Group Successful?

1. The **size** of the group
- **Smaller groups** are more effective than large groups.
- Smaller groups can organize more easily.
- A member of a small group is more likely to experience the group's success and, therefore, is more likely to work harder than a member of a large group.
2. The **intensity** of the group members' feelings about the issue
- **Single-issue groups** form around a specific policy and tend to pursue it uncompromisingly.
    - Single-issue groups often deal with moral issues that people feel strongly about.
    - Members of single-issue groups often vote according to a candidate's stand on the group's issue.
3. The **financial resources** at the group's disposal
- Politicians are most likely to serve the needs of people or groups with money.
- Money allows groups to mobilize, conduct research, and maintain an administration.

How Groups Try to Shape Policy

Lobbying: Professional lobbyists attempt to persuade lawmakers to act on behalf of their group. The more helpful a lobbyist is, the more power he or she has with a politician. Lobbyists
- serve as policy experts in their interest area
- act as consultants who advise legislators on how to approach policy issues and debates
- mobilize support for politicians during reelection
- suggest innovative policy ideas

Electioneering: Interest groups endorse a candidate who supports their interests and work to get that candidate elected. The groups

- encourage people to vote for the candidate
- help finance the candidate's campaign through **PACs**
  - Congressional candidates have become largely dependent on PAC money.
  - Most PAC money goes to **incumbents** rather than challengers.

Litigation: Interest groups use lawsuits to change policies that have already gone through the legislative process.

- Any member of the public is allowed to sue the government.
- Even the threat of a lawsuit may be enough to influence policymaking.
- Groups can file *amicus curiae* **briefs** to state their side in a court case and to assess the consequences of the decisions the court might make.
- Groups can also file **class action lawsuits,** which allow them to file suit on behalf of a larger group in the electorate.

Mobilizing public opinion: Interest groups try to influence the public because they know that politicians' careers depend on public opinion.

- Groups cultivate a positive image of themselves in the eyes of the public.
- Groups encourage public participation to advance interests from the point of view of the constituency.

Types of Interest Groups

Economic interests: business, labor, farmers

- against regulations and tax increases
- want tax advantages, subsidies, and contracts for work
- Labor is the second largest organized group under the **AFL-CIO** after senior citizens under the **AARP.**
- Business interests are the most widely represented interests in Washington.

Environmental interests: the fastest-growing type of interest group

- favor wilderness protection, pollution control, energy alternatives
- oppose policies that damage the environment

Equality interests: civil rights, women, social welfare

- Concerns center around fair treatment in jobs, housing, and education.

Consumers' interests and **public interests:** the whole public benefits from certain policy actions

- product safety, which was introduced by Ralph Nader
- groups that cannot assert their interests themselves: children, the mentally ill, animals
- fair and open government; government reform

For Additional Review

Make a table of several interest groups that have made the headlines recently. First define the interests of each one. Then evaluate them in terms of size, intensity, and financial resources. Was each group successful in influencing policy?

Multiple-Choice Questions

1. Elite theorists believe that the power of interest groups
   (A) is derived from their equal access to the government
   (B) comes mostly from public support
   (C) is evenly distributed among them
   (D) reinforces a more democratic government
   (E) is held by only a few wealthy groups

2. Smaller interest groups often meet with more success because
   (A) they have highly developed methods of fund-raising
   (B) their members are more active
   (C) they make large campaign contributions
   (D) they have more resources with which to mobilize the public
   (E) they pursue only less-politicized issues

3. Citizens concerned about a proposal to redistribute federal funding to public schools would form which of the following groups?
   (A) Public interest group
   (B) PAC
   (C) Consumer interest group
   (D) Single-issue group
   (E) Class action group

4. Lawmakers often rely on lobbyists for all of the following reasons EXCEPT
   (A) to come up with new policy ideas that they can introduce in Congress
   (B) for advice on strategies to advance or prevent a piece of legislation
   (C) for money that would allow them to travel to their constituencies
   (D) to encourage group members to vote for them during reelection
   (E) for expertise on a certain issue

5. Iron triangles are composed of
   (A) a cabinet department, a legislative committee, and a federal judge
   (B) a corporate board, an interest group, and the speaker of the House
   (C) a PAC, an interest group, and a congressional candidate
   (D) an interest group, a legislative committee and a federal agency
   (E) a local civic group, a state legislator, and a federal department

6. Proponents of the pluralist theory argue that for the most part power is evenly distributed among interest groups because
   (A) the public participates equally in different types of interest groups
   (B) all interest groups receive the same amount of federal funds
   (C) each policy area is assigned a limited number of related interest groups
   (D) interest groups each get the same attention from politicians
   (E) competition prevents any one group from becoming more influential

7. Which of the following statements accurately describe methods interest groups employ to influence policymaking?

    I. Class action lawsuits allow interest groups to sue in the name of a larger section of the public.

    II. Interest groups meet with judges about cases that affect their policy area.

    III. Interest groups make almost all of their PAC contributions to incumbents rather than challengers.

    IV. Lobbyists use their policy expertise to make themselves indispensable to politicians.

    V. Interest groups pay committee members to review proposed legislation from a legislative point of view.

(A) III only
(B) I and IV only
(C) II and V only
(D) I, III, and IV only
(E) II, IV, and V only

8. Which of the following interest groups has become the most influential in recent years?

(A) NRA
(B) AARP
(C) AFL-CIO
(D) AFSCME
(E) HIAA

9. Interest groups differ from political parties in which of the following ways?

(A) Interest groups link the public to the political process.
(B) Interest groups pursue general policy goals in the political arena.
(C) Interest groups try to shape specific policy goals primarily through legislation.
(D) Interest groups are not allowed to play any part in political campaigns.
(E) Interest groups unite politicians with the same political ideology.

10. Which of the following causes would most likely be taken up by a single-issue group?

(A) Abortion
(B) Corporate taxation
(C) International trade
(D) Workers' compensation
(E) Campaign finance reform

Free-Response Question

Choose ONE interest group from the following list.

- National Association for the Advancement of Colored People (NAACP)
- Health Insurance Association of America (HIAA)
- National Rifle Association (NRA)
- National Education Association (NEA)

For the group you selected, answer BOTH of the following questions.

    a. Which government institution or institutions would this group appeal to in order to pursue its policy interests?

    b. What is one resource that the group has at its disposal and how does it use it to influence policy?

Multiple-Choice Questions

▌ **1. (E) is correct.** Elite theorists believe that power, influence, and access are not distributed evenly among interest groups. Only those with money to promote themselves and to contribute to campaigns have any significant influence on policymaking. Half of all PAC contributions, for example, come from the wealthiest 3 percent of PACs.

▌ **2. (B) is correct.** Members of a small interest group are more likely to feel the benefits of membership if the group is successful. They therefore are likely to participate more actively in order to maintain the group's success. In contrast, the success of a large group is divided among many more people and might be less apparent to them.

▌ **3. (A) is correct.** Public education is an issue that affects all Americans. An interest group that focuses on this area of policymaking would therefore be a public interest group. Any successes achieved by the group would benefit the public as a whole.

▌ **4. (C) is correct.** Lobbyists are forbidden by law from contributing any money directly to lawmakers for any reason. They must establish a PAC in order to make campaign contributions, and this money, in theory, can be used only for general party purposes; it cannot go to a specific candidate. All interest group donations, moreover, are closely monitored by the Federal Election Commission.

▌ **5. (D) is correct.** An iron triangle, or subgovernment, is composed of an interest group, the federal agency, and the legislative committee, which all handle a specific policy. They work closely together to create policies. Hyperpluralists argue that iron triangles give interest groups too much access to the government.

▌ **6. (E) is correct.** Pluralists believe that interest groups have about the same amount of power because they must compete with each other for influence. If, for example, one group increases its efforts to reach politicians, other groups will quickly follow suit to catch up and will therefore balance out the system again.

▌ **7. (D) is correct.** Interest groups frequently file class action lawsuits in an attempt to reverse policy decisions. They also solidify their relationships with members of Congress by channeling most of their campaign contributions to incumbents. Interest groups also know that policymakers are more easily influenced if they must rely on a lobbyist for information and advice about a policy.

▌ **8. (B) is correct.** The AARP has the largest membership of any interest group and is extremely active in politics, especially in matters of health care policy. This indicates that senior citizens are becoming an influential group among the electorate.

▌ **9. (C) is correct.** Interest groups concentrate most of their efforts on shaping policy during the political process. They maintain frequent contact with lawmakers while Congress is in session. Political parties, on the other hand, try to shape the policy agenda by having their candidates elected to office. They therefore apply their efforts mostly to campaigns.

10. (A) is correct. Members of single-issue groups usually feel incredibly strongly about the issue that concerns them. Such issues often appeal to their emotions. Abortion is one such issue about which some voters feel strongly.

Free-Response Question

The National Association for the Advancement of Colored People has been an influential interest group since the early twentieth century, when it formed to fight for the rights of African Americans. It has become a powerful and prestigious interest group.

This group works with the Department of Justice to make sure civil rights are enforced, but otherwise it pursues its interests primarily in the legislative arena. It is most likely to win the attention and cooperation of members of Congress whose constituencies include a high percentage of African Americans. It would also be most likely to concentrate its efforts on a few key committees in the House and Senate that handle urban housing, education, and labor policy. For example, the NAACP might lobby members of the Senate Labor and Human Resources Committee about the minimum wage or the House Education and the Workforce Committee about after-school programs in low-income school districts. With the help of the NAACP, in fact, Congress passed the Civil Rights Act of 1964, the Voting Rights Act of 1965, and the Fair Housing Act of 1968. These legislative victories also demonstrate the success of the NAACP in pursuing its interests and representing a major group of Americans.

The most powerful resource of the NAACP is the body of people whom it represents, African Americans. They are one of the largest minority groups in the United States and, when organized under the NAACP, have had significant political successes. However, only about half of all African Americans vote. To encourage African Americans to exercise this right and thus wield their power, the NAACP has initiated voter registration and education efforts. If voter turnout were higher among this portion of the electorate, more African Americans might be elected to influential governmental positions to work directly for the group. They would also gain political clout because politicians, in order to win their votes, would have to pay attention to their concerns. An interest group is, in part, as powerful as its members are vocal.

This is an in-depth discussion of the NAACP. The student identifies specific targets of the interest group and cites some of its policies' victories as a result of its interaction with congressional committees and the Justice Department. The student also clearly identifies one of the NAACP's most important resources—the group of people it represents. Furthermore, the student explains in detail why this group is not reaching its full potential and how it could be more powerful if more African Americans voted. This essay quickly and clearly links each paragraph to the question. The reader will have no difficulty identifying parts of the question in the response.

CHAPTER 12

Congress

The federal government is divided into a number of institutions, each with its own political role and responsibilities. The legislative branch is composed of both houses of Congress and the legislative committees, the executive branch comprises the president and the federal bureaucracy, and the system of courts makes up the judicial branch. At least one-third of the questions on the AP U.S. Government and Politics Exam will address the duties of each institution and how it functions to carry out those duties.

The Representatives and Senators

Congress is composed of 435 representatives and 100 senators, for a total of 535 members.

- **Average age:** representatives—54, senators—60
- **Occupation:** Most are lawyers or businesspeople.
- **Party:** Both houses are about evenly split between Democrats and Republicans, with one or two Independents in each.
- **Race:** The members of both houses are largely Caucasian. The House has some diversity, but the Senate is almost exclusively white.
- **Gender:** The ratio of men to women in the House is about 6 to 1; in the Senate it is about 7 to 1.
- **Committee work:** Most members serve on at least five committees and subcommittees; senators usually serve on more committees than representatives do.

Congressional Elections

Congressional elections are held every two years in November. The most important factor that determines which candidate wins an election is incumbency. **Incumbents** already hold office and are running for reelection, and they win reelection more than 90 percent of the time. Senatorial races are usually intense because incumbents, who tend to have **higher profiles,** are more likely to be held accountable for public policy successes or failures. Their challengers are also more likely to be known already in the political arena, because senatorial races often draw former representatives or governors. Still, incumbents usually win, though by a narrower margin. In fact, turnover in Congress usually occurs only when members retire. Some other factors also influence who wins an election.

The Advantages of Incumbents

▌ **Advertising:** Advertising makes a candidate visible to many constituents. The number of votes a candidate receives is fairly proportional to his or her air time on television and the frequency of his or her public appearances. Advertising requires a great deal of campaign funds, particularly for senators, which explains in part why Congress is composed mostly of wealthy men.

▌ **Credit claiming:** Incumbents have the benefit of being able to present their **congressional record** to their constituents in order to demonstrate their hard work in service of the district or state. They may have helped specific people or groups sidestep bureaucratic red tape, or they have helped with federal programs and institutions. From this record of service to the constituency, incumbents can build a more clearly defined **public image,** whereas challengers new to politics are less likely to be able to convey their position on issues to the public.

▌ **Position taking:** Incumbents' public image is strengthened because they have already taken a stand on issues relevant to their constituency. At election time, this can work in their favor to identify them in the minds of the public.

▌ **Party identification:** Voters for the most part cast their ballots along **party lines.** Thus, a predominantly Democratic district, for example, is most likely to elect and then reelect a Democratic candidate.

Money in Congressional Elections

Most congressional campaign funds come from individual contributions, but about one-third come from **political action committees,** which are special financial bodies set up by interest groups to channel contributions into elections. PACs usually support incumbents or candidates most likely to win because they are hoping to gain influence in Congress. Money spent is almost always proportional to votes received. A challenger must spend a great deal of money to be seen and heard over an incumbent, and in races for open seats, the highest spender usually wins.

How Congress Is Organized to Make Policy: American Bicameralism

The House

A state's **population** determines how many representatives it has. A state is divided into **congressional districts,** each with an equal population. Every ten years, district lines must be redrawn according to the population data supplied by the national **census.** States therefore can lose or gain a seat in the House, but total membership remains at 435. Other characteristics of the House:

▌ Members tend to vote along party lines.

▌ Power is usually hierarchical.

▌ Special responsibilities include introducing revenue bills and articles of impeachment.

The Senate

▌ Power is more evenly distributed among senators.

▌ Senators act more independently of their parties.

- Special responsibilities include approving presidential nominations, ratifying treaties, and the trial of impeached federal officials.
- Senators can **filibuster.** This power of unlimited debate means that they can talk so long that they delay or even prevent voting on a piece of legislation.
- Senators can stop a filibuster by voting for **cloture,** which halts debate. This rarely happens because it requires 60 votes.

Congressional Leadership

- The leader of the House is the **speaker of the House,** who is chosen by the majority party. The speaker presides over each session and is largely responsible for assigning representatives to committees or party positions.
- The vice president of the United States is **president** of the Senate. This role is more formal than active, however. Most authority rests with party leaders in the Senate.
- The **majority leader** in both the House and the Senate is usually the most active or seasoned member of the majority party. The majority leader manages the schedule of debate and rallies party votes for party legislation or against proposals of the minority party.
- The **minority leader** rallies the support of the minority party around legislation and acts as its spokesperson.
- **Party whip**s assist party leaders in generating support for party legislation.

The Committees and Subcommittees

Committees are the nuts and bolts of Congress. They are responsible for researching, assessing, and revising the thousands of bills that are introduced by members of Congress each year. They also conduct **legislative oversight,** which is the monitoring of federal agencies and their execution of the law. Oversight usually takes the form of investigation—often committees **hold hearings** to question agency officials about the activities of their departments. As the federal bureaucracy has grown over the last few decades, so has the process of legislative oversight.

There are four basic types of committees.

1. **Standing committees** handle a **specific policy area,** such as agriculture, finance, energy, and commerce. Both the House and Senate have standing committees. Each committee is often divided into **subcommittees.**
2. **Joint committees** are responsible for legislation that **overlaps policy areas.** They are composed of both senators and representatives.
3. **Select committees** are appointed to handle a **specific issue,** such as an investigation or impeachment trial.
4. **Conference committees** iron out the differences between the House and Senate version of a bill. They also consist of members of both houses.

The Congressional Process

Policymaking is a slow and laborious process, and often a final bill has changed significantly from the original. The authors of the Constitution intentionally devised a complicated legislative system, however, as a means to prevent hasty decisions and to encourage compromise in policymaking. The diagram below shows how proposed legislation usually follows a path through Congress.

1. A single member of Congress or a small group in either the House or Senate formally introduces a bill.

↓

2. The bill goes to a subcommittee of the appropriate standing committee.

↓

3. The subcommittee conducts research and holds hearings on the proposal and rewrites it as necessary.

↓

4. The approved bill then moves to the standing committee, which assesses the legislation in a formal report, rewrites the bill as necessary, and ultimately decides whether to pass it on for debate or to kill it.

↓

5. The bill is introduced for debate on the floor of the chamber. Committee members usually serve as authorities on the proposal to whom their colleagues turn, and they often rally support for it. Amendments may be added to the bill.

↓

6. If passed by both houses, the bill goes to the president for final approval as law. If different versions are passed in each house, the two bills go to a conference committee that resolves the differences between them. Then both houses vote on the final version of the bill and it is sent to the president.

Some important committees to know:
- The **House Rules Committee** reviews all bills submitted by committees before they go to the House floor, assigns them a slot on the calendar, **allocates time for debate,** and even **decides whether the bill may be amended** or not. This committee is unique to the House and has a significant degree of power.
- The **House Ways and Means Committee** writes **tax codes,** which are subject to the approval of both houses.
- The **Senate Finance Committee** works in conjunction with the House Ways and Means Committee to write **tax codes.**
- The **Appropriations Committee in each house** decides how government money will be **apportioned** to federal agencies.

Party, Constituency, and Ideology

- Members of Congress do not always vote with their party. Partisanship tends to be strongest on economic and welfare issues. On other issues, members of Congress may act more independently, especially in order to fulfill the needs of their constituents. Thus, although whips actively attempt to garner support for certain legislation, they are not necessarily successful.

▌ When representatives or senators do act independently, what influences their vote? If the issue is of significance to their constituency, or is likely to be highly publicized, members of Congress tend to vote as the constituency would want them to. On the many other issues about which the public is less informed, congressmen and -women are more likely to vote according to their own personal ideology.

Lobbyists and Interest Groups

With lobbyists dominating Washington, how effective is Congress in representing the people? You should be familiar with both sides of this debate.

Congress Represents the Interests of the Electorate	Congress Serves the Interest Groups, Not the Public
▪ Interest groups are organized by groups of "the people" to make their views known so that policymakers will act on their behalf.	▪ Critics argue that those interest groups with enough money to buy influence dominate the policy agenda and distract policymakers from the needs of the public.
▪ As pluralists contend, the competition among groups for the support of members of Congress ensures that compromise will play a part in policymaking.	▪ So many competing interests prevent the formation of cohesive policy. In fact, different committees may handle the same policy issue in drastically different ways.
▪ The issues on which Congress focuses are as diverse as the interests pushing them to the forefront, thereby decentralizing the political agenda and power in each house.	▪ Ultimately the government wastes a significant amount of money by attempting to appease so many interests.

For Additional Review

As you read your textbook, keep a list of all the committees you come across. Jot down what kind of committee each is and what its role or policy specialty is. Not only will this information help prepare you for Section I of the AP U.S. Government & Politics Exam, but also it may contain good examples for use in your free-response answers.

Multiple-Choice Questions

1. The task of joint committees in Congress is to
   (A) register bills to be introduced to the floor and schedule debate
   (B) handle proposed legislation that deals with more than one area of policy
   (C) merge each house's version of a bill into a single bill
   (D) combine members of both the House and Senate to consider overlapping policy areas
   (E) educate the public about the activities of Congress

2. Incumbents have all of the following advantages over their challengers EXCEPT
   (A) incumbents receive more campaign donations than challengers
   (B) challengers' positions on most issues are not likely to be known by the public
   (C) incumbents have well-established relationships with their constituencies
   (D) incumbents have higher visibility than challengers
   (E) challengers have a clean political record, and incumbents do not

3. In which of the following ways does Congress conduct legislative oversight?
   I. Appoints select committees to investigate the actions of the bureaucracy
   II. Controls the spending of federal agencies
   III. Holds hearings to question agency officials
   IV. Issues inspections of government offices
   V. Passes laws to limit the powers of the bureaucracy
   (A) I and III only
   (B) II and IV only
   (C) III and V only
   (D) I, II, and IV only
   (E) I, III, and V only

4. Which of the following statements accurately describe legislative committees?
   I. Committees are in session only when preparing bills to be introduced onto the floor.
   II. Committee recommendations largely influence members' votes on a piece of legislation.
   III. Junior members of Congress have few opportunities to sit on committees.
   IV. The speaker of the House has a great deal of influence in appointing members to committee chairmanships.
   V. Conference committees are composed of senators whose task is to amend bills that are in danger of being killed in Congress.
   (A) I and III only
   (B) II and IV only
   (C) III and V only
   (D) I, II, and IV only
   (E) I, III, and V only

POLITICAL PARTY AFFILIATIONS IN CONGRESS AND THE PRESIDENCY, 1953–2001						
		House		Senate		
Year	Congress	Majority party	Principal minority party	Majority party	Principal minority party	President
1953–1955	83rd	R-221	D-211	R-48	D-47	R (Eisenhower)
1955–1957	84th	D-232	R-203	D-48	R-47	R (Eisenhower)
1957–1959	85th	D-233	R-200	D-49	R-47	R (Eisenhower)
1959–1961	86th	D-283	R-153	D-64	R-34	R (Eisenhower)
1961–1963	87th	D-263	R-174	D-65	R-35	D (Kennedy)
1963–1965	88th	D-258	R-177	D-67	R-33	D (Kennedy)
						D (L. Johnson)
1965–1967	89th	D-295	R-140	D-68	R-32	D (L. Johnson)
1967–1969	90th	D-247	R-187	D-64	R-36	D (L. Johnson)
1969–1971	91st	D-243	R-192	D-57	R-43	R (Nixon)
1971–1973	92nd	D-254	R-180	D-54	R-44	R (Nixon)
1973–1975	93rd	D-239	R-192	D-56	R-42	R (Nixon)
						R (Ford)
1975–1977	94th	D-291	R-144	D-60	R-37	R (Ford)
1977–1979	95th	D-292	R-143	D-61	R-38	D (Carter)
1979–1981	96th	D-276	R-157	D-58	R-41	D (Carter)
1981–1983	97th	D-243	R-192	R-53	D-46	R (Reagan)
1983–1985	98th	D-269	R-165	R-54	D-46	R (Reagan)
1985–1987	99th	D-252	R-182	R-53	D-47	R (Reagan)
1987–1989	100th	D-258	R-177	D-55	R-45	R (Reagan)
1989–1991	101st	D-259	R-174	D-55	R-45	R (Bush)
1991–1993	102nd	D-267	R-167	D-56	R-44	R (Bush)
1993–1995	103rd	D-258	R-176	D-57	R-43	D (Clinton)
1995–1997	104th	R-230	D-204	R-53	D-47	D (Clinton)
1997–1999	105th	R-227	D-207	R-55	D-45	D (Clinton)
1999–2001	106th	R-222	D-211	R-55	D-45	D (Clinton)

SOURCES: U.S. Bureau of the Census, *Historical Statistics of the United States, Colonial Times to 1970* (Washington, D.C.: Governement Printing Office, 1975); U.S. Congress, Joint Committee on Printing, *Official Congressional Directory* (Washington, D.C.: Government Printing Office, 1967–); CQ Weekly, selected issues.

Note: Figures are for the beginning of the first session of each Congress.

5. Which of the following conclusions may be drawn based on the data in the table above?
   (A) The party of the president does not necessarily determine the majority party in either house of Congress.
   (B) Since the 1950s, the Republican Party has usually been the majority party in the House of Representatives.
   (C) In the Senate, the majority party almost always outnumbers the minority party by two to one.
   (D) Voters typically do not reelect presidents who do not work well with the majority party in Congress.
   (E) Most representatives in the House would probably support presidential proposals.

6. A senator can effectively prevent the Senate from voting by
   (A) conducting oversight
   (B) filibustering
   (C) introducing another bill
   (D) holding hearings
   (E) no known process, because the rules are very structured

7. Membership in the House is determined by which of the following methods?
   (A) States are divided into congressional districts of equal population, with one representative per district.
   (B) Electors from each state cast their vote based on the popular vote.
   (C) Political parties elect their representatives internally.
   (D) The public elects two representatives from each state.
   (E) Seats are divided among regions of the United States, each with the same number of representatives.

8. On a major piece of health care legislation, members of Congress are most likely to vote
   (A) along party lines
   (B) according to their personal ideology
   (C) in a presidential coalition
   (D) in keeping with the needs of their constituency
   (E) according to the pressures of lobbyists

9. After a House committee reviews a bill and writes its report, the bill goes to the
   (A) Senate
   (B) appropriate subcommittee
   (C) president
   (D) floor for debate
   (E) House Rules Committee

10. Senators are often unwilling to vote for cloture on a debate because
   (A) their constituents would disapprove
   (B) the bill under discussion would most likely be killed
   (C) they want support when they filibuster
   (D) they would be less likely to be appointed to an influential committee seat
   (E) the president would probably veto the bill

Free-Response Question

The committee system in Congress distributes the responsibility of assessing proposed legislation to smaller groups of congressmen and women, allowing them to specialize in fewer policy areas. This system, however, is composed of dozens of committees and subcommittees in both houses, each attempting to generate new policies from the perspective of their different policy areas. Does the committee system do more harm than good, or does it contribute to effective policymaking? Cite THREE advantages or disadvantages of the committee system in your argument.

ANSWERS AND EXPLANATIONS

Multiple-Choice Questions

❚ 1. **(D) is correct.** Joint committees composed of House and Senate members deal with issues that overlap both houses, such as budgets or special investigations. By starting with a joint committee, each house begins with common information, provided by the joint committee.

❚ 2. **(E) is correct.** Remember to trust your common sense. Challengers, just because they are new to the potential governmental position, do not necessarily have a clean record. Many challengers have held other posts, and ones who have not would have no record at all. Furthermore, incumbents, just because they have already served in Congress, do not necessarily have a poor record. In fact, it is to their advantage to demonstrate to the public their record of service to the constituency.

▌ **3. (C) is correct.** Standing committees conduct legislative oversight primarily by holding hearings in which they question bureaucrats. Each committee conducts oversight of the federal departments that fall within its policy area. The budgets of these departments are controlled by Congress, so agency heads must account for their yearly spending. They also must report on the actions their departments have taken to enact or enforce laws that Congress has passed.

▌ **4. (B) is correct.** Evaluate each of the given statements as you would the answer choices. Look at statement II. Members of Congress do pay a lot of attention to a committee's recommendation. The committee formulates its recommendation after a thorough examination of the proposal and an extensive assessment of its impact. Moreover, congresspeople are busy with the work of their own committees and may not have had time to be briefed on the piece of legislation before a vote is called. Statement IV is also true. The speaker has a great deal of influence in the House, guiding the party leaders in assigning positions on House committees.

▌ **5. (A) is correct.** Look at the figures for each of the majority parties. In both houses, the majority party has usually been the Democrats. However, presidents actually have been Republican more often than they have been Democratic during the time period shown in the table. Therefore, the majority party does not necessarily have any bearing on which party's presidential candidate will be elected. Remember to consider only those answer choices that address the given data. Eliminate answer choices that go beyond the scope of the chart or graph that is shown.

▌ **6. (B) is correct.** In the Senate, there is no limit to debate over a piece of legislation. A senator who has the floor is free to talk for as long as he wishes. He or she may attempt to stall by talking a bill to death. This tactic, called a filibuster, prevents senators from calling for a vote. It also causes senators to lose interest and adjourn without voting. This was a popular strategy of southern senators who held out against civil rights legislation.

▌ **7. (A) is correct.** The number of seats a state receives in the House depends on its population. Congressional district lines are drawn to divide the state's population equally, and each district elects one representative. Every ten years, seats in the House are reapportioned according to shifts in the population as reported by the national census. California, for example, recently gained seven seats because its population had grown, whereas New York lost seats because its population had decreased.

▌ **8. (D) is correct.** This is one of the harder questions that you might find on the AP exam. A number of different factors may influence a representative's vote. A major piece of welfare legislation is likely to be a highly publicized issue. With reelection in mind, congresspeople would *most likely* vote as their constituency would want them to. Moreover, healthcare is a key issue among the elderly, who make up a large part of the electorate.

▌ **9. (E) is correct.** After a bill has been reviewed by a committee in the House, it is ready to be debated on the floor of the House. However, the bill must first be submitted to the House Rules Committee, which registers the bill, assigns it a limited time for debate, and sometimes decides whether the bill can be amended during discussion. This gives the House Rules Committee a significant degree of influence over proposed legislation.

▌ **10. (C) is correct.** Senators are unlikely to vote for cloture, which brings a filibuster to a halt, because they want to be able to filibuster too. A senator who moves for cloture is more likely to have it called on him or her when filibustering, so most senators back down. This makes the filibuster an especially strategic maneuver.

Free-Response Question

Here is a list of advantages and disadvantages that you might have brainstormed for use in your response.

Advantages

- The burden of research and in-depth analysis is evenly distributed among senators and representatives.
- No representative could possibly be an expert in all policy areas.
- Committees weed out bills that would ultimately not succeed, thereby saving Congress time and energy.
- A committee can also use its specialization to conduct oversight of the corresponding agencies and departments.
- Serving on committees makes members of Congress better policy-makers by giving them a chance to learn more about policy areas and how policies will actually affect the people.

Disadvantages

- Time and money are wasted by so much bureaucracy.
- Different committees might be generating conflicting policies.
- Competition for committee positions could lead to an unequal distribution of power among members of Congress and could create a hierarchy within each house.
- The desire to control committees leads to partisanship rather than consensus between members of different parties.
- Committees keep congresspeople so busy that they don't have time to think about policies beyond their scope, and ultimately have to vote according to the opinions of other members.

The congressional committee system contributes to a more effective and efficient method of policymaking. Each year Congress must review thousands of bills in many different policy areas. Committees assess each proposal so that the whole of Congress is not burdened with this daunting task. While the number of committees in operation does contribute to a more sprawling legislative branch, their role in honing policy ultimately makes them more helpful than problematic.

Each committee conducts important research and analysis to determine if a proposal is feasible. Committees are able to concentrate their resources on a single piece of legislation more effectively than the whole of Congress could. In doing so, they are able to kill bills that ultimately would not succeed, thereby saving Congress the time and energy of debating an ultimately weak or impractical proposal.

Committee reports and recommendations are also helpful because they provide information on which senators and representatives can base their opinion of the legislation. Most members of Congress do not have the time or resources to be experts in all areas of policy. Committees conduct the basic research on a bill for them, also saving time and energy. Moreover, by serving on a committee, each member of Congress is able to specialize in a few policy areas. This makes them more effective policymakers in those areas and distributes the responsibilities of policymaking equally among all representatives.

Because committees specialize in a specific policy area, they are better equipped to conduct legislative oversight of those agencies and departments that are responsible for enacting pertinent legislation. For example, the Senate Labor and Human Resources Committee would be best equipped to conduct oversight of the Labor Department. It would have more information about labor policy at its disposal, and it would have already assessed the labor legislation that became the laws that the Labor Department enacts and enforces.

Ultimately, the federal government conserves its resources by dividing the many tasks involved in policymaking among committees. In fact, committees perform a significant part of the legislative process before bills even reach the floor. Without them, Congress would have a difficult time fashioning strong, useful policies that best fulfill the needs of the public.

This essay thoroughly explains three advantages to the committee system. The student displays a good understanding of the legislative process and the role that committees play, and provides a useful example by mentioning the Senate Labor and Human Resources Committee. The student also demonstrates an understanding of the conditions under which representatives work to make policy. The student presents a well-structured essay, clearly stating his or her position in an introduction, devoting a paragraph to each of advantage or disadvantage, and introducing each one with a clear topic sentence. Finally, the student sums up his or her argument in the last paragraph.

CHAPTER 13

The Presidency

While many representatives and senators are content with a long, successful congressional career, many others harbor intentions of running for president. The presidency as a government institution has changed dramatically since the writing of the Constitution. At that time, the president had few powers and, because he was chosen directly by the **Electoral College** without a popular vote, was far removed from the populace. Today the president is elected by the people—via electors—after a long and expensive campaign. Presidential powers have increased in the last few decades as, thanks to television, the president has become a more public figure. Questions on the AP U.S. Government & Politics Exam will test your knowledge of the powers of the president and the relationship between the president and other governmental institutions.

The Presidents: How They Got There

- **Presidents** can reach the oval office in different ways:
  - Many are former congressmen or governors who have been nominated by their party, campaign, and win the election. Others served as vice presidents who took over on the death of the president.
  - **Vice presidents** also assume the role when the president is impeached or has resigned.
- The Constitution sets forth the process of **impeachment** of a president who has abused his powers or committed a "high crime or misdemeanor" worthy of removal from office.
  1. The House may vote for the impeachment of the president by a simple majority.
  2. The Senate tries the president, and the chief justice of the Supreme Court presides over the trial.
  3. A two-thirds vote in the Senate removes the president from office.
- Only two presidents have been impeached, though neither was removed from office.
  - Andrew Johnson was tried but not convicted in 1868.
  - William Clinton was acquitted by the Senate in 1999.

Presidential Powers

The Constitution grants the president fairly limited powers that were designed to prevent him or her from gaining too much authority and thus to maintain the balance of power among government institutions. A partial list of the president's powers appears below.

- Veto proposed bills
- Report to Congress in the State of the Union address
- Nominate government officials and federal judges
- Grant pardons for certain offenses
- Act as commander in chief of armed forces
- Make treaties
- Serve as diplomatic representative for the United States
- Oversee the departments and agencies that make up the executive branch

This last power is one of the more overlooked responsibilities of the president. As the bureaucracy has grown, it has become nearly impossible for the president to execute and enforce all laws. Instead, the president now appoints numerous administrative officials, including cabinet members, and department heads.

Running the Government

- **Vice presidents** traditionally have few responsibilities and little political prominence.
    - They are second in line to assume the presidency if anything happens to the president.
    - They act as the president of the Senate and cast a vote whenever there is a tie.
    - Today, vice presidents assume more responsibilities, depending on how the president they are serving entrusts functions to them. They may serve as diplomats representing the president, take part in important policy meetings, or help raise funds for their party.
- The **cabinet** is a group of officials who act as advisers to the president. The cabinet is not mentioned in the Constitution, but it quickly became an institution that has accompanied every presidency. The modern cabinet is composed of the attorney general and the heads, or secretaries, of the thirteen executive departments. The president has the power to appoint all of these officials, but each appointment must be confirmed by Congress.
- Each cabinet member heads a **department** that deals with a different policy area. The departments, created by Congress, carry out all the administrative work necessary to enforce laws or assist the president in his executive duties.

The Executive Office

This is another collection of administrative and advisory bodies which assist the president in overseeing policy.

- The **National Security Council** coordinates matters of national security across agencies.
- The **Council of Economic Advisors** advises the president on economic issues.
- The **Office of Management and Budget** reviews the budgetary implications of federal programs and legislation.

Presidential Leadership of Congress: The Politics of Shared Powers

Presidents do not have legislative powers, but they have ways of pursuing their own policy agendas.

1. **Acting as chief legislator:** Presidents usually have the last word in the legislative process.

   - The power to veto legislation can be an effective tool of intimidation. Because a veto rejects a bill in its entirety, the president can have a good deal of influence over the shaping of each specific provision. If the president does veto a bill, it goes back to Congress, which, by a two-thirds vote, can override the veto. However, this rarely happens.
   - The president also has the power to reject any legislation submitted at the end of the congressional session without the possibility of his veto being overruled. If he does not sign a bill submitted by Congress within ten days of its adjourning, the bill is automatically rejected. This is a **pocket veto.**

2. **Relying on party support:** In order to influence policy, presidents must work closely with Congress. Specifically, they rely on party ties. Political parties help bridge the gap between the legislative and executive branches.

   - A president and a representative of the same party were most likely elected by the same body of people, or by voters who have similar political views, so they probably share political priorities.
   - Congresspeople who support the president are likely to receive support in return, such as the approval of their legislation. A close relationship with a popular president also sits well with the public during reelection.
   - The president must rely on members of Congress to introduce legislation for him and to win support for it during the legislative process. He therefore must work closely with party leaders to convince representatives to vote with the party line. Even if his party is the majority party in either house, he may not necessarily have the full support of representatives, who often do not vote along the party line.

3. **Public support:** Public support for the president factors heavily in his congressional support. Representatives are much more likely to vote in favor of the initiatives of a president who is popular with the electorate, and presidents are well aware that public opinion is an incredibly powerful tool of persuasion.

   - Public approval gives a president more leeway in pursuing policy goals, because representatives are more likely to support his objectives in the hope of being reelected by an electorate that has confidence in him. Public support lends a president a greater degree of legitimacy.
   - The policies of a president who is perceived as weak are more likely to be cast into doubt by Congress, making it harder for the president to garner legislative support.

   Congress is more likely to respond to the will of a president who was elected by a large margin, especially on legislation proposed early in his term.

4. Legislative skills: Presidents may also exert their influence over the political agenda by employing specific strategies at key times in the legislative process.

- To strengthen a presidential coalition, presidents often bargain with representatives by offering support on one piece of legislation in exchange for receiving it on another. Congresspeople may also receive certain presidential favors, such as joint public appearances during campaigns.
- Presidents present many proposals to Congress soon after their election during what is called the "honeymoon period," when there is a fresh sense of community in Washington.
- Presidents work hard to focus the attention of Congress on their own specific agendas. By setting priorities, they are able to concentrate their resources to push through a few key policy objectives.

The President and National Security Policy

The president is both the commander in chief of the armed forces and the head of American diplomacy. The diplomatic powers of the president include the following.

- Establishing formal recognition of other governments or terminating it
- Negotiating treaties
- Formulating **executive agreements** with other foreign leaders, which, unlike treaties, do not require congressional approval; most executive agreements are administrative in nature
- Using U.S. influence to arbitrate conflicts between other nations

Military powers include the following.

- The decision to use weapons of mass destruction
- Authorizing military actions during war
- Sending troops into specific areas of conflict

The **War Powers Resolution,** passed in 1973, intended to limit this power by requiring that these troops be withdrawn within 60 days unless Congress declares war or issues an extension.

Power from the People: The Public Presidency

Because presidents know that public approval works enormously in their favor, they work hard to sell their agenda to the public. A voter's approval of the president is determined by several factors.

- Whether the voter identifies with the political party of the president
- How the president responds to economic shifts or handles other current issues
- How effective a public speaker the president is, and his appearance in front of the cameras
- Whether the president appeals to the public directly, in which case the public usually responds positively
- How the media interpret the actions of the president

The efforts of the White House to influence public opinion are not always successful, however. The public tends to be fickle in its approval, and the media often mislead the public by oversimplifying political and economic issues.

For Additional Review

As you read the chapters in your textbook about the president and presidential campaigns, keep a list of notable events or issues surrounding particular presidents to look over before the exam. The more details you have on hand during the free-response section, the higher your score will be.

Multiple-Choice Questions

1. A bill that is vetoed by the president
   (A) goes to a conference committee for revision
   (B) must be rewritten by the representative who authored it
   (C) will never become law
   (D) goes to a federal court for approval of the veto
   (E) can become law if Congress overrides the veto

2. Which of the following statements accurately describe a step in the process of removing a president from office?
   I. The accused president is tried by the Senate.
   II. The chief justice of the Supreme Court decides if the president is guilty of the crime with which he is charged.
   III. The House of Representatives votes to impeach the president.
   IV. A two-thirds vote in the Senate removes the president from office.
   V. A conference committee holds hearings to consider public opinion of the president's performance.
   (A) I and II only
   (B) I and IV only
   (C) I, III, and IV only
   (D) II, III, and V only
   (E) III, IV, and V only

3. The War Powers Resolution checks the president's power by
   (A) prohibiting him from issuing executive agreements that engage the country in war
   (B) increasing the power of Congress to control the military budget
   (C) preventing him from sending troops into crisis situation without congressional approval
   (D) mandating that Congress approve the president's decision to use weapons of mass destruction
   (E) requiring troops to be withdrawn in 60 days unless Congress declares war or issues an extension

4. Presidents attempt to influence policymaking in all of the following ways EXCEPT by
   (A) appealing directly to the public for support
   (B) proposing legislation in congressional committees
   (C) offering favors such as backing during reelection
   (D) exchanging support for policies with representatives
   (E) building coalitions among party members

5. A presidential candidate is most likely to choose a vice presidential running mate who
   (A) has charisma and an appearance that will appeal to the public
   (B) has made substantial campaign contributions
   (C) will be able to preside impartially over the Senate
   (D) will attract voters from a part of the electorate that is otherwise not as likely to favor the president
   (E) has highly specialized diplomatic skills with which to advise the president in foreign relations

6. Which of the following factors is the greatest influence on a citizen's approval of the president?
   (A) His or her political party affiliation
   (B) The president's success in working with Congress
   (C) His or her state of residence
   (D) The president's public image
   (E) His or her understanding of the Constitution

7. The presidency has become a more powerful institution for all of the following reasons EXCEPT
   (A) the United States has become more active in foreign affairs
   (B) the bureaucracy has expanded as the government has taken on more regulatory responsibilities
   (C) new technology requires a more immediate response to crises than Congress can offer
   (D) the Supreme Court has increasingly interpreted the Constitution in favor of the president
   (E) the advent of television has made the presidency more public

8. Which of the following statements about the presidential veto is true?
   (A) Presidents rarely veto legislation.
   (B) Congress rarely overrides a veto.
   (C) The pocket veto has proved to be an effective tool of intimidation.
   (D) Presidents can use a line-item veto to reject only part of a bill.
   (E) Presidents are more likely to veto legislation at the beginning of their first term.

9. All of the following are powers of the president EXCEPT
   (A) conducting diplomatic relations
   (B) granting pardons
   (C) dismissing Supreme Court justices
   (D) negotiating treaties
   (E) appointing administrative officials

10. As set forth in the Constitution, the order of presidential succession is the vice president, then the
    (A) speaker of the House
    (B) secretary of state
    (C) Senate majority leader
    (D) attorney general
    (E) chief justice of the Supreme Court

Free-Response Question

The Constitution makes several provisions for the case of war. However, modern technology has radically changed the way the government goes about engaging in war. The president, who serves as commander in chief, now has instant decisions to make, affording him the opportunity to bypass Congress. How do the new conditions of war affect the system of checks and balances between the executive and legislative branches? Address each of the following points in your response.

- What are the military powers of the legislative and executive branches?
- How have these powers changed as a result of modern technology?
- Discuss one example of a president's use of expanded power to act independently in a crisis.

ANSWERS AND EXPLANATIONS

Multiple-Choice Questions

■ 1. **(E) is correct.** While a presidential veto usually effectively kills proposed legislation, Congress can override the veto and has done so in about in about 4 percent of the vetoes. The Constitution gives the president the power to veto as a means to check Congress, and it gives Congress the power to override a veto as a means of checking the president.

■ 2. **(C) is correct.** As sanctioned by the Constitution, the process of removing a president from office is as follows: 1) the House votes to impeach the president; 2) the Senate carries out the impeachment trial; and 3) the Senate must have a two-thirds vote to convict and remove the president. Statements I, III, and IV describe these steps.

■ 3. **(E) is correct.** The War Powers Resolution maintains a president's ability to act quickly and decisively by sending troops to a trouble spot, but it prevents him from sidestepping Congress's power to declare war by requiring that those troops be withdrawn after 60 days. Congress is, by virtue of its size, a slow institution. The time limit gives Congress time to debate and declare war if it chooses to. If it does not, the president must withdraw the troops.

■ 4. **(B) is correct.** If the answer doesn't leap out at you, try eliminating those ways that you know presidents *do* try to influence policy decisions. They do appeal directly to the electorate through public appearances or televised addresses. They also offer to support the legislation of a representative in exchange for that representative's vote, and they do work closely with party leaders in Congress to build coalitions. There is also an understanding between presidents and Congress that representatives who support the president's agenda receive small favors. While presidents often do push their own proposals through Congress, they cannot introduce a bill themselves—they must find a member of Congress to endorse it for them. This enforces the separation of powers set forth in the Constitution.

5. (D) is correct. The selection of a running mate is a very strategic move for a presidential candidate. In order to win the election, the candidate must draw in as much of the electorate as possible. Candidates often choose a running mate who attracts a part of the electorate that the candidate might not otherwise reach. For example, a conservative candidate might choose a more liberal running mate. Choices *A* and *E* are desirable qualities in a vice president, but the questions asks for the *most likely* characteristic.

6. (A) is correct. A citizen's approval of the president is often derived from party affiliation. A president of his or her preferred party most likely acts in keeping with the platform of which the citizen already approves. By relying on party identification, a person is able to make a judgment about the president, even if he or she is not well informed about the president's performance.

7. (D) is correct. Again, since this is an "except" question, first try to eliminate any answer choices that you know are reasons that the presidency has become more powerful. The United States *has* become more active in world politics since World War II. This has enlarged the president's scope or responsibilities substantially, since he is commander in chief of the armed forces. The bureaucracy has also grown in the last few decades, thus increasing the president's executive duties. New technologies in communications and warfare often necessitate immediate decisions or quick responses, and Congress is by design a large, slow institution. A single president with numerous advisers at hand, however, can make such decisions quickly. Because television has made the president a more public figure, the electorate has invested him with greater authority. The Supreme Court, however, has not favored the president's views in its decisions.

8. (B) is correct. While presidents do not exercise their power to veto very often, they do use it more than rarely. Recent presidents have vetoed an average of 35 bills in each term. However, it is fairly unusual for Congress to override a president's veto. Less than 5 percent of vetoed bills are overridden, largely because it is difficult to achieve a two-thirds vote in both houses of Congress.

9. (C) is correct. Presidents can nominate justices, but they cannot remove them from their seats on the Supreme Court. In fact, justices, once they have been nominated by the president and approved by Congress, hold their positions for life. The Constitution specifies that justices have no term limit. Justices can be impeached, but this has happened only once.

10. (A) is correct. The Constitution authorizes the vice president to take over the office of the presidency if the president dies, resigns, is impeached, or is otherwise unable to perform his duties. If the vice president is also unable to serve for any of these reasons, the speaker of the House assumes the presidency until the next election.

Free-Response Question

This free-response question requires an analysis rather than an argument, so you do not need to choose a position and defend it. Instead you are asked to assess the system of checks and balances in relation to the changing responsibilities of the president as commander in chief. The best approach is to brainstorm about each of the points listed and then write a body paragraph for each (in addition to an introduction and conclusion). Be sure to write a topic sentence that ties your three paragraphs together.

As commander in chief, the president is primarily responsible for the country's engagement in war. However, because the system of checks and balances was designed to prevent one branch of government from gaining too much power, Congress does have some military powers. The nature of warfare, however, has changed dramatically since the writing of the Constitution, and consequently so has the president's role as commander in chief. Ultimately, in the case of military involvement, the system of checks and balances is somewhat outdated.

The Constitution grants the president the power to lead the armed forces, but only Congress can actually declare war. In theory, then, the president cannot act until Congress has voted on the matter. Only then does the president have the authority to make all decisions about how a military situation should proceed.

With the development of advanced technology, military situations today are much different from those at the time of the writing of the Constitution. Crises develop rapidly, since troops can move about quickly and perform extensive military operations in just a few hours. Such situations therefore require a quick response from the president. His concentrated authority allows for decisions to be made quickly and decisively. This need for immediate action has significantly expanded the president's military powers. Today, a president can bypass Congress and send troops to a trouble spot for a limited length of time. He also authorizes the use weapons of mass destruction.

Congress, which must debate and agree to declare war, by virtue of its size cannot act quickly. However, to check the power of the president, it passed the War Powers Resolution in 1973. This law requires any troops that the president has deployed to be withdrawn within 60 days unless Congress in that time declares war. The War Powers Resolution helps to maintain the system of checks and balances despite the changing nature of military action.

Recent presidents have taken full advantage of their power to deploy troops without the prior approval of Congress. President Clinton used the threat of invasion to persuade the military regime in Haiti to step down. Violence had erupted, and it was necessary for the president to respond quickly. The threat of invasion worked, and President Clinton then sent troops in to keep the peace as Haiti prepared to hold elections for a democratic government. Congress did not vote to declare war. In this case, regardless of the success of President Clinton's strategy, the system of checks and balances failed to check the power of the president. Essentially, modern warfare does not allow enough time to maintain the balance of power within the government.

This response clearly addresses each of the bulleted questions. The student explains each legislative and executive military power and understands the relationship between them in maintaining checks and balances. Specifically, the student includes the following pertinent points:

- *Congress declares war.*
- *The president acts as commander in chief after Congress has declared war.*
- *The president authorizes the use of weapons of mass destruction.*
- *The president may send a limited number of troops into a crisis situation temporarily.*

The student also demonstrates how the president's role and military powers have expanded as a result of modern warfare and correctly describes the War Powers Resolution. Finally, the student discusses a pertinent example of the president's unauthorized use of force.

CHAPTER 14

The Congress, the President, and the Budget: The Politics of Taxing and Spending

The president and Congress are responsible each year for creating the federal budget. In a balanced budget, **revenues** are equal to **expenditures.** Balancing the budget is extremely difficult, however, especially when Americans favor more federal programs but disapprove of increasing **taxes.** Spending more money than the government takes in results in a budget **deficit,** which is difficult to avoid given the demands on a large government.

Sources of Federal Revenue

Income taxes: A percentage of what a person earns goes directly to the government.

▊ The **Sixteenth Amendment** (1913) officially authorized Congress to collect income taxes.

▊ The **Internal Revenue Service** collects income taxes.

  ▪ monitors people's payments through **audits**

  ▪ investigates and prosecutes in cases of tax evasion

▊ The income tax is **progressive**—people with higher incomes pay a greater percentage in taxes.

  ▪ Opponents suggest a flat tax in which everyone pays an equal rate.

  ▪ Others propose a sales tax to replace the income tax.

▊ Corporations also pay taxes on their income, but most tax money comes from individual income taxes.

Social insurance taxes: Social Security taxes are paid both by businesses and their employees.

▊ Money collected from this tax is used specifically to pay current monthly benefits to senior citizens.

▊ These taxes have grown significantly and now account for about one-third of the federal revenue.

▊ As the population ages, more people will be expecting payments from the government. Economists are concerned that the baby boom generation main drain the system.

Borrowing: The federal government has borrowed a huge amount of money over the years.

- It borrows from foreign investors, foreign governments, and the American people.
  - People can buy government bonds. The government gets the money but must pay it back to the bondholder with interest.
- The money the government owes is the **federal debt.** Today the federal debt is more than $5 trillion.
  - About 10 percent of the federal budget is allocated to pay just the interest on this amount.
  - Future generations will have to pay for many policies enacted today.
- Lawmakers have considered proposing a **balanced budget amendment,** which would require Congress and the president to balance the budget each year.
  - Critics argue that it is too difficult to predict a balanced budget because of the uncertainties of the economy.

Taxes and Public Policy

Tax loopholes: Any tax breaks that allows a person to benefit from not paying some part of his or her taxes.
- Deductions for specific items are considered loopholes.
- Not everyone has the same access to loopholes.

Tax expenditures: The losses in federal revenues that result from tax breaks, deductions, and exemptions.
- They function like built-in subsidies—the government loses money by excusing a homeowner from paying taxes on a mortgage, but then the government does not have to pay for something like a homeowners' assistance program.
- Middle- and upper-income people benefit the most because they usually have more deductions and write-offs.

Tax reform: How much to tax is almost always a point of contention among Congress and the public.
- The most significant tax reform was President Reagan's **Tax Reform Act of 1986,** which cut taxes for everyone.
  - eliminated many deductions and exemptions
  - exempted many low-income families from paying
  - Many cite these reforms as the cause of the enormous national debt.
- President Clinton raised tax rates on the wealthy.

Federal Expenditures

The government must pay its own operational costs, which make up a significant percentage of its overall expenditures.
- **National security** was the biggest expenditure during the Cold War and Reagan era, but it had begun to decline before September 11, 2001.
- **Social services** are now the biggest expenditure: programs for people of low income and senior citizens make up one-third of the budget.
  - Social Security began with the **Social Security Act,** part of the New Deal.
  - **Medicare,** initiated in 1965, extends medical coverage to senior citizens.

- Because people are living longer and the current generation of senior citizens is large, Social Security taxes have risen.
- **Uncontrollable expenditures** are a form of mandatory spending.
  - Pensions and payments toward the national debt are fixed and thus not subject to budgetary cuts or changes.
  - **Entitlements** are benefits the government must pay to people who are eligible according to federal rules, such as veterans' aid, Social Security, and welfare.
- **Incrementalism** is the basis on which the budget is adjusted every year.
  - A budget is calculated by assuming that the expenditures included in the budget of the previous year will rise for the next year.
  - One issue is how large the increment should be, and another concern is that this creates a system of an ever-increasing budget.

The Budgetary Process

The budget affects and involves agencies and departments in the federal, state, and even local governments.
- Budget requests are submitted to the **Office of Management and Budget (OMB)**.
- Interest groups and agencies often team up when making budgetary requests.
- Based on all of the agency requests, the president formally proposes a budget plan to Congress in February.
- The **House Ways and Means Committee** and the **Senate Finance Committee** write the tax codes that will determine how much revenue the government will have for the year.
- The House and Senate Budget Committees and the **Congressional Budget Office** review the proposal for its feasibility.
- Congress must agree on a **budget resolution,** the final amount of expenditures not to be exceeded for the year.
- The **Appropriations Committees** in both houses determine how federal funds within the total expenditure will be allotted among agencies and departments.
- Congress might make changes to existing laws in order to meet the budget resolution.
  - **reconciliation:** Program authorizations are revised.
  - **authorization bill:** The expenditures allowed for discretionary programs or the requirements for entitlement programs are changed.
- Congress must pass the final budget bill and the president must sign it for it to become law.

For Additional Review

Make a table of each step in the budgetary process. List the institutions involved in that step and their specific responsibilities. Make a note of any political motivations that influence each participant's role in making the budget.

Multiple-Choice Questions

1. A progressive income tax authorizes wealthy people to
   (A) pay the same amount in taxes as people in other income brackets
   (B) pay taxes at more than twice rate as people in the lowest-income bracket
   (C) pay taxes at a slightly lower rate than people in the middle-income bracket
   (D) pay taxes slightly higher than the rate of people in the lowest-income bracket
   (E) pay taxes at the same rate as people in the middle-income bracket

2. Which of the following institutions is responsible for compiling the president's budget proposal?
   (A) Department of the Treasury
   (B) Congressional Budget Office
   (C) Senate Appropriations Committee
   (D) Office of Management and Budget
   (E) Council of Economic Advisors

3. Which of the following are accurate statements about the federal debt?
   I. The rising cost of public education has contributed significantly to the federal debt.
   II. The debt allows the government to displace the cost of current policies onto the shoulders of future generations.
   III. President Reagan's major tax cuts in the 1980s caused the national debt to grow to an unprecedented size.
   IV. The government will erase the national debt as soon as it succeeds in balancing the fiscal budget.
   (A) II only
   (B) IV only
   (C) I and II only
   (D) II and III only
   (E) I, III, and IV only

THE FEDERAL GOVERNMENT DOLLAR
(Fiscal Year 2003 Estimate)

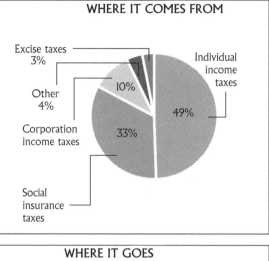

WHERE IT COMES FROM

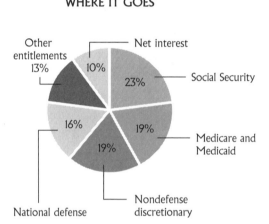

WHERE IT GOES

SOURCE: *Budget of the United States Government, Fiscal Year 2003: Historical Tables* (Washington, D.C.: U.S. Government Printing Office, 2002), 32, 125, 132.

4. All of the following statements accurately describe the data in the graphs EXCEPT
   (A) individuals pay five times more income taxes than corporations
   (B) the cost of social services for senior citizens outweighs the income from social insurance taxes
   (C) 10 percent of the budget is used to pay off interest on the national debt
   (D) national defense spending is only slightly less than the total spending for all other discretionary programs
   (E) the amount earned from corporate income taxes is enough to fund Medicare and Medicaid

5. Which of the following is an uncontrollable expenditure?
   (A) National security
   (B) Public education
   (C) Entitlement programs
   (D) Highway systems
   (E) Energy research

6. All of the following are steps in the budgetary process EXCEPT
   (A) the Congressional Budget Office works closely with the president to finalize the budget that he will propose to Congress
   (B) the House Ways and Means Committee and the Senate Finance Committee work together to write the tax codes
   (C) the OMB reviews and assesses the budget proposals submitted by each agency
   (D) Congress passes a budget resolution to set a cap on expenditures for the fiscal year
   (E) the Appropriations Committee decides how to divide federal resources among the departments and agencies

7. The federal government borrows money from citizens through
   (A) income taxes
   (B) bonds
   (C) Social Security
   (D) authorization bills
   (E) entitlement programs

8. What is one factor that has contributed most to the expansion of the government and, consequently, the budget deficit?
   (A) Globalization
   (B) Expanding suffrage
   (C) Incrementalism
   (D) Tax reforms
   (E) National security

9. The government receives most of its revenues from
   (A) excise taxes
   (B) social income taxes
   (C) personal income taxes
   (D) public bonds
   (E) sales taxes

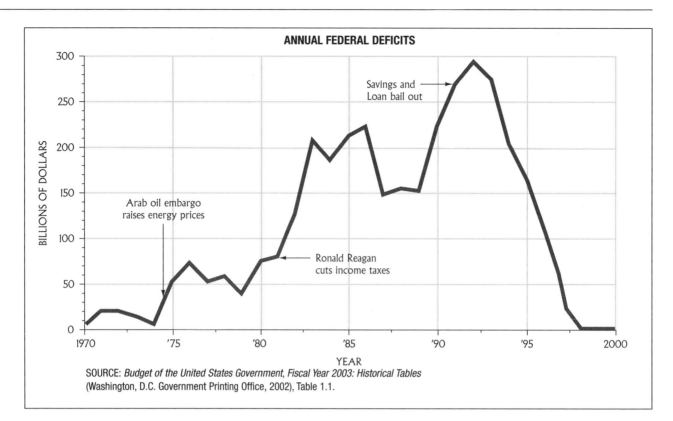

ANNUAL FEDERAL DEFICITS

Savings and
Loan bail out

Arab oil embargo
raises energy prices

Ronald Reagan
cuts income taxes

BILLIONS OF DOLLARS

YEAR

SOURCE: *Budget of the United States Government, Fiscal Year 2003: Historical Tables*
(Washington, D.C. Government Printing Office, 2002), Table 1.1.

10. Which of the following conclusions may be
drawn from the graph above?
(A) The Clinton administration closed the
budget deficit to reach a balanced budget in 1998.
(B) The federal deficit decreased dramatically
during the Reagan administration.
(C) Between 1972 and 1992, the deficit grew
by about five times the 1972 deficit.
(D) The federal deficit decreased significantly
between 1975 and 1980.
(E) The administration of George W. Bush is
primarily responsible for reversing the
deficit and balancing the federal budget.

Free-Response Question

Each year the president and Congress must determine the fiscal budget for the
federal government. Describe the process by which the budget is created. In
your answer, discuss the roles of ALL of the following groups:
■ Office of Management and Budget
■ Appropriations Committee
■ federal agencies
■ interest groups

ANSWERS AND EXPLANATIONS

Multiple-Choice Questions

▌ **1. (B) is correct.** People in the lowest income bracket pay taxes at about a rate of 15 percent. People in the highest income bracket pay taxes at a rate of about 36 percent. This makes the system of taxation more fair according to the distribution of wealth among Americans.

▌ **2. (D) is correct.** The Office of Budget and Management was established to coordinate the budget proposals of all government agencies into the president's final proposal. It has a significant amount of budgetary power, but this is checked by Congress's approval of the president's nominee for its director.

▌ **3. (D) is correct.** Ronald Reagan instituted enormous tax cuts while dramatically increasing defense spending at the same time. During his eight years as president, the national debt tripled. It continued to grow but has recently leveled off at more than $5 trillion.

▌ **4. (E) is correct.** Corporate taxes generate only about 10 percent of federal revenues. Expenditures for Medicare and Medicaid, according to the second graph, are about 19 percent of all expenditures. Corporate taxes are therefore too low to finance Medicare for senior citizens.

▌ **5. (C) is correct.** Entitlement programs are a form of mandatory spending because everyone entitled to the benefits of the program must be paid. Congress cannot control these expenditures unless it changes the eligibility requirements of the program, which it is unlikely to do unless such measures are absolutely necessary.

▌ **6. (A) is correct.** The president works closely with the Office of Management and Budget, an executive office, to formulate his budget proposal. The Congressional Budget Office works with congressional committees to review and amend the president's proposal.

▌ **7. (B) is correct.** Bonds function like loans—people buy them from the government, and the government must pay them back with interest. Bonds are usually a good source of income for the federal government.

▌ **8. (E) is correct.** Defense spending increased rapidly after World War II and as a result of the Cold War. This is one major reason for the growth of the budget deficit. However, since the end of the Cold War, both national security spending and the deficit have decreased.

▌ **9. (C) is correct.** Nearly half of all federal revenues are generated by personal income taxes. Social Security revenues have been increasing and also count for a large portion of federal revenues. Corporate income tax revenue has decreased, however.

▌ **10. (A) is correct.** The deficit was at its peak when President Clinton was elected in 1992. It decreased dramatically throughout the 1990s, however, and disappeared completely in 1998, when the United States experienced its first budget surplus in thirty years.

All federal departments and agencies have a stake in the federal budget because it dictates how much money each will receive for its own budget. Therefore, almost every group in Washington plays at least some part in the budgetary process.

In the executive branch, the main vehicle through which the president's budget proposal is prepared is the Office of Management and Budget. First the OMB assesses the current economic situation and works with the agencies to make projections for the budget of the next fiscal year. It sends its recommendations to the president for his input. With these guidelines, each agency then submits a detailed budget for the upcoming year to the OMB. Agencies frequently overshoot their figures in the expectation that they will not receive as much as they are asking for. They also enlist the help of interest groups to lobby Congress on their behalf. The more money the Department of Agriculture receives, for example, the better an interest group endorsing farmers' subsidies is likely to fare. The interest group reminds Congress of how necessary funding for that department is. After the OMB receives all of the proposed budgets, it weighs them and makes specific recommendations to the president. The president reviews this information and makes final decisions about the budget plan. Each agency must revise its budget accordingly. Finally, the president formally presents his budget proposal to Congress.

The Constitution grants Congress the ultimate authority in all budgetary matters. Congress must make the budget for the upcoming year feasible. First, the Congressional Budget Office makes its own projections. The CBO then reviews the president's proposal and reports its findings to the Budget Committees in each house. The standing committees also submit reports on the spending of the agencies over which they conduct legislative oversight. The Budget Committees tally the expenditures and revenues so that Congress as a whole can establish the budget resolution for the year. This is the ceiling for the total budget. With this bottom line, the Appropriations Committee then sets the budget for each agency. If necessary, Congress can change laws that affect the funding of a particular agency's program. This is called budget reconciliation. Finally, all of the numbers are adjusted before the new fiscal year begins in the fall.

This essay correctly touches on each major step in the budgetary process. The student clarifies the roles of all of the important players required in the question. The essay is very well organized, with one paragraph dedicated to the executive branch's development of a budget proposal and another to Congress's final allocation of federal funds. The student provides specific examples to fully demonstrate a grasp of the budgetary process.

CHAPTER 15

The Federal Bureaucracy

The federal **bureaucracy** is composed of all of the agencies, departments, offices, and bureaus in the executive branch. These bodies are primarily responsible for implementing and enforcing laws.

The Bureaucrats

- Bureaucrats are hired in one of two ways:
  1. through the **civil service system**
    - entrance exam
    - promoted by **merit** rather than **patronage**
    - must be politically impartial and treated as such
  2. presidential recruitment
    - Each new administration fills about 3,000 of the top posts.
    - The president chooses people who will support the administration's policies.
    - Many presidential nominees must be **approved by Congress.**
- The **Department of Defense** has the largest number of civil employees, followed by the **U.S. Postal Service.** Overall, federal civilian employment has not increased in decades, indicating that the federal bureaucracy is not actually growing.
- Bureaucrats are not easily removed from office

How Bureaucracies Are Organized

1. Cabinet departments

- Fourteen cabinet departments oversee and administer various policy areas.
- Each is supervised by a secretary.
- Each has its own staff and budget.

2. Regulatory agencies

- oversee a particular aspect of the economy
- create regulations that protect people
- can enforce regulations by judging disputes
- headed by a commission (confirmed by Congress) rather than a secretary
- closely involved with interest groups that want to influence regulations

3. Government corporations

- perform services for a fee, like a private business
- The U.S. Postal Service is the largest.

4. Independent executive agencies

- all other executive bodies—most created for specific purposes, such as NASA
- heads appointed by the president, so these usually have some partisan motivation

Bureaucracies As Implementors

- Enact and enforce rules and procedures for putting Congress's policy decisions into practice
  - work out details and guidelines, and assign responsibilities among bureaucrats
- Oversee day-to-day operation of the federal government
- **Policy implementation** is not always successful once a program is up and running for various reasons.
  - Program design is flawed.
  - Congress was not clear enough about policy goals.
  - A department lacks staff or resources to carry out implementation.
  - An agency is so mired in its **standard operating procedures** that it fails to see what else needs to be done.
  - Administrators use their discretion differently when the standard operating procedures do not sufficiently address a particular situation.
  - There can be confusion when several departments are involved in the implementation of a particular policy.
- Reorganization of the bureaucracy for the sake of efficiency is unlikely, because this would disrupt well-established **iron triangles** of congressional committees, the agencies they oversee, and the affiliated interest groups.

Bureaucracies As Regulators

- Oversee policies once they are in place through regulation
  1. establish guidelines for a program or project
  2. enforce guidelines
     - through complaints registered by the public
     - through inspections
     - by issuing permits and licenses to people who meet the guidelines
  3. **bureaucratic institutions have the authority to change rules of a policy and apprehend violators**
- All products and even many daily activities are shaped by regulation.

Bureaucracy and Democracy

- The governmental bureaucracy hires the most civilians but is not elected by the public.
- The governmental bureaucracy answers ultimately to the president.
  - President appoints agency heads who will support his policies.
  - issues **executive orders** to change or implement statutes
  - manages budget of each agency (at least in his budget proposal)
  - can reorganize an agency

- The governmental bureaucracy is partially controlled by Congress.
  - Congress ultimately determines each agency's budget.
  - can refuse to confirm a presidential appointment
  - performs legislative oversight through hearings
  - can change the legislation behind a program
- The governmental bureaucracy is full of **iron triangles,** which may produce conflicting guidelines or regulations.

For Additional Review

Look through your textbook and make a list of federal agencies and departments. For each one, note the policy area that it handles and any other relevant information, such as which type of bureaucratic institution is or how its administrators are selected.

Multiple-Choice Questions

1. Which of the following statements accurately describes the size of the federal bureaucracy?
   (A) The U.S. Postal Service is the largest department in the bureaucracy.
   (B) The federal bureaucracy grew at a rapid rate due to the expansion of national defense during the Cold War.
   (C) The federal bureaucracy experienced no significant change in size throughout the second half of the twentieth century.
   (D) The federal bureaucracy expands at the same rate that the American population grows so that the two remain proportional.
   (E) Washington, D.C., houses the largest group of federal bureaucrats.

2. Most federal bureaucrats are hired in which of the following ways?
   (A) They are awarded positions by the political party in power.
   (B) They take an examination to prove their qualifications.
   (C) They are appointed to a position by the president.
   (D) They work in the legislative branch and then move to the bureaucracy.
   (E) They pay a fee to apply for a position.

3. What is the main function of the federal bureaucracy?
   (A) To develop and enforce procedures for implementing policy
   (B) To make policy recommendations
   (C) To create new policies
   (D) To review policies
   (E) To research policy initiatives

4. Policy implementation is sometimes a matter of trial and error and may not succeed for any of the following reasons EXCEPT
   (A) administrators may make poor judgments
   (B) bureaus often are short staffed or lack resources
   (C) miscommunication among departments that share responsibility for a program
   (D) failure to establish standard operating procedures
   (E) legislation may not clearly convey Congress's policy goals

5. Which of the following statements accurately describe relationships in an iron triangle?
    I. Federal agencies bear most of the policy implementation burden, including handling complaints from constituents, and as a result may receive favorable treatment from Congress.
   II. Interest groups provide both agencies and legislative committees with information about the industries and groups of people they represent in order to influence legislation.
  III. Courts base their rulings on federal briefs such as committee recommendations and agency requests.
   IV. Agencies influence the policy decisions of congressional committees by determining each committee's budget.
   (A) II only
   (B) IV only
   (C) I and II only
   (D) III and IV only
   (E) I, II, and III only

6. Federal agencies perform their regulatory task of enforcing industry standards by
   (A) setting budgets for private industries
   (B) issuing executive orders to factories
   (C) hiring civil servants to head industry offices
   (D) requiring industries to report directly to the president
   (E) sending agency officials to inspect facilities

7. The president exercises his influence over the federal bureaucracy in which of the following ways?
   (A) By hiring interest groups to influence certain agencies
   (B) By appointing administrators sympathetic to his policy agenda
   (C) By writing guidelines for agency programs
   (D) By removing administrators from office
   (E) By having federal judges disband agencies

8. Federal agencies differ from legislative committees in all of the following ways EXCEPT
   (A) agencies enact policies; committees formulate policies
   (B) agencies make budget requests; committees determine budgets
   (C) agencies can prosecute in order to enforce policies; committees have no power to enforce laws
   (D) agencies focus on specific policy areas; committees handle only general fiscal policies
   (E) agencies establish specific guidelines for policies; committees make policy decisions

9. Federal departments are most likely to receive help from interest groups in which of the following cases?
   (A) When the department is being restructured by the president
   (B) When the department prosecutes industry violations
   (C) When the president appoints new cabinet secretaries
   (D) When the department is enforcing a regulation
   (E) When the budget proposal is under congressional review

10. A citizen would best express his or her concern about airport safety in which of the following ways?
   (A) Filing a complaint with the National Transportation Safety Board
   (B) Voting for a new secretary of the Department of Transportation
   (C) Abstaining from voting in the next congressional election
   (D) Writing a letter to the president
   (E) Hiring federal agents to inspect automobile plants

Free-Response Question

Iron triangles, or subgovernments, often form around a specific policy area to shape and administer relevant policies.

Select ONE of the following policy areas.

- agriculture
- the environment
- product safety
- oil

For the policy area you selected, describe how an iron triangle might form. Who would the political participants be and what are their roles and their responsibilities to each other?

ANSWERS AND EXPLANATIONS

Multiple-Choice Questions

1. **(C) is correct.** Despite the common misconception, the federal bureaucracy actually has *not* grown. In fact, the American population has grown and the social responsibilities of the government have increased without the size of the federal bureaucracy changing much. State and local bureaucracies have grown, however, as the burden of implementing many federal programs has fallen to them. Answer *A* is a trick—the U.S. Postal Service is not a department; it is an agency.

2. **(B) is correct.** Civil service is based on the merit system. Applicants must take an exam, and only qualified individuals are hired. Most bureaucratic positions are filled this way, though the president does appoint some people to high-level positions.

3. **(A) is correct.** As the federal bureaucracy makes up the bulk of the executive branch, its job is to execute the laws passed by Congress. It establishes the budget, personnel, and other resources necessary to translate policy goals into practice. Then it is responsible for regulating and enforcing those programs.

4. **(D) is correct.** All agencies have some form of standard operating procedures. These provide uniformity and help streamline the agency's activities. Implementation might falter, however, in unusual cases for which the standard operating procedures do not apply.

5. **(C) is correct.** Federal agencies deal with the day-to-day operations of federal programs and therefore shoulder the burden of most technicalities so that Congress does not have to. For their part in an iron triangle, interest groups provide both agencies and committees with information about how policies are or might have an impact on the public or on a certain industry. With this information, they are able to influence Congress's policy decisions and agencies' guidelines for regulation.

6. **(E) is correct.** Federal agencies often send experts to investigate plants, factories, and other industry facilities. For example, the Food and Drug Administration has government officials inspect and report on activities at

meatpacking plants. They may also test products and inspect working conditions to ensure that all standards of quality and safety regulations are being met.

▌ **7. (B) is correct.** Each new president has the task and the privilege of filling countless bureaucratic posts. He therefore solicits individuals who not only are well qualified but also are likely to endorse the president's policy proposals and work to advance his agenda. The constitutional system of checks and balances, however, requires that all appointees be confirmed by Congress.

▌ **8. (D) is correct.** Both federal agencies and congressional committees specialize in specific policy areas. In fact, the committee that creates a policy also conducts legislative oversight over the agency or agencies responsible for enacting and regulating the policy as law.

▌ **9. (E) is correct.** Interest groups are particularly vocal on behalf of federal departments during the budgetary process. The more money an agency receives, the more an affiliated interest group is likely to benefit. Furthermore, if an interest group actively endorses an agency, that agency will look more favorably on the interest group and may be more inclined to return the favor.

▌ **10. (A) is correct.** One of the ways federal agencies assess the effectiveness of their policy implementation is by gauging public reaction. Citizens' complaints also help agencies enforce regulations and prosecute violators.

Free-Response Question

Iron triangles often form among an interest group, a federal agency, and a legislative committee or subcommittee in order to shape policies in a particular policy area. One example of an iron triangle that deals with environmental issues might include an interest group such as Greenpeace, the Environmental Protection Agency, and the Senate Environment and Public Works Committee or one of its subcommittees.

For example, suppose hundreds of residents near a few different power plants have developed chronic asthma from the plants' emissions. They may take their case to the EPA and seek assistance from Greenpeace, which has the resources to draw attention to their cause. Greenpeace brings the issue into the political arena by demanding tighter federal regulation of plant emissions. It issues many reports to the EPA showing a link between the chemicals emitted by the plants and the illnesses of the residents. The EPA may also become involved if citizens register their complaints directly with the agency. As a result of these claims, the EPA may send inspectors to test the air quality in the neighborhoods around each plant. The EPA, with the help of Greenpeace, has gathered enough information to prompt the need for new regulations. However, suppose federal law prohibits EPA from making certain industry changes to power plants. The EPA and Greenpeace then must enlist the help of a sympathetic committee, such as the Senate Environment and Public Works Committee.

The interest group now lobbies the committee—it provides information about the effects of plant emissions and pledges support for committee members in the next congressional election. The EPA also appeals to the committee and can argue that it has already done its best to shoulder the complaints of the public, thereby shielding committee members from angry voters. The committee, in order to appease the voters and Greenpeace, may revise the law to allow further regulation by the EPA. Alternatively, it may increase the budget of the EPA so that the agency can develop some kind of solution on its own.

Either way, each member of the iron triangle benefits. The interest group has succeeded in influencing policy. The agency, with the help of Greenpeace's resources, has done its job of enforcing regulations or may have increased its budget in order to do so. The members of the committee are allowed to remain out of the fray; voters are not likely to take out their anger on the committee members at the polls, and the committee is absolved of most of the responsibility of resolving the issue by handing the practicalities over to the EPA. Finally, by working together, these three participants have solidified their relationships with each other in case another issue arises.

This essay identifies the participants in an environmental iron triangle and describes how the iron triangle forms during various steps of the policy process. The student successfully applies a theoretical concept to a real-world situation in order to demonstrate a knowledge of iron triangles and the way they operate in politics.

CHAPTER 16

The Federal Courts

In the American judicial system, courts apply the law to a conflict between two parties. Federal courts hear cases of federal law and cases involving two parties of different states. This amounts to only about 2 percent of all trials—most cases are heard in state and local courts.

The Nature of the Judicial System

▌ **Criminal law:** Used when a person has violated a law and must be punished.
Civil law: Used to settle disputes between parties; no law has been broken.

▌ Only about 3 percent of all cases actually go to trial; most are settled out of court.

▌ **Litigants:** The parties involved in a case
  ▪ The **plaintiff** brings the charges (this name is listed first in the name of the case).
  ▪ The **defendant** is the party who has been charged (this name is listed second).
  ▪ Plaintiffs must have **standing to sue,** or sufficient legal reason to bring charges.
  ▪ Litigants in a **class action suit** sue on behalf of all citizens who are in the same situation.

▌ **Groups:** Interest groups become involved with court cases to influence decisions about the law.
  ▪ May have their lawyers take up an appropriate litigant's case
  ▪ Can submit *amicus curiae* briefs to influence a judge's decision
    • Explain the possible effects of the judge's decision
    • Bring new points of view to the case
    • Provide additional information not presented in the case
    • The federal government can also submit them.

▌ **Attorneys:** Lawyers present a case in court.
  ▪ Every citizen is guaranteed a lawyer in a criminal case.
  ▪ **Public interest lawyers** and **legal aid groups** may represent poor people in some civil and criminal cases.
  ▪ State and local governments hire public defenders to represent poor defendants in criminal cases.
  ▪ Usually people with more money can hire lawyers with more time and resources, and therefore may have an unfair advantage.

The Structure of the Federal Judicial System

▋ Courts of **original jurisdiction** are the first courts to hear a case, usually when it goes to **trial.**
  - ▪ The court assesses and decides a case based on the **facts of the case.**
  - ▪ Most cases do not continue after their first ruling.

▋ Courts of **appellate jurisdiction** hear cases that have been **appealed.**
  - ▪ The court interprets the case as it relates to the law; it does not review the facts.
  - ▪ The litigants do not appear before the court, and there is no jury.

▋ **District courts:** there are 91 federal district courts
  - ▪ Have original jurisdiction
  - ▪ Hold trials in which the litigants appear before the court
  - ▪ Federal district courts primarily handle the following types of cases:
    - • Cases violating federal law or involving federal civil law
    - • Civil suits in which the litigants are of different states
    - • Bankruptcy proceedings and process of naturalization
  - ▪ The **U.S. attorney** in each district serves as the government's lawyer.
    - • The government is a plaintiff when prosecuting violators of federal laws.
    - • The government can be a plaintiff or defendant in a civil suit.

▋ **Courts of appeal:** Twelve courts of appeal review cases appealed from the district courts.
  - ▪ Have appellate jurisdiction
    - • Do not focus on the facts of the case
    - • Evaluate the treatment of the case in the district court in terms of errors of procedure or the law
  - ▪ Usually three judges hear a case
  - ▪ Their ruling sets a **precedent** for the district courts.

▋ **Supreme Court:** The ultimate authority on the law
  - ▪ Has original jurisdiction in cases between two states, the federal government and a state, or a state and a foreign country
  - ▪ Most cases fall under its appellate jurisdiction
    - • It can choose which cases to hear.
  - ▪ Consists of nine justices who rule on cases together

The Politics of Judicial Selection

▋ All federal judges and justices are appointed by the president.
▋ Nominations must be confirmed by the Senate.
  - ▪ Confirmation of state-level judges is determined by **senatorial courtesy,** which actually gives Congress significant influence in appointing judges.
▋ Justices are carefully selected by the president when there is a vacancy on the Supreme Court.
  - ▪ Supreme Court cases set precedents for the law.
  - ▪ Justices serve much longer than a president's term.
  - ▪ The Court will be more closely aligned with the president's ideology.

The Courts as Policymakers

1. **Accepting cases:** The Supreme Court shapes policy by selecting which cases to hear.

   ▪ Most likely to choose cases involving civil rights and civil liberties, a discrepancy in the lower courts' interpretation of the law, or disagreements between justices and the lower courts

2. **Making decisions:** The Court follows a regular process.
   - ▪ Justices read briefs pertaining to the case.
   - ▪ Hear **oral arguments**
   - ▪ Meet to discuss cases and vote on decision
   - ▪ Write and announce opinions

   ▪ Decisions are based heavily on **precedent;** lower courts must follow precedents set by higher courts.
   - ▪ The Supreme Court has overruled its own precedents 200 times.

   ▪ Decisions often must clarify ambiguities in the law.

   ▪ Justices usually rule *stare decisis:* "let the decision stand."

3. **Judicial implementation:** Decisions must be translated into policy.

   ▪ This is accomplished by policymakers, the president, lower courts, lawyers, administrators.

   ▪ The public must become aware of its rights under the new decision.

   ▪ Often implementors disagree with the decision and try to hinder implementation.

The Courts and the Policy Agenda

▪ Some justices have had a significant impact on the shaping of policy.
   - ▪ **John Marshall:** Initiated the practice of judicial review in the case of *Marbury* v. *Madison* and expanded the power of the Supreme Court significantly
   - ▪ The **Warren court:** The Supreme Court became actively involved in expanding civil rights and civil liberties.
   - ▪ The **Burger court:** Appointed by Nixon, Burger made the Court more conservative, though it still allowed abortion in *Roe* v. *Wade.*
   - ▪ The **Rehnquist court:** The Court became even more conservative with Reagan's appointments and began to limit (though not reverse) previous rulings.

▪ Some critics think the Supreme Court is too powerful and favor **judicial restraint.**

▪ Others favor **judicial activism** to allow justices the freedom to forge new policies, especially concerning people largely underrepresented in the political process.

▪ Power of the courts is checked by the president's appointments and by Congress's ability to amend the Constitution despite—or in order to overrule—a Supreme Court decision.

For Additional Review

Select two Supreme Court cases that are of particular interest to you, or that had a major impact on politics or society. Read the opinion or opinions associated with the cases to better understand the reasoning on which the justices make important decisions.

Multiple-Choice Questions

1. A plaintiff cannot bring suit unless he or she has fulfilled which of the following requirements?
   (A) Paid bail
   (B) Filed an *amicus curiae* brief
   (C) Appealed the case
   (D) Hired a public defender
   (E) Established standing to sue

2. Which of the following statements are true about the cases on the Supreme Court's docket?
   I. The Supreme Court tries to hear every case that is appealed to it.
   II. Cases pertaining to civil liberties are likely to be placed on the docket.
   III. The U.S. solicitor general decides which cases the Supreme Court will hear.
   IV. The Supreme Court has original jurisdiction in cases involving civil disputes among residents of a particular state.
   (A) II only
   (B) IV only
   (C) I and II only
   (D) II and III only
   (E) III and IV only

3. Courts of appeal focus their attention on which aspect of a case?
   (A) The facts presented by both parties in the original case
   (B) The *amicus curiae* briefs registered with the court
   (C) The backgrounds of the jury members in the original case
   (D) The procedures and interpretation of the law in the original case
   (E) The testimonies of both sides given before the Supreme Court

4. Congress influences the ideology of the Supreme Court by
   (A) passing laws to limit judicial review and prohibit judicial activism
   (B) issuing recommendations through the Senate Judiciary Committee
   (C) approving or rejecting the president's nomination of justices
   (D) choosing which cases the Supreme Court will hear
   (E) nominating justices for the president's approval

5. All of the following statements accurately describe the federal court system EXCEPT
   (A) very few federal cases actually go to trial
   (B) federal courts do not handle cases involving state laws
   (C) all federal judges must be nominated by the president and confirmed by Congress
   (D) lower courts must adhere to the precedents set by higher courts
   (E) some federal courts have original jurisdiction, whereas others have appellate jurisdiction

6. What is the final step in the Supreme Court's decision-making process?
   (A) Taking a vote
   (B) Writing the opinion
   (C) Hearing oral arguments
   (D) Reading briefs
   (E) Setting the agenda

7. Which of the following is the most frequent outcome of a Supreme Court case?
   (A) It significantly alters current policies.
   (B) The justices vote unanimously.
   (C) It reverses the decision of the lower court.
   (D) It overrules the Court's own precedent.
   (E) It agrees with the decision of the lower court.

8. The decision of a federal court is most likely determined by
   (A) the argument put forth by the prosecution
   (B) the argument put forth by the defense
   (C) precedents set by similar cases
   (D) the political ideology of the judge
   (E) briefs submitted by the federal government

9. Interest groups become involved in the judicial process in all of the following ways EXCEPT by
   (A) running advertisements endorsing a judicial nominee
   (B) lobbying the Judiciary Committee about a judicial nominee
   (C) filing *amicus curiae* briefs
   (D) having their lawyers represent a plaintiff
   (E) filing a class action suit

10. The Warren court had the greatest impact on which area of policy?
    (A) Abortion
    (B) Labor
    (C) Welfare
    (D) Civil rights
    (E) Environment

Free-Response Question

The selection of Supreme Court justices is a complex matter involving many participants. Explain this process AND discuss the various motivations that lie behind judicial appointments.

ANSWERS AND EXPLANATIONS

Multiple-Choice Questions

■ **1. (E) is correct.** A plaintiff must have sufficient standing to sue. This means that he or she has a legitimate personal stake in the case. It must be evident that the plaintiff has suffered as a result of another person's actions or of a government action. A citizen cannot simply bring a suit against a law with which he or she disagrees.

■ **2. (A) is correct.** The Supreme Court justices, not the solicitor general, select the cases they will hear. However, very few appeals are chosen. Civil liberties is usually one policy area in which the Supreme Court is willing to become involved.

■ **3. (D) is correct.** Courts of appeal do not become directly involved with the facts of a case. Rather, they review how a case was handled in a lower court—how the ruling was decided and whether or not that ruling appropriately applied the law to the case.

■ **4. (C) is correct.** The Constitution authorizes Congress to confirm the president's nominees for federal judgeships as part of the system of checks and balances. The

Senate Judiciary Committee is fairly active in this role; about one-fifth of the nominees have been denied a position on the bench.

■ **5. (B) is correct.** Federal courts do sometimes interpret state laws. In some cases, the court must decide if a state law violates the Constitution. Federal courts also have jurisdiction over cases in which the litigants reside in different states; federal judges weigh the state laws without bias.

■ **6. (B) is correct.** After the justices vote to decide the ruling, the task of writing the opinion is assigned to one of the justices who was in the majority. The chief justice usually writes the opinion in a major case. In the opinion, the Court officially states the reasons for its ruling.

■ **7. (E) is correct.** Most Supreme Court rulings uphold the decision made by the lower court. This is the principle of *stare decisis,* meaning "let the decision stand."

■ **8. (C) is correct.** Most court rulings are based on precedents set by previous cases that addressed a similar issue. Judges are not required to rule by precedent, but precedents do serve as a guide and help to make the law more uniform.

■ **9. (A) is correct.** Interest groups do attempt to influence the appointment of judges, but not by running advertisements. The process of filling judgeships is far removed from the public—the only means of influence it has is by its election of the president and of members of Congress, who, in turn, choose judges. Advertisements aimed at swaying public opinion therefore have little use in this case.

■ **10. (D) is correct.** Earl Warren was appointed by President Eisenhower and presided as chief justice over the Supreme Court through the 1950s. The Warren court was extremely active in the cause of civil rights and handed down one of the most important decisions in American history in the case of *Brown* v. *Board of Education.* Eisenhower, a conservative, considered his appointment of Warren one of the worst failures of his presidency.

Free-Response Question

The nomination and appointment of Supreme Court justices is extremely important, because the nine justices serve life terms. Therefore they have a great deal of influence over political, social, and even economic issues in the United States.

The president has the power to nominate justices if a seat on the Supreme Court becomes available during his term. This provides an opportunity for the president to choose someone of a similar ideology to sit on the Court. An appointment can change the leaning of the Court to a more liberal or a more conservative position. Also, because justices serve such long terms, the president has an opportunity to influence policy long after his own term has ended. Lastly, the president may be remembered for his bold choice—Reagan, for example, appointed the first woman to the Supreme Court. The president first solicits recommendations from other judges affiliated with the Department of Justice. The attorney general screens candidates and the Federal Bureau of Investigation conducts background checks on them. Senators also play a small role in endorsing candidates from their states. After careful scrutiny of each candidate's personal and political ideology, the president chooses a nominee.

The Senate is responsible for confirming the president's nomination. Senators have a good deal of leeway to oppose the president and heavily interrogate judicial nominees. This is especially likely if the president is of a different political party from the majority in Congress; in this case, the senators are more likely to oppose the ideology of the nominee whom the president has selected. In a series of hearings, the Senate Judiciary Committee probes the nominee about his or her previous experience and political views. Interest groups also sometimes become involved at this stage in the process. They may lobby committee members for or against the president's nominee. The Judiciary Committee takes all of this into account and makes its recommendation to the Senate. Finally, the Senate votes, and a simple majority determines if the nominee has gained the seat.

If the Senate fails to confirm the nominee, the president must make another nomination and the process begins again. This has happened several times in American history. These instances when the Senate disagrees with the president ultimately serve to show that the system of checks and balances is still an effective force in the shaping of politics.

This essay correctly identifies each step in the process of selecting Supreme Court justices. The student discusses the roles and motivations of the key participants—the president, the Senate, and interest groups. The essay is well-organized and contains a sufficient amount of detail.

CHAPTER 17

Economic Policymaking

The U.S. government and economy have always been closely entwined. The American economy is based on the principles of **capitalism** and **laissez-faire,** but in practice it is a **mixed economy** because the government plays a regulatory role.

Government and the Economy

Social problems arise as a result of economic downturns.

- **Unemployment** occurs when there are not enough jobs.
  - Measured by the **unemployment rate**
  - The Democratic coalition consists of groups concerned with unemployment (labor and the lower classes).
  - Voters, especially Democrats, take the state of the economy into account when choosing candidates.
  - Democrats generally sacrifice higher inflation to keep unemployment down.
- **Inflation** occurs when prices rise.
  - Measured by the consumer price index
  - The Republican coalition includes businesspeople who are concerned about the cost of goods and services.
  - Republicans generally try to prevent inflation, even at the risk of rising unemployment.

Instruments for Controlling the Economy

- **Monetary policy:** Monitoring and controlling the amount of money in circulation
  - If there is too much available cash or credit, inflation occurs.
  - The **Federal Reserve System** was created to manage monetary policy. Its Board of Governors is appointed by the president and confirmed by the Senate but operates fairly independently. It regulates monetary policy by
    1. influencing the rate at which loans are given, which influences decisions about borrowing;
    2. controlling the amount of money banks have available, and, in turn, the rate at which people can borrow;
    3. adding to the money supply by selling bonds.

- **Fiscal policy:** Regulating revenues and expenditures through the federal budget; determined by Congress and the president
  - **Keynesian economic theory** (liberal)
    - Encourages government's active participation in the economy
    - Government spending stimulates the economy by creating demand.
  - **Supply-side economics** (conservative)
    - By decreasing government involvement in the economy, people will be forced to work harder and save more.
    - Cutting taxes increases the money supply.

Obstacles to Controlling the Economy

- It is difficult to predict the economy far enough in advance to make and implement policy.
- Events abroad can affect the economy.
- The economy is grounded in the private sector, which is harder to regulate.

Arenas of Economic Policy

Business Policy

- A few **transnational corporations** control most of the country's assets and play a large role in the world economy.
- Formed through **mergers**
- **Antitrust laws** allow the Justice Department to bring suit against companies that have **monopolized** a certain product or service.
  - Breaks up the company
  - Opens the market to competition
- The government participates in the economy by assisting failing industries with subsidies and loans and by funding product research.
- Business lobbies are well established and influential.

Consumer Policy

- Consumer groups are fairly new.
- Have successfully lobbied for increased regulation over product safety and advertising
  - The **Federal Trade Commission** regulates trade and now enforces truth in advertising.
  - The **Food and Drug Administration** monitors the health safety of food and approves new drugs for sale.

Labor and Government

- Prior to the twentieth century, the government traditionally favored business over labor.

- In the twentieth century, labor won some economic protection of the law.
    - Unions have the power of **collective bargaining** with management.
    - Unemployment compensation
    - Minimum wage
    - Safety standards
    - The regular workweek

New Economy, New Policy Arenas

- The Internet is creating an economy based on information.
- The **"digital divide"** describes the inequality of access among socioeconomic groups.

For Additional Review

Unemployment and inflation are two social consequences of economic downturns. Brainstorm a list of some other social problems that may arise as a result of these two situations. What other consequences might result from a poor economy? Can you think of anything consumers can do to avoid or alleviate these problems?

Multiple-Choice Questions

1. According to Keynesian economic theory, increasing government spending
   (A) threatens the economy by raising the federal deficit
   (B) stimulates the economy by creating demand among consumers
   (C) does little to curb unemployment
   (D) creates a supply among consumers and encourages them to save
   (E) prevents the Federal Reserve System from managing banks

2. All of the following factors indicate that the United States has a mixed economy EXCEPT
   (A) there is an established minimum wage
   (B) the Justice Department can sue monopolistic companies
   (C) Congress sets tariffs on imported goods
   (D) the federal government owns the means of production
   (E) there is a federal minimum age requirement for employment

3. Which of the following is one reason why Republican presidents usually focus their attention on controlling inflation?
   (A) Keeping the cost of production low does the most to help the economy.
   (B) They hope to attract the votes of the middle- and lower-class Americans.
   (C) They endorse Keynesian economics.
   (D) Controlling inflation keeps people from buying too much.
   (E) They want to avoid having to solve the problem of high unemployment.

4. The economy suffers inflation when there is too much money in circulation. To overcome this problem, the government could do which of the following?
   (A) Decrease loan rates to make them more available to the public
   (B) Increase the amount of credit available to the public
   (C) Decrease the amount of money in banks in order to raise loan rates and discourage people from borrowing
   (D) Limit the number of bonds sold to the public to discourage people from buying
   (E) Increase the amount of money in banks to help people acquire spending capital

5. Which of the following statements accurately describe significant trends in recent economic policy?
   I. Consumer groups have become more active in lobbying Congress for product safety.
   II. Congress has been able to regulate the growth and expansion of the Internet.
   II. The influence of business interest groups has declined steadily as the government has taken on more regulatory responsibilities.
   IV. The Federal Trade Commission has tightened its regulation of advertisements.
   (A) I only
   (B) III only
   (C) II and III only
   (D) I and IV only
   (E) I, II, and III only

6. Which of the following government institutions has the greatest impact on the economy?
   (A) Senate Finance Committee
   (B) Federal Reserve Board
   (C) Office of Management and Budget
   (D) Council of Economic Advisors
   (E) House Appropriations Committee

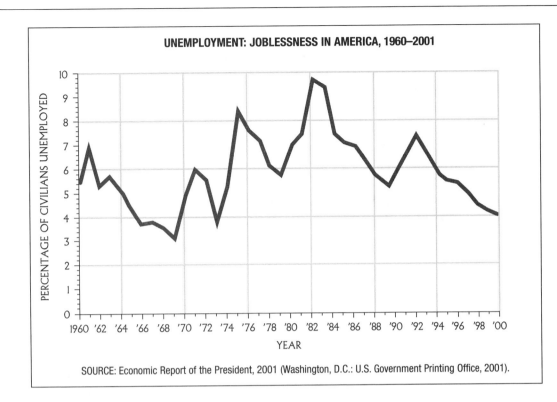

UNEMPLOYMENT: JOBLESSNESS IN AMERICA, 1960–2001

SOURCE: Economic Report of the President, 2001 (Washington, D.C.: U.S. Government Printing Office, 2001).

7. Which of the following statements accurately describes the data in the graph above?
   (A) Unemployment decreased during the Clinton administration.
   (B) Unemployment increased steadily through the 1970s.
   (C) Unemployment rises only during a Republican presidency.
   (D) Unemployment is higher in the United States than in other countries.
   (E) Unemployment declined by about 50 percent during the 1980s.

8. Antitrust laws are designed to prevent
   (A) large companies from having a monopoly over a specific good or service
   (B) the expansion of large multinational corporations
   (C) the government from interfering in international business transactions
   (D) the spread of dot-com businesses into traditional economic spheres
   (E) the Federal Reserve Board from gaining too much power over economic policy

9. The government can increase the money supply in which of the following ways?
   (A) Increasing agricultural subsidies
   (B) Issuing fewer loans
   (C) Limiting the money in bank vaults
   (D) Selling bonds
   (E) Raising income taxes

10. Congress and the president have little influence over the Federal Reserve Board, because
   (A) its members are elected directly by the public
   (B) it is not subject to congressional over sight
   (C) it is part of neither the executive nor the legislative branch
   (D) its members are required by law to remain strictly nonpartisan while in office
   (E) its members are appointed for 14-year terms in order to remain isolated from politics

Free-Response Question

The evolution of the Internet has produced what some economists call the "new new economy." For the first time, information is the commodity being traded on the Internet. The expansion of this new economic medium, however, has happened so quickly that the government has not yet been able to develop guidelines for its use and continued growth.

What are THREE problems that might arise as the Internet continues to expand without government regulation?

ANSWERS AND EXPLANATIONS

Multiple-Choice Questions

1. (B) is correct. Keynesian economic theory endorses an active government, because government spending creates demand among consumers. The government can create jobs for the unemployed and help businesses expand; in so doing, it keeps money circulating in the economy and keeps consumers actively involved.

2. (D) is correct. In a Communist system, the government owns the means of production; in a capitalist system, the government plays no part at all in the economy. The United States has a mixed economy that falls between these two extremes. The private sector is large, but the government has established many measures to regulate it.

3. (A) is correct. Republican presidents focus on keeping inflation down because this helps business to remain steady by easing costs to business owners and other producers. Moreover, Republicans usually attract the votes of middle- and upper-class businesspeople rather than of lower-class labor.

4. (C) is correct. The Federal Reserve Board controls how much money is issued from the Federal Reserve Bank to all other banks. When it limits those available funds, banks are forced to offer loans at higher rates. This discourages people from applying for loans, which are one cause of the over-circulation of money.

5. (D) is correct. Since the 1960s, the government has become increasingly involved in regulating product quality and safety. This is because consumer groups have lobbied more actively for government intervention in business practices. One result of this is the Federal Trade Commission's close monitoring of advertisements.

6. (B) is correct. The Federal Reserve Board has the most direct influence over the economy because it controls the money supply. It is also able to act quickly and decisively because it is a relatively nonpartisan government institution.

7. (A) is correct. Bill Clinton was president from 1993 to 2001. The unemployment rate dropped from 7.4 percent to 4 percent in his first seven years.

8. (A) is correct. Antitrust laws were developed at the turn of the twentieth century to check the power of such business magnates as J. P. Morgan and John D. Rockefeller. These laws prevent any one company from monopolizing a particular market. One recent instance of trust-busting occurred when the government forced AT&T to sell off parts of its telephone empire to create smaller businesses and allow room in the marketplace for competition.

▌ **9. (D) is correct.** If there is not enough money in circulation, the government sells bonds. These loans from citizens to the government help stimulate the flow of money. When people invest in the government, it has more money to spend in return, and, ultimately, bond holders earn money off the interest.

▌ **10. (E) is correct.** Long terms for members of the Federal Reserve Board allow them greater independence. They do not have to appeal to anyone in order to be reelected, and they do not necessarily have to please the president or Congress once they have been guaranteed a 14-year post on the Board.

Free-Response Question

In the past several decades, the government has increased its regulatory responsibilities in the economic arena. Numerous federal agencies monitor the quality and exchange of products. However, the advent and explosive expansion of the Internet, an entirely new economic concept, has thus far eluded federal regulation. It remains to be seen if this will have any serious economic or social implications, but it is possible that some problems may arise as a consequence of the complete freedom of the Internet.

One major concern is the security of information on the Internet. Because a user can buy virtually anything over the Internet, a large amount of credit or other personal information is transferred. Although almost all sites have security measures to protect users, there have been many cases of computer hackers successfully accessing private information illegally. Companies that conduct business over the Internet must spend a great deal of money on security programs, and each may institute such programs or security protocol differently. It is the government's job to protect consumers, but no solution has completely secured all information available on the Internet, especially because there are thousands of points of access through different sites.

Another concern that Congress thus far has unsuccessfully pursued is regulation of the content of the Internet. Whereas it can set standards for products people buy, it cannot control what information they access over the Internet. Congress has concentrated its efforts on controlling the access of minors to pornography, but others view this as censorship. Twice the Supreme Court has struck down laws as unconstitutional violations of users' First Amendment rights. The government has therefore been unsuccessful in its attempt to play this particular regulatory role.

Finally, there are social consequences of the Internet that have yet to be fully realized. The Internet has become an instrumental tool—it provides users with access to businesses, services, and products, and with the ability to learn and communicate. However, not everyone has equal access, because many Americans cannot afford a computer or Internet service. Furthermore, internet service providers decide where to lay the phone and cable lines for service. These two factors have led to the digital divide: people with more money or in urban areas have better access than do poorer people or those who live in more rural areas. These people are at a disadvantage, especially as education becomes increasingly dependent on the Internet. The government has not yet devised a way to prevent the digital divide from growing, so the new Internet-based economy continues to advance a society of haves and have-nots. It remains to be seen just how far the Internet can go without the controlling force of federal regulations.

This essay clearly and explicitly describes three examples of consequences of the government's failure to regulate the Internet: the security of information available, the content of Internet sites, and the inequality of access. The student explains terms such as the "digital divide" and includes details such as the two laws found unconstitutional by the Supreme Court. Overall, the student demonstrates an understanding of the government's regulatory role in a mixed economy.

CHAPTER 18

Social Welfare Policymaking

The United States has one of the largest income gaps in the world because **income distribution** is extremely unequal among different economic classes. The degree of government involvement in issues of **poverty** has resulted in a major political debate. The biggest factor in this debate is how people view the poor—as lazy people who are avoiding work, or as disadvantaged people with no opportunity to advance their economic situation. This policy area plays a key role during elections, because Americans feel strongly about it.

Income: Defining the Rich and the Poor

The rich have not only more **income** but also greater **wealth** in the form of stocks and other assets.

- A small number of Americans—1 percent of the total population—possess more than one-third of all wealth in the United States.
- The assets of that 1 percent are actually higher than the total worth of 90 percent of Americans.

The social welfare debate hinges on **how people view the poor.**

- As receiving too much government money
    - Most government funds are given through **entitlement programs** to people who are not poor.
    - Eligibility for **means-tested programs** depends on how narrowly poverty is defined.
- As "deserving" if a family has lost its breadwinner or has a legitimate reason, such as a disability, for not being able to work.
- As "undeserving" if they abuse the system or have created conditions of poverty themselves.

Poverty is defined by the government as a family income that falls below the **poverty line.**

- Counts underestimate poverty, because millions of people hover around the line and continually fall just below or rise just above it.
- African Americans, Hispanic Americans, people living in inner cities, and unmarried women tend to be the groups most afflicted with poverty.

Income: Defining Government Involvement

Through **taxation**
- Types of taxes
    - **Progressive**: The wealthy are taxed at a higher rate.

- **Proportional:** Everyone is taxed at the same rate.
- **Regressive:** People of lower incomes are taxed at a higher rate.

■ State sales taxes are somewhat regressive, but the effect is counterbalanced by progressive federal income taxes.

Through **expenditures**

■ **Transfer payments** are given by the government directly to citizens.
- Food stamps
- Student loans
- Social Security and Medicare benefits

■ The elderly receive the most in transfer payments.

The Evolution of American Social Welfare Programs

■ The **Great Depression** proved that poverty can be beyond anyone's control and encouraged the government to become more involved in welfare.

■ Social Security began under the **New Deal;** the poor become a part of the Democratic coalition.

■ President Johnson initiated many **Great Society** programs to fight the **War on Poverty** during the civil rights era.

■ President Reagan cut the growth of many of these programs in the 1980s.

■ The system underwent a major overhaul during the Clinton administration.
- Families receive small payments with a maximum of two years to find employment.
- People have a lifetime maximum of five years on welfare.
- States operate their own welfare programs.

The Future of Social Welfare Policy

Social programs have become a major component of government. How they will continue to fare depends on future presidents, members of Congress, interest groups, and voters.

■ **Social Security:** It is highly likely that the system will go bankrupt during the twenty-first century.
- More people will be of retirement age.
- The cost of living is rising, so monthly payments will increase.
- Either taxes will have to be raised or benefits will have to be cut.

■ **Means-tested programs:** Their future is even more tenuous.
- Results of antipoverty programs show that poverty has not decreased.
- Some argue that federal benefits encourage people to remain in poverty.
- Others contend that other problems such as recessions have distorted the results.

Understanding Social Welfare Policy: Democracy and Social Welfare

Social welfare can be an emotionally charged issue.

■ Influences voters' decisions

■ Is a factor in choosing party identification

■ The public participates in many active interest groups.

Welfare for the elderly receives much more political and public support than welfare for the poor.

■ Interest groups for senior citizens are much better organized and funded than groups for the poor.

■ Senior citizens are more likely than the poor to vote.

■ The size of the bureaucracy has grown in order to support such sweeping welfare programs.

For Additional Review

Do some research and then create a list of some of the key public and political institutions involved in making and implementing social welfare policy. Briefly describe the role of each one and then note any ideological motivations that might influence the actions or decisions of the institution.

Multiple-Choice Questions

1. Which of the following statements best explains why social welfare is usually a main issue on both presidential and congressional platforms during elections?
   (A) Politicians feel significant pressure from antipoverty interest groups.
   (B) Both parties vie for the votes of lower-income groups.
   (C) Presidents are most often remembered for their legacy of social policy.
   (D) A congressional candidate's stand on social policy often influences his or her committee assignment.
   (E) Voters have strong opinions about how much the government and taxpayers should help the poor.

2. All of the following statements accurately describe social welfare policy EXCEPT
   (A) the current system encourages beneficiaries to seek employment
   (B) programs usually have expanded under Republican presidents
   (C) beneficiaries have little input in program goals
   (D) the vast majority of social funds go to Social Security and Medicare
   (E) the poorest Americans receive federal money rather than having to pay income taxes

3. Welfare programs are administered primarily by
   (A) state governments
   (B) the Bureau of Labor
   (C) charitable organizations
   (D) Equal Employment Opportunity Commission
   (E) the Senate Committee on Banking, Housing, and Urban Affairs

4. Which of the following is one major impact of social programs on the federal government?
   (A) A new federal court has been established to handle cases addressing poverty.
   (B) The responsibilities and size of the bureaucracy have increased.
   (C) The Federal Reserve Board now determines entitlement eligibility.
   (D) They have led to the election of Democratic presidents for most of the twentieth century.
   (E) The bureaucracy has come under the jurisdiction of the Department of Justice.

WHO GETS WHAT? INCOME SHARES OF AMERICAN HOUSEHOLDS					
Income Quintile	1960	1970	1980	1990	2000
Lowest fifth	4.9	5.5	5.1	4.6	3.7
Second fifth	11.8	12.0	11.6	10.8	8.9
Third fifth	17.6	17.4	17.5	16.6	14.9
Fourth fifth	23.6	23.5	24.3	23.8	23.0
Highest fifth	42.0	41.6	41.6	44.3	49.6
SOURCE: U.S. Census Bureau.					

5. Which of the following statements accurately describe the data in the chart?
   I. The highest fifth was the only group to benefit from the economic boom of the 1990s.
   II. Overall, all groups fared well in the 1970s and 1980s.
   III. The third fifth has had the steadiest income of all of the groups.
   IV. The lowest three fifths have fared the worst since the 1960s.
   (A) II only
   (B) I and II only
   (C) I and III only
   (D) I and IV only
   (E) II, III, and IV only

6. The poor are largely at a disadvantage in the political process because they
   (A) are represented by too many antipoverty interest groups that are competing for influence
   (B) have been denied access to policymakers by an executive order from the president
   (C) make up only a small percentage of voters
   (D) usually vote for Democrats, but the power of the Democratic Party has declined sharply
   (E) do not pay enough in income tax to gain the attention of policymakers

7. The Social Security program is likely to falter in the mid-twenty-first century for all of the following reasons EXCEPT
   (A) people are living longer
   (B) the cost of living is rising
   (C) the baby boom generation will be receiving benefits
   (D) expenditures will exceed revenues
   (E) rising unemployment will drain the program's income

8. Which of the following is an accurate comparison of social welfare in the United States and welfare in European countries?
   (A) Americans pay higher taxes to fund social welfare programs.
   (B) Americans receive greater benefits from social welfare.
   (C) Americans are less supportive of social welfare.
   (D) The American government is better equipped to handle issues of poverty.
   (E) The American government is more actively involved in social welfare.

9. The census count of people below the poverty line is not an accurate estimation of poverty in the United States because
   (A) many people hover just around the poverty line
   (B) the income at which the poverty line is set is too high
   (C) the income at which the poverty line is set is too low
   (D) the sample is not evenly distributed across different regions
   (E) many people in poverty refuse to participate in the census

10. Social Security fares better than welfare in budget battles for all of the following reasons EXCEPT
    (A) Social Security is an entitlement program, not a means-tested program
    (B) everyone will benefit from Social Security at some point in his or her life
    (C) senior citizens are more organized and better represented
    (D) Social Security is administered by state governments
    (E) senior citizens vote in greater numbers

Free-Response Question

The following data shows poverty rates for each racial group in the United States. Based on this information and on your knowledge of American politics, answer the following questions.

a. What does the data indicate about the poverty rate among each racial group in the United States?

b. Explain TWO ways that the federal government has attempted to assist people in poverty.

c. Evaluate the success of both of these governmental programs.

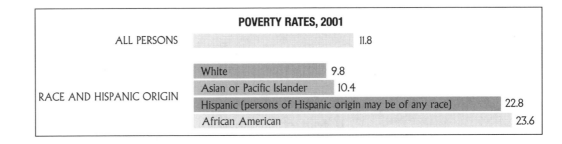

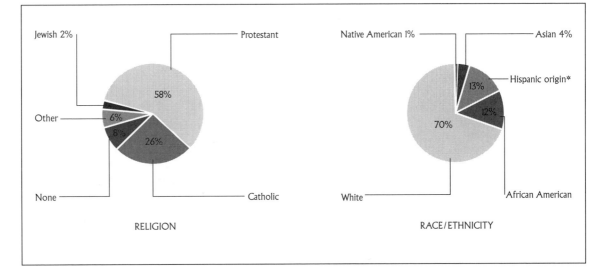

ANSWERS AND EXPLANATIONS

Multiple-Choice Questions

▌ **1. (E) is correct.** Americans feel strongly about social welfare, in part because their taxes are being used to help other people. This makes social welfare a highly charged issue, one on which both presidential and congressional candidates are often pressed to take a stand. In choosing candidates, voters are more likely to consider candidates' ideas about social welfare than about energy policy.

▌ **2. (B) is correct.** Welfare programs have expanded most under Democratic presidents. The government first became actively involved in social welfare under Roosevelt's New Deal and expanded its antipoverty efforts after the civil rights movement under Democrat Lyndon Johnson.

▌ **3. (A) is correct.** The reforms enacted under President Clinton shifted the administration of welfare programs to state governments. Each state is allotted federal funds but can decide within broad federal guidelines how best to run its welfare program with the money.

▌ **4. (B) is correct.** Social programs now account for about one-third of all government expenditures. To organize and administer the hundreds of programs that are federally funded, the bureaucracy has expanded. However, the federal bureaucracy itself has not grown substantially since the Johnson era, when many of these social programs began because the states administer many of the programs.

▌ **5. (D) is correct.** The income of all groups declined during the 1990s except for that of the highest fifth. Overall, the income of the lower three fifths declined between the 1960s and 1999.

▌ **6. (C) is correct.** Because people in poverty don't vote in very high numbers, they do not have a significant political voice. Politicians are more likely to respond to the needs of those people who elect them to office, such as senior citizens.

▌ **7. (E) is correct.** Unemployment, while it may have some impact on Social Security revenues, is the least likely factor to threaten the Social Security program. The biggest problem that will inevitably arise is the increase in beneficiaries, both because people are living longer today and because the baby boom generation will be of age.

▌ **8. (C) is correct.** Americans view social welfare with a greater degree of skepticism than do Europeans, who pay as much as 50 percent of their income in taxes to fund a wealth of social programs. Americans are generally more suspicious of big government and also tend to believe that poverty is more the fault of the individual than of society at large.

▌ **9. (A) is correct.** The census count of people below the poverty line is not wholly accurate because millions of people have incomes just above it. Any small event could cause them to fall below it, and many people do fall just below, rise just above, and fall below again. Census data, therefore, underestimates the amount of poverty in the United States.

10. (D) is correct. Social Security is administered by the federal government through the Social Security Administration. Welfare programs are, however, administered individually by each state. This allows each state to set regulations and implement antipoverty initiatives in ways best suited to the residents of the state.

Free-Response Question

Poverty is a major problem in the United States and, as the data above shows, it is unevenly distributed among racial groups in the United States. Most noticeably, the poverty rates among African Americans and Hispanic Americans are twice that of whites and Asian Americans. Whites and Asian Americans have poverty rates just below the national average at 9.8% and 10.4% respectively. However, Hispanic Americans and African Americans have rates of 22.8% and 23.6% respectively—twice the national average. These groups are much smaller than whites, who make up 70% of the population. Poverty is therefore much more concentrated among these two groups, since about one in every four or five African Americans and Hispanic Americans experiences poverty. In contrast, only one in every ten whites does.

The government has devised some programs to extend social welfare to these groups in poverty. One is the Earned Income Tax Credit. To those people with especially low incomes as reported on their tax returns, the government issues a check instead of collecting taxes. This tax break benefits poor people directly. Moreover, because it is paid to working people, it encourages employment. However, the federal government loses a good deal of money by not being able to collect taxes but having to make transfer payments to beneficiaries instead.

Medicaid is a means-tested program that pays for the medical care of the poorest people in America. While this benefits those who otherwise would have no access to health care, Medicaid is expensive for the federal government. This is largely because the cost of medical care is so high in the United States. At best, the government can make the eligibility requirements more strict so that even fewer people have access to federally funded health care. Finally, while this program does help the needy receive medical treatment, it does nothing to end poverty or to encourage people to work and save money.

Debate continues over what role the government should play in alleviating poverty. The amount of poverty has not decreased much, despite federal assistance programs. About one in ten Americans experiences poverty, and about half of those are Hispanic Americans or African Americans. As these are the least active groups in the electorate and the least powerful, politicians may not be particularly responsive to this cause despite its prevalence in America.

This essay answers each component of the question with clear, specific examples. The student accurately interprets the data in the graphs and uses this information to illustrate the problem of poverty in the United States. He or she also explains the basic premise of two federal assistance programs—the Earned Income Tax Credit and Medicaid—and notes some advantages and disadvantages of each. Overall, the student demonstrates a good understanding of social welfare in the United States as represented by the given data.

CHAPTER 19

Policymaking for Health Care and the Environment

Both health care policy and environmental policy are becoming important issues on the public and political agendas. Many competing interests vie to influence these policies. The health care system is expensive, and not all people have access to it. Politicians and the public agree that the system needs major reforming, but no one has yet agreed on what those reforms should be. Environmental policies, while they help protect the environment, may hinder business. Furthermore, these two policy areas require a fair amount of technical expertise in order to be fully understood, so most Americans are unable to make informed policy choices and most decisions are left to policymakers, interest groups, and the industries.

Health Care Policy

The cost of health care in the United States is very high and is growing.

▊ Funding has focused on **technological advances,** which are extremely expensive.

▊ More facilities have been built than are being used, but their upkeep must be paid for.

▊ New drugs and procedures have been developed to treat more illnesses than ever before.

▊ The public is not pressed to be concerned about the cost of health care, since most of it is paid for by the **government, employers, and insurance companies.**

▊ **Malpractice lawsuits** are becoming more common, which raises doctors' insurance premiums and, in turn, raises the cost of their services.

Americans do not all have equal access to health care.

▊ Health care and insurance are mostly **privatized,** not **nationalized,** so they are not provided for everyone.

▊ Most people get **insurance** through their jobs.

  ▪ Unemployed people have to pay for health care themselves, and most cannot afford to.

  ▪ Companies feel they are bearing too much of the health care burden, but they do get significant tax breaks for contributing to their employees' insurance policies.

  ▪ Part-time employees are usually not eligible for benefits.

  ▪ Small companies cannot afford to pay for their employees' health care.

- **Accessibility** is unequal among people of different races and incomes.
  - A greater percentage of minorities and lower-income families do not have insurance.
  - Members of minority groups and lower classes have poorer health because they often do not have regular family doctors.
  - Health maintenance organizations (**HMO**s) have lowered the cost of health care but have not alleviated the problem of inaccessibility.

Debate continues over **who should pay for health care.**
- The **government** pays for about 50 percent of health care costs.
  - A nationalized system in which the government pays all health care costs has been proposed and rejected after lobbying by insurance and doctors' interest groups.
  - The government pays for Medicare and part of Medicaid, but the Medicare system is in danger of running out of money in the next decade.
- **Insurance companies** pay for about 30 percent of health care costs.
  - Have lobbied against **socialized medicine** because it would put them out of business
- Individuals pay about 20 percent.

Policymaking for Health Care

Policymaking for health care involves several political players and a highly charged issue.
- Senior citizens actively pursue federal funding for Medicare.
  - Lawmakers must fulfill the needs of their constituents, especially of those who vote.
- Interest groups representing the medical profession and insurance companies are well funded and very active in the political arena.
- Business groups try to persuade the government to take on more responsibility for health care so that businesses do not have to pay for it.
- Many groups, particularly the poor, are largely underrepresented in the health care policy debate.
- Policymakers in some cases choose which medical procedures to fund, because the money necessary to perform just a few very expensive procedures could be distributed more widely to provide basic services to more people.

Environmental Policy

Environmental policy and **economic policy** often conflict with each other.
- Industrial processes can harm the environment.
- Environmental restrictions may inhibit economic growth and expansion.
- Environmental and business interest groups lobby strongly for conflicting policies.
  - Environmental groups call for preservation of wildlife and natural resources and for greater regulation of pollution.

- Business groups demand fewer regulations and restrictions that inhibit industrial expansion.
- Private companies and federal agencies must file a report with the **Environmental Protection Agency** citing the possible effects on the environment of every project they plan to undertake.
    - Interest groups have access to the reports, and even the threat of a lawsuit brought by one of them deters many companies from proposing projects that may be challenged by the environmental lobby.

Environmental and **energy policy** also may conflict but are dependent on each other.

- There is a growing demand for energy, but most energy is derived from sources that harm the environment.
    - The government has tried to make industries more responsible for cleanups and environmental protection.
    - Energy providers argue that such restrictions are costly to the industry.
- The government funds research on **alternative energy** resources and sets standards for environmentally safe energy production and consumption.
- Policy debates continue over how to dispose of **nuclear waste.**
- Debate also continues over the possible consequences of **global warming** and what the government should do to prevent it.
- **"Environmental racism"** refers to the placing of factories and power plants in poor, minority neighborhoods, which meets with less organized opposition.

For Additional Review

Make a table of the advantages and disadvantages of the current health care system. Then, in a third column, note reforms that have been attempted or suggested. Can you think of any other possibilities?

Multiple-Choice Questions

1. Voters tend to be less informed about environmental politics because
   (A) they are not familiar with the highly technical motivations and consequences of environmental policies
   (B) most people are not concerned about environmental issues
   (C) most reports on environmental policies are not accessible to the public because they contain sensitive material
   (D) most environmental issues go unreported by the news media
   (E) most environmental issues and policies are too new to be familiar to voters

2. The cost of health care in the United States is very high for all of the following reasons EXCEPT
   (A) more illnesses are curable by medical treatment today
   (B) the frequency of malpractice suits is leading to higher insurance rates
   (C) the cost of upkeep for excessive medical facilities
   (D) more people are getting sick than ever before
   (E) new medical technologies are expensive

3. In the American health care system, who pays most of the costs for medical research and treatment?
   (A) Taxpayers
   (B) Employers
   (C) Medical professionals
   (D) Insurance companies
   (E) The government

4. Energy companies and environmentalists usually have opposing political goals because
   (A) no alternative energy sources have been discovered yet
   (B) factories that produce electricity pollute the environment
   (C) environmentalists are liberal, whereas energy producers tend to be conservative
   (D) environmentalists want to put an end to energy production
   (E) energy companies refuse to comply with federal environmental protection procedures

5. Which of the following statements accurately describe the health care policy debate?
   I. Senior citizens are the most active portion of the electorate in the health care debate because they stand to gain the most.
   II. Medicare is the one policy on which most congresspeople, health care professionals, and voters agree because it has proven to be the most cost-effective program.
   III. Groups like the American Medical Association lobby successfully for privatized health care because they are well funded and highly organized.
   IV. Many new interest groups have arisen to lobby for more health care assistance to people in poverty.
   V. Business interest groups represent employers who want the government to take greater responsibility for health care.
   (A) I only
   (B) II and V only
   (C) III and IV only
   (D) I, III, and V only
   (E) II, IV, and V only

6. Environmental interest groups are particularly powerful because
   (A) most politicians can personally identify with environmental problems
   (B) they have more money than most business interest groups
   (C) they work with specialists who fully understand the environmental impact of policy decisions
   (D) public participation is higher in environmental groups than in any other type of interest group
   (E) environmental groups lobby members of Congress more aggressively than any other type of interest group

7. Which of the following is an accurate comparison between the American health care system and those in most European countries?
   (A) Management of the American system is concentrated in one federal institution.
   (B) The American system provides all needed assistance to lower-income families so that they receive regular medical care.
   (C) The American system is more cost effective because employers, insurance companies, and the government all work together.
   (D) In the American system, everyone has equal access to health care.
   (E) Under the American system, people pay more, and many are not covered by insurance.

8. Businesses oppose environmental regulations for all of the following reasons EXCEPT
   (A) they are unclear because they conflict with earlier environmental policies
   (B) they discourage employment because they prevent factories from moving into new areas
   (C) they force businesses to buy raw materials from other countries
   (D) they usually force companies to pay high cleanup costs
   (E) they inhibit the expansion and growth of industry

9. Businesses offer insurance benefits to their employees mainly because
   (A) they are forced to by federal law
   (B) they receive a sizable tax break
   (C) they are concerned about the health of their employees
   (D) they receive subsidies
   (E) the health system is designed so that all people must get insurance through their workplace

10. Interest groups battle environmental racism because
   (A) people in neighborhoods where factories are located have an unfair economic advantage
   (B) the energy industry practices job discrimination when hiring employees for new power plants
   (C) factories that pollute the air and water are usually located in poorer neighborhoods
   (D) environmental activists usually lobby for environmental protection of only more affluent suburban neighborhoods
   (E) minority neighborhoods tend to create more pollution than other neighborhoods do

The American health care system is criticized for being both inefficient and expensive. For these reasons, health care reform is an extremely pressing issue on both the public and political agendas. However, so many conflicting interests are at stake that policymakers have not been able to agree on the nature of the reforms, so the system continues to cost billions of dollars.

Select ONE of these groups in the electorate.

- Senior citizens
- The poor

Select ONE of these businesses.

- Medical profession
- Insurance companies

For each group you selected, explain its involvement in the health care debate. Specifically, answer ALL of the following questions.

a. What is the group's perspective on health care reform?
b. What does the group stand to gain or lose through reforms?
c. How does the group influence policy decisions?

ANSWERS AND EXPLANATIONS

Multiple-Choice Questions

1. **(A) is correct.** Voters have a hard time making decisions about environmental policy because of the technical expertise needed to fully understand the impact of political policies on the environment. For a time the government had more flexibility because it had only specialists reporting to it. Today, however, many active interest groups include environmental specialists who are able to argue effectively against programs that are harmful to the environment.

2. **(D) is correct.** More people are undergoing medical treatment because more types of illnesses can be treated today, but people are not actually getting sick in greater numbers. The main reason health care is so costly is that medical treatments are extremely expensive to perform and medical facilities are extremely expensive to maintain.

3. **(E) is correct.** Despite the common misconception that the American health care system is entirely privatized, the government is actually the greatest financial contributor. It funds nearly 50 percent of health care, while insurance companies pay about 30 percent and individuals pay about 20 percent.

4. **(B) is correct.** Energy companies and environmentalists have a fundamental conflict. Factories and power plants cause most of the pollution to lakes, rivers, soil, and the air. The companies must meet Americans' increasing demand for energy, however. As a result of this conflict, energy policy is shifting toward researching alternative energy sources.

5. **(D) is correct.** Many different interest groups are extremely active in the health care debate, because so many groups stand to gain or lose in policy decisions. Senior citizens lobby for Medicare and federal funding to assist them in

the high cost of medical treatments for the elderly. Doctors and insurance companies attempt to block reforms that move the system toward socialized medicine and away from privatization because they would lose profits. Employers, on the other hand, push for greater federal responsibility in the health care system so that they do not have to pay insurance for their employees.

▌ **6. (C) is correct.** Environmental groups have gained a significant degree of political power by employing specialists who understand the environmental impact of federal policies. These groups are particularly important, because this is one policy area about which the public is less informed because it lacks technical expertise. Vocal interest groups, however, prevent government and industry from making economic decisions without considering the environmental consequences.

▌ **7. (E) is correct.** In most European countries, the government funds upward of 70 percent of health care costs. Most of these countries have nationalized health care systems in which all people have equal access to health care at virtually no cost. In contrast, the American government funds only about 46 percent of health care costs, leaving the rest to insurance companies and individuals. Many Americans, however, cannot afford to buy insurance or pay for medical treatment, so Americans tend to be less healthy than people in European countries.

▌ **8. (A) is correct.** Current environmental policies do not necessarily conflict with earlier policies; rather, they have become much more stringent. Environmental regulations now control where new factories can be located and affect new industrial processes by setting strict emissions standards. Recent environmental policies have also put the burden of environmental clean-up on the industries that created the pollution.

▌ **9. (B) is correct.** The government encourages employers to help finance health care by offering tax breaks to companies. This appeases many large companies and allows most employees to be insured. However, small businesses do not have as many resources to offer insurance to their employees, so they are more actively opposed to the role business plays in the health care system.

▌ **10. (C) is correct.** Power plants tend to be located in poorer neighborhoods for two reasons: Land is cheaper there, and residents have less political clout with which to oppose new plants. Environmentalists have taken up the cause of environmental racism because pollution from the plants affects mostly people of low income who cannot afford medical care.

Free-Response Question

The American health care system is costly, inefficient, and in need of reform. However, instituting reforms is very difficult, because so many groups have different needs. Politicians must listen to and weigh all of these interests but hesitate to make any decisions that would upset their constituents or campaign contributors and therefore cost them reelection.

Senior citizens are one powerful group in the electorate—and one with much at stake in the health care system. Because people are living longer (with the costly advances in health care), the number of senior citizens is rising. This group is therefore becoming the largest consumer of health care. Senior citizens want to see the continuation of the federally funded Medicare program, even though in just a few years expenditures for Medicare will begin to exceed revenues. Furthermore, senior citizens not only need more regular medical care than younger Americans, but they are also more likely to endorse advanced, highly technical medical procedures that will help them live longer. Such extremely expensive procedures, however, skew the costs of health care. The money spent on just one procedure on an ailing 85-year-old could be used to finance regular medical care for a number of low-income families. However, senior citizens are more likely to win their policy battles because they are more active than other groups in the electorate. The AARP is the largest and one of the most influential interest groups, and senior citizens vote in greater numbers than do most other Americans. Politicians are therefore very aware of how health care reform will affect senior citizens.

Medical professionals, such as doctors and hospital administrators, also have much at stake in the health care debate. Their profession requires a great deal of money for upkeep of facilities and new technology. This is the main reason why health care is so expensive. Although too many facilities have been built and are now wasting money, cutbacks to the health care profession cannot be so restrictive that they prevent doctors from saving lives. Money is also required for medical research so that doctors can develop cures and new treatments. Moreover, medical professionals, who make a lot in profits and point to concerns about the quality of socialized systems, are proponents of privatized health care. They are therefore likely to oppose any reforms that might lead to socialized medicine. In fact, it was the American Medical Association, a large, well-funded interest group, that prevented Woodrow Wilson from enacting a nationalized health care system in the early twentieth century. Today, this and other groups continue to protect doctors from losing part of their salaries for the benefit of the system. Such interests have essentially brought health care reform to a standstill. Health care is an especially difficult policy area because it is both a social concern and a widespread, lucrative business.

This essay clearly explains the interests of two groups in the health care reform debate. The student demonstrates a knowledge of health care policy by relating the needs and policy preferences of each group. The student also correctly explains each group's role in shaping health care policy and therefore shows a good understanding of the policymaking process as a whole.

CHAPTER 20

Foreign and Defense Policymaking

Foreign policy has become crucial to governmental affairs in the past century, as the United States made the transition from isolationist country to world superpower. In this global era of high-speed connections, brief but deadly missile strikes, and free trade, it is apparent that this policy area will continue to hold an important place on every politician's agenda and in the public's mind as well.

American Foreign Policy: Instruments, Actors, and Policymakers

International organizations are becoming more necessary in today's global political and economic arenas.

▌ The **United Nations** is a global legislative body.
- Nearly 200 countries are members, each with one vote in the General Assembly.
- Mainly responsible for **peacekeeping**, but also international economic, education, and welfare programs
- The **Security Council** makes the most pressing decisions.
  - Five permanent members, each with veto power: **the United States, China, Russia, France,** and **Great Britain**
  - Ten other seats are rotated each session.

Regional organizations combine blocs of countries in military and economic alliances.

▌ The **North Atlantic Treaty Organization (NATO)** is a military alliance formed by the United States and western European countries during the Cold War.
- Since the end of the Cold War, some former Eastern bloc countries have been admitted.
- Members pledge to support each other in times of war.
- Helps prevent the threat of war

▌ The **European Union** is an economic alliance.
- Most Western European countries share a common currency.
- No trade barriers
- No employment restrictions among countries

Multinational corporations contribute to about one-fifth of the global economy.

▌ Have significant influence over taxes and trade regulations

▌ Can be as powerful as governments

Non-governmental organizations (NGOs) unite people globally for common causes or goals.

▌ Churches, labor unions, environmental groups, human rights groups

American foreign policy is conducted mostly by the president and the executive branch, though Congress has some important responsibilities.

▌ The president serves as chief diplomat.

- Commander in chief of the armed forces
- Negotiates treaties and make executive agreements
- Appoints ambassadors
- Can act quickly and decisively

▌ The bureaucratic arm of foreign policy is the **State Department.**

- The **secretary of state** is the president's top foreign policy adviser.
- American embassies fall under its jurisdiction.

▌ The **Department of Defense** works closely with the State Department in matters of national security.

- The **Joint Chiefs of Staff** represent each branch of the armed forces in an advisory committee.

▌ The **Central Intelligence Agency** collects information to help the departments make policy decisions.

- Sometimes plays a covert role in the governmental affairs of other nations.

▌ **Congress** helps to oversee foreign policy.

- Ratifies treaties
- Declares war
- Appropriates funds for national security

American Foreign Policy: An Overview

▌ The United States practiced **isolationism** until World War I.

▌ During the ideological **Cold War,** the United States focused on the **containment** of **communism.**

- The Department of Defense grew in terms of size and responsibilities.
- The **military-industrial complex** came to play a major role in politics.
- The **arms race** between the United States and the Soviet Union caused an international arms buildup.

▌ The United States became involved in the **Vietnam War** to contain the spread of communism in Asia.

- The prolonged conflict resulted in massive troop commitments and heavy bombing of the north.
- Protests erupted at home, and Americans' faith in the government was shaken.

▌ The policy of **détente** brought greater cooperation among nations.

▌ Defense spending went up enormously under Reagan, higher than it had been through the whole Cold War.

▌ The Cold War came to an end with the fall of the Soviet bloc in the early 1990s, but international relations have yet to stabilize completely in a new, more cooperative system.

The Politics of Defense Policy

▌ Defense spending has decreased significantly to one-sixth of the federal budget.
  ▪ There is some concern that defense spending detracts from social spending.
  ▪ Decreasing spending means fewer jobs for weapons builders.
▌ The standing army is large and costly, though it has been decreasing.
▌ The extremely costly arms buildup has stopped.
  ▪ Treaties have reduced nuclear weapons reserves among most nations.

The New Global Agenda

Attention has shifted away from long wars and formal military actions and alliances.

▌ **Economic sanctions** have become a powerful tool of foreign policy.
  ▪ Embargoes, cutting off economic aid, and restricting imports are all forms of sanctions.
  ▪ Are safer and cheaper than military alternatives
  ▪ Are often initiated as a result of the efforts of human rights, environmental, and other political groups
▌ Stopping the proliferation of **nuclear weapons** is high on the international agenda.
▌ **Terrorism** has become a pressing international issue.

The international economy is now the highest priority on the international agenda.

▌ International trade has increased dramatically in the past few decades.
▌ Capital can move more easily across borders with the Internet and advanced communications systems.
▌ The use of tariffs has declined to allow free trade among nations.
  ▪ International protests against free trade have become common, because people fear the exploitation of less-developed countries by multinational corporations and because workers fear the loss of jobs.
▌ In the United States, imports exceed exports, so there is a **balance of trade deficit.**
  ▪ Labor is cheaper in other countries.
  ▪ This leads to unemployment, especially in blue-collar jobs.
▌ The North-South divide of wealthy nations and third world countries is becoming increasingly apparent.
  ▪ Less-developed countries are millions of dollars in debt to developed countries.
  ▪ Countries that receive aid usually have desirable natural resources.
▌ **Oil** and energy supplies are making economies more interdependent.
  ▪ The United States imports most of its oil from the Middle East.
▌ The **environment** is a global concern that affects all nations, but economic progress usually dominates environmental priorities.

For Additional Review

Make a time line of some of the most important foreign policy events of the twentieth century. Note important political actors and briefly describe the consequences of each event.

Multiple-Choice Questions

1. Which of the following institutions would be most likely to press for international environmental regulations?
   (A) Multinational corporations
   (B) NATO
   (C) Congress
   (D) Nongovernmental organizations
   (E) Joint Chiefs of Staff

2. Free trade among nations has all of the following consequences EXCEPT
   (A) less-developed countries lose some control over their natural resources
   (B) tariffs are increased to protect American business
   (C) products move easily between nations
   (D) multinational corporations gain profits and power
   (E) developed countries lose jobs in production

3. Economic sanctions typically fail to affect the targeted nation when
   (A) they are unilateral
   (B) the economy of the targeted nation is weak
   (C) the nation imposing sanctions is not part of NATO
   (D) the oil market is doing well
   (E) they are proposed by humans rights groups

4. Congress exercises the most influence over foreign policy in which of the following ways?
   (A) Declaring war
   (B) Confirming ambassadors
   (C) Appropriating money
   (D) Ratifying treaties
   (E) Recognizing nations

5. Which of the following statements best explains why defense spending has decreased?
   (A) Most resources have been channeled into increasing the standing army, which costs less to maintain than military equipment does.
   (B) Weapons can be produced more cheaply today as a result of new technology.
   (C) The United States has succeeded in containing communism in all parts of the world.
   (D) There have been fewer missions in the past two decades to require new military technologies.
   (E) The arms race, which required the building of expensive weapons, has ended.

6. All of the following are characteristic of foreign policy during the Cold War EXCEPT
   (A) the expanding Department of Defense
   (B) an end to détente
   (C) the arms race
   (D) containment
   (E) the rise of the military-industrial complex

7. The president has which of the following advantages in the area of foreign policy?
   (A) Authority to set the defense budget
   (B) Power to declare war
   (C) Ability to act quickly and independently
   (D) Power to impose sanctions
   (E) Access to United Nations funds

8. Some of the most important global treaties that the United States has entered into recently have focused on
   (A) the removal of weapons of mass destruction
   (B) global environmental protection
   (C) alleviating the debt of less-developed countries
   (D) protecting jobs from the globalization of industry
   (E) the containment of communism

9. Which of the following bureaucratic institutions is primarily responsible for gathering information from foreign governments?
   (A) Department of Defense
   (B) Federal Bureau of Investigation
   (C) Federal Communications Commission
   (D) Central Intelligence Agency
   (E) State Department

10. Which of the following was a major consequence of the Vietnam War?
    (A) The United States failed to stop the spread of communism throughout Asia.
    (B) The Cold War came to an end, leaving the United States as the sole superpower.
    (C) NATO was created to protect the United States and Western nations from the threat of communism.
    (D) The United States adopted the philosophy of détente as the new cornerstone of its foreign policy.
    (E) American citizens lost faith in the government after being lied to about the progress of the war.

Free-Response Question

The landscape of foreign policy has changed significantly in the past 50 years. Power and responsibility have shifted, both within and without the government. Discuss the roles that BOTH of the following entities play in foreign policy, citing how and why those roles have changed.

- The president
- Multinational corporations

ANSWERS AND EXPLANATIONS

Multiple-Choice Questions

- **1. (D) is correct.** Nongovernmental organizations such as Greenpeace and Amnesty International form to advance particular causes across nations. They are not funded by or answerable to any one government, but they do influence governments to take up their causes, much as interest groups do in the United States.
- **2. (B) is correct.** Trade barriers such as tariffs have been reduced, not increased, as a result of free trade. They once protected American businesses

from competition with imported goods, and without them, imports have increased and created a balance of trade deficit. However, at the same time, exports have soared without tariffs.

▌ **3. (A) is correct.** Sanctions brought by only one country against another are doomed to failure because the sanctioned country can simply divert its trade elsewhere. Sanctions are thus effective only when a group of countries agree to impose trade restrictions on a country together. Sanctions therefore also contribute to global interdependency.

▌ **4. (C) is correct.** Because the pace of foreign policy does not allow Congress much time for making important decisions, its powers have diminished somewhat. However, it does have full authority over all military expenditures, including foreign aid and the budgets of the State Department, the Department of Defense, and the CIA.

▌ **5. (E) is correct.** The arms race slowed down substantially as the United States adopted the policy of détente toward the Soviet Union. In the past two decades, treaties such as the Strategic Arms Reduction Treaty have actually encouraged nations to destroy many of their weapons of mass destruction.

▌ **6. (B) is correct.** Détente was a policy adopted by the United States and the Soviet Union to help both superpowers make the transition out of the Cold War. This new approach eased tensions between the two countries and led them to new cooperation with each other.

▌ **7. (C) is correct.** The president's power has increased in recent decades, because new technologies have sped up military and other foreign policy processes. Unlike Congress, the president is an independent actor who is able to make decisions quickly in order to respond to situations that arise suddenly in the global arena.

▌ **8. (A) is correct.** The United States has entered into many treaties, but some of the most significant are ones that reduce nuclear weapons stores in countries possessing them. The United States is scheduled to reduce its nuclear weapons to no more than 2,200 by 2012. Some countries, such as Ukraine, have given up their nuclear weapons, and others, such as Brazil and Sweden, have discontinued their nuclear weapons programs.

▌ **9. (D) is correct.** Although the CIA has a somewhat glorified image of conducting espionage and covert operations, it actually collects most of its data from legitimate sources, such as foreign governmental reports. This information is then used to help make foreign policy decisions.

▌ **10. (E) is correct.** The Vietnam War had a great impact on American attitudes toward government. Not only did the public feel betrayed by President Johnson's breaking his campaign promise not to send American draftees into the war, but people felt they had been lied to about the progress of the long, drawn-out war that ended more in defeat than in success. Watergate further shook public opinion, and even today people view the government with some suspicion.

Free-Response Question

Foreign policy has become increasingly important in today's global era. Communications and transportation have created closer relationships among countries, and free trade has entwined their economies. These changes have encouraged a new style of foreign policy in which the president and multinational corporations have come to play powerful roles.

Globalization calls for diplomacy, so as the nation's chief diplomat, the president now devotes more time and energy to foreign policy. During the era of isolationism, the president was not highly visible beyond American borders. Now, however, the president must regularly serve as the representative of the United States abroad. Moreover, the president has the constitutional power to recognize nations formally, and hundreds of new nations have formed in the past century. These increased responsibilities, in turn, concentrate more power in one person, especially because media technology now makes the president even more visible. The president also has more leeway as commander in chief than ever before. The speed at which crises arise and wars are fought requires quick decision making. The 535 members of Congress are not well equipped to act with haste, but a single president can respond to situations almost instantly. As commander in chief, the president also has the power to determine the nature of military operations and even can authorize the use of nuclear weapons without restraint from any other governmental institution. Though presidents have always authorized the use of weapons, weapons were never as enormously destructive as they are today. Furthermore, because the United States has the most military might in the world, in this sense the president can be seen as the most powerful person in the world.

Foreign policy, while still dealing with military crises all over the world, is shifting its focus to the international economy. Trade barriers have declined, allowing for the free and easy movement of products across borders. Companies too now extend beyond the borders of any one country. Multinational corporations have offices, plants, and labor forces all over the world. They exert a major influence over the economies of less-developed countries, where they can set up factories, hire labor, and acquire raw materials cheaply and without the restraints of governmental regulation. Not only are they extensive, but they are incredibly powerful because these corporations are now responsible for about 20 percent of the world's economy. Multinational corporations therefore have significant political power. They are bound only by laws of countries in which they operate and can use their influence to pressure those governments as well as our own. They may even play a key role directly in the government of less-developed nations. Multinational corporations can exert their influence to pressure a country to open its borders to free trade, as was done when several worked together to overthrow the resistant Chilean government in 1973. If their power continues to go unchecked, multinationals stand to become the next rogue governments. Regardless, their presence indicates that foreign policy actors will continue to be of great power and importance in this global era.

The student demonstrates an understanding of the new global era of foreign policy by clearly illustrating the roles that the president and multinational corporations play. He or she conveys both general concepts, such as the increasing predominance of the global economy in foreign policy, and strong, specific examples to explain both how and why the roles of these two foreign policy actors have changed.

CHAPTER 21

The New Face of State and Local Government

State and local governments employ thousands of people to perform all kinds of regular daily tasks, many of which are often taken for granted. In the past few decades, the responsibilities of both state and local governments have grown. The governments themselves have become increasingly diverse and more active in social policy than ever before.

State Constitutions

Each state is governed by a constitution that lays out the structure of the government and the laws of the state.

- Most state constitutions authorize a **governor** and a **bicameral legislature.**
- Most provide for the separation of powers and include a **bill of rights.**
- The U.S. Constitution has supremacy over all state constitutions.

State Elections

Citizens usually have the opportunity to vote for many political officials, including state judges.

- Some states allow residents to vote on laws directly during elections.
- Gubernatorial elections, like presidential elections, are becoming more candidate-centered.
    - Political parties are declining in influence in state elections.
    - Voters are less likely to vote by **party identification.**
    - Gubernatorial campaigns are fairly independent and rely heavily on television advertising.
    - This leads to **ticket splitting** and **divided government** at the state level.
- Voters also elect their state's lieutenant governor, attorney general, treasurer, and often many department secretaries.
- In *Baker* v. *Carr,* the Supreme Court decreed that state House (and later Senate) districts must be based on population counts.
    - Shifted political focus away from rural agendas
    - Suburban areas win new political representation.
- State representatives tend to be less known, because their campaigns are smaller and receive less media attention.
    - Incumbents usually have a great advantage over challengers.

- Some states have attempted to set **term limits** for state legislators and executive officers.
- More women and minorities are being elected to state-level positions.

The Job of Governor

Each state's governor has different powers and responsibilities, and some governors have more power than others.

- Governors in most states have become more powerful as the decreasing number of elected officials has **concentrated power.**
  - Their power is checked by a large, merit-based civil service.
- Governors exercise a great deal of power through the **line-item veto**.
  - Can veto specific parts of an appropriations bill, which gives the governor the last word in legislation
- Governors also have significant **budgetary** power.
  - State legislatures do not have the time and the staff to devote much effort to amending the governor's budget proposal.
  - The **line-item veto** allows governors to fine-tune budgetary legislation.

State Legislatures

State legislatures are becoming increasingly important to the political activity of each state.

- They have undergone a great deal of reform to make them more professional and more representative of their constituents.
  - **Legislative sessions** have been lengthened to allow legislatures to be more critical and more active in policymaking.
  - A raise in salaries allows legislators to devote more attention to policymaking rather than relying on another job.
  - Legislatures now have **larger administrative staffs.**
  - Many people criticize the reforms for engineering too much politicking and failing to achieve greater representation.
- State legislatures have many of the **same responsibilities as Congress.**
  - Pass laws in the same process
  - Appropriate money
  - Confirm the governor's appointments
- State legislators are more closely in contact with their **constituents** than federal politicians are.

State Court Systems

State court systems developed with little organization but have recently been reformed to mirror the federal court system.

- **Trial courts** oversee civil and criminal cases.
- **Intermediate courts of appeal** hear routine appeals.
- The **state supreme court** handles appeals that may have a greater impact on state law.
- In some states, voters elect judges; in others, judges are appointed.

- Many states are adopting the **merit plan.** According to this plan, judges are appointed from a list of recommendations, serve a trial term, and then are put on a ballot for voters to decide if they should stay in office.

Direct Democracy

Some states, particularly in the West and Midwest, offer voters the ability to participate in politics directly.

- **Initiatives** allow citizens to propose a piece of legislation, petition to have it placed on the ballot, and then vote on whether to make it law.
    - Elected politicians are bypassed in the legislative process.
    - Not all initiatives are well planned, and some do not succeed.
    - Many initiatives are backed by interest groups, not groups of citizens.
- A **referendum** is a proposal passed by the state legislature that is then placed on the ballot to be approved by voters rather than by the governor.
- Voters can use a **recall** to call for a special election to remove a politician from office.
    - This is difficult and costly and therefore occurs infrequently.

Local Governments

Local governments are completely subservient to the state government. However, because they work closely with constituents, they still have significant political clout.

- **County**—mostly administrative
    - Keep birth, death, marriage, and property records
    - Responsible for law enforcement, roads, education, elections, collecting taxes
    - Usually have only limited legislative powers to make laws
- **Township** — also administrative
    - Most have limited responsibilities assisting county governments.
    - Some function like city governments, but they have no lawmaking powers.
- **Municipality**—the most common type of government, which does have legislative capabilities
    - Responsible for all public works, education, and public services
    - **Mayor-council government:** Both a mayor and city council are elected.
    - **Council-manager government:** The city council is elected and chooses a manager to implement policies.
    - **Commission government:** Members of the commission are elected by voters. Each has an area of jurisdiction over which he or she has both legislative and executive authority.
    - **School district:** A special type of government that deals specifically with public education
        - Residents elect a board of education, pay taxes toward their schools, and make decisions about their schools.

There are many pressing issues about social and economic inequalities among school districts.

■ **Special district**: Any other special government set up to handle a specific issue, such as waste disposal or public libraries

State and Local Finance Policy

▌ States get most of their revenues from sales and income taxes.

▌ State expenditures go mostly to statewide social programs and public services or to local governments.

▌ Local governments get most of their funds from the state, local taxes, and certain service fees for residents.

For Additional Review

Draw a diagram of the major federal, state, and local governmental institutions. Draw arrows to show where authority is directed and briefly describe the responsibilities of each institution you have included.

Multiple-Choice Questions

1. Governors have more power over state legislatures than the president has over Congress for which of the following reasons?
   (A) Governors can use a line-item veto.
   (B) Governors assign state legislators to committees.
   (C) State legislatures do not have any budgetary power.
   (D) Governors must be of the same party as the majority party in the legislature.
   (E) The system of checks and balances does not apply to state governments.

2. Citizens have more democratic access to state and local governments than to the federal government through all of the following means EXCEPT
   (A) passing laws by initiative
   (B) using recalls to remove officials from office
   (C) more frequent elections because state officials have shorter terms
   (D) proposing and voting on initiatives
   (E) electing numerous executive officials

3. Which of the following political trends are being experienced by both the federal and state governments?
   (A) Increasing focus on foreign policy
   (B) Divided government
   (C) Budget surpluses
   (D) Stronger party identification
   (E) Substantially growing bureaucracies

4. State legislators have significantly less power than members of Congress primarily because they
   (A) are appointed by the governor, not elected by the people
   (B) receive more media attention, and therefore are more constrained by public opinion
   (C) cannot overrule a gubernatorial veto
   (D) are held accountable to a greater degree by their constituents
   (E) usually work only part-time as legislators

5. Which of the following statements accurately describe municipal governments?
   I. The special district is the least democratic type of local government because its officials might not be elected and its activities are not publicized much.
   II. Counties are the most powerful type of municipal government because they are invested with both legislative and executive powers.
   III. The most prevalent and fastest-growing type of municipal government is the commission government.
   IV. School districts have proved to be highly effective forms of government that have successfully overcome the difficulties of desegregation.
   (A) I only
   (B) IV only
   (C) I and II only
   (D) III and IV only
   (E) II, III, and IV only

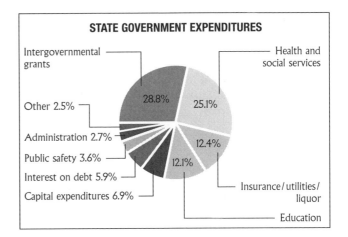

STATE GOVERNMENT EXPENDITURES

Intergovernmental grants — 28.8%
Other 2.5%
Administration 2.7%
Public safety 3.6%
Interest on debt 5.9%
Capital expenditures 6.9%
Health and social services — 25.1%
12.4%
12.1%
Insurance/utilities/liquor
Education

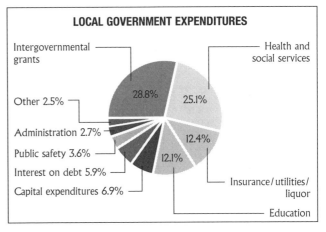

LOCAL GOVERNMENT EXPENDITURES

Intergovernmental grants — 28.8%
Other 2.5%
Administration 2.7%
Public safety 3.6%
Interest on debt 5.9%
Capital expenditures 6.9%
Health and social services — 25.1%
12.4%
12.1%
Insurance/utilities/liquor
Education

SOURCE: U.S. Bureau of the Census, *Statistical Abstract of the United States, 2001* (Washington, D.C.: U.S. Goveernment Printing Office, 2002), 284–287.

6. Which can you infer from the data in the two graphs above?
   (A) The cost of health and social services is divided almost equally between state and local government.
   (B) Thirty-four percent of local government's revenue is from state grants.
   (C) Local government's debt is larger than state government's.
   (D) A school that wants money to buy computers should ask the local government for funds.
   (E) State government has fewer administrators than local government does.

7. The relationship between local and state governments differs from the relationship between state and the federal governments in that
   (A) local governments have powers equal to those of the state government, but states are subordinate to the federal government
   (B) states and the federal government share powers, whereas local governments are subordinate to the powers of the state
   (C) local and state governments share powers, whereas state governments have no powers in relation to the federal government
   (D) local and state governments share powers, whereas states and the federal government do not
   (E) state governments have powers equal to those of the federal government, but local governments are subordinate to the powers of the state

8. Which of the following statements accurately describes the organizational structure of courts in most states?
   (A) All state courts are specialized to handle cases in certain administrative or legal fields.
   (B) State courts have only original jurisdiction and do not hear appeals.
   (C) Most state court systems are organized in the same way as the federal court system.
   (D) All cases from the general trial courts are appealed directly to the state supreme court.
   (E) The intermediate courts of appeal are the highest courts in the state.

9. Many state legislatures have undergone reforms in order to
   (A) cut spending by reorganizing the government
   (B) give governors more power
   (C) involve citizens more directly in the legislative process
   (D) decrease the use of the patronage system in state governments
   (E) make them more professional, full-time governmental bodies

10. A county government differs most from a municipal government in which of the following ways?
   (A) Only county governments can hold and regulate federal elections.
   (B) Municipal governments oversee a greater number of citizens.
   (C) County governments are responsible for keeping all public records.
   (D) County governments do not have the power to make broad policy.
   (E) Municipal governments generate more revenues.

Free-Response Question

In a federal system of government, authority over and responsibility for a nation's citizens are shared among different levels of government institutions. Citizens vote for officials and receive the benefits of a federal, state, and local government.

Select TWO of the following government activities.

- Collecting taxes
- Holding elections
- Providing public education
- Administering welfare programs

For EACH of the activities you selected, explain how responsibility is shared among the levels of government in order to perform the activity or provide the service to citizens.

ANSWERS AND EXPLANATIONS

Multiple-Choice Questions

1. **(A) is correct.** The line-item veto is a powerful tool. With it, governors truly have the final say in every budget because they can simply remove parts of it with which they disagree. State legislatures must accept the governor's final version of the legislation since they rarely have the votes to override it.

2. **(C) is correct.** Generally, state politics are more democratic than federal politics because citizens have more opportunities to vote for their leaders and sometimes even for their laws. However, they do not necessarily vote more frequently; in fact, many states have extended the term of office for governors from two to four years.

3. **(B) is correct.** Due to an overall decrease in party identification among the electorate, both levels are experiencing the difficulties that arise with divided government. Governors who are of a different party from the majority party in the state legislature encounter many of the same frustrations as the president. Consequently, both levels of government are also more frequently grappling with policy gridlock.

4. **(E) is correct.** State legislatures usually convene for only a few months or even just a few weeks a year. They have small staffs, and most legislators receive only a small salary and therefore hold other jobs during the rest of the year. For these reasons, being a state legislator is only a part-time job and carries less power against the full-time, fully-staffed governor.

5. **(A) is correct.** Special districts are unique governmental bodies. They may span other district lines to serve a single purpose, such as waste management. Because they are designed to provide only one service, their officials are frequently not elected by the public, which generally knows little about them and their activities.

6. **(D) is correct.** Remember that circle (or pie) graphs compare parts of a whole (100 percent); the figures do *not* describe dollar amounts. Since the state

"pie" is so much bigger than a local "pie," 3 percent of state expenses can be much more than 6 percent of local expenses. Education is by far the biggest priority of local governments, and they would be in charge of the needs of individual schools.

7. **(B) is correct.** Under federalism, the state and federal governments have concurrent powers. Local governments, however, are completely subject to state governments. A state government has full authority to establish or dissolve a local government.

8. **(C) is correct.** The court systems in each state evolved differently, and often haphazardly. However, reforms have brought them more in line with the federal system. Now most states have general trial courts, intermediate courts of appeal, and a state supreme court.

9. **(E) is correct.** As part-time governmental bodies, state legislatures can be ineffective. Many states have enacted reforms to encourage more full-time legislative participation in statewide policymaking. These reforms include extending the length of the legislative session, increasing the salary of legislators, and increasing their administrative staffs.

10. **(D) is correct.** County governments serve primarily administrative functions. They keep public records and provide many public services, but they have limited policymaking authority.

Free-Response Question

Under the Constitution, the United States was established as a federal system in which power is shared among the federal, state, and local levels of government. In some policy areas, each level has its own responsibilities and functions; in others, the three levels have concurrent powers. Collecting taxes and providing public education are two such policy areas.

Local, state, and federal governments all collect taxes for their own use. In fact, taxes are usually their primary source of revenue. The federal government collects income taxes from all employed people. This money funds federal programs such as Social Security and national defense, but some of it is also given in aid to the states. Each state, in turn, earns nearly half of its revenues through sales taxes and other taxes (though a few states do not have sales tax). These taxes are used to fund statewide social programs, build roads, pay the government's administrative costs, and provide aid to local governments. Local governments, which rely heavily on state funding, supplement their revenues with property taxes. Each level of government, then, earns money to help sustain itself and the other levels through taxes. This also means that citizens pay many different taxes, but, at the same time, they receive some services from each level.

Public education is one example of an expenditure on which each level of government spends some part of its revenue. Public education has always been a responsibility of the states, but all states receive federal aid to help fund new schools, hire teachers, and buy supplies. There is a trade-off in this system: in order to receive the funds, states must comply with federal standards. Schools statewide therefore receive both federal and state funding. While most money comes from the state, the state itself turns the responsibility of administration over to local governments. Most cities have established school districts in which citizens of a particular neighborhood pay additional taxes to and have some say in the administration of the schools in their area. They choose members of the board of education, decide on the building of new schools, and may even have a say in the hiring of teachers and school administrators. Schools, then, ultimately receive funding from all three levels of government and must adhere to the program requirements of each. Public education, even if it is not wholly successful, is a good example of how three levels of government share authority over and responsibility for a public service in a federal system.

This essay describes the role each level of government plays in both of the activities the student has chosen: collecting taxes and administering public education. The student clearly understands the relationships among levels of government in a federal system, and he or she also demonstrates a good understanding of the basic revenues and expenditures of each level of government. Finally, the student offers some good insights into the advantages and disadvantages of a federal system.

Part III

Sample Tests with Answers and Explanations

On the following pages are two sample exams. They mirror the actual AP exam in format and question types. Set aside a time to take these exams, timing yourself as you will be timed when you take the real test, to prepare you for your actual test-taking experience.

United States Government & Politics AP Exam Practice Test 1

United States Government & Politics Section I

Time: 45 minutes
60 Questions

Directions: Each of the questions or incomplete statements below is followed by five suggested answers or completions. Select the one that is best in each case and then fill in the corresponding oval on the answer sheet.

1. Political action committees were created by campaign reform laws to
   (A) involve the public more directly in presidential campaigns
   (B) regulate how groups such as business and labor contribute to campaigns
   (C) finance challengers' campaigns in order to eliminate the advantages of incumbency
   (D) pay for candidates' air time because it has become the most expensive feature in a campaign
   (E) limit the influence of political parties over election outcomes

2. All of the following are examples of the system of checks and balances EXCEPT
   (A) the president's power to veto
   (B) Congress's confirmation of presidential appointments
   (C) the Supreme Court's power of judicial review
   (D) Congress's authority to impeach the president
   (E) the president's control over the budget

GO ON TO THE NEXT PAGE

Political Action Committees—Number by Committee Type: 1980 to 2001

[As of December 31]

Committee type	1980	1985	1990	1995	1997	1998	1999	2000	2001
Total	2,551	3,992	4,172	4,016	3,844	3,798	3,835	3,706	3,907
Corporate	1,206	1,710	1,795	1,674	1,597	1,567	1,548	1,523	1,545
Labor	297	388	346	334	332	321	318	316	317
Trade/membership/health	576	695	774	815	825	821	844	812	860
Nonconnected	374	1,003	1,062	1,020	931	935	972	902	1,026
Cooperative	42	54	59	44	42	39	38	39	41
Corporation without stock	56	142	136	129	117	115	115	114	118

Source: U.S. Federal Election Commission, press release of January 2002.

3. Which of the following generalizations is supported by the information in the chart above?
   (A) Nonconnected PACs formed more frequently between 1980 and 2001 than any other kind of PAC.
   (B) The most dramatic change in the number of PACs occurred between 1980 and 1985.
   (C) There are only a few cooperative PACs because these are the most difficult type to meet the approval of the Federal Election Commission.
   (D) Business PACs spend the most money on congressional elections.
   (E) All types of PACs have increased in number dramatically since 1980.

4. Most of the cases that reach the Supreme Court do so through
   (A) congressional approval
   (B) *certiorari* appeals from lower federal courts
   (C) review and selection by the solicitor general
   (D) original jurisdiction
   (E) assignments by the president

5. The government began to pursue civil rights in the 1950s when
   (A) Congress passed the Voting Rights Act
   (B) civil rights activists marched on Washington to demand government action
   (C) the Supreme Court declared segregation unconstitutional
   (D) states agreed to discontinue their use of poll taxes as a means of preventing people from voting
   (E) the president issued an executive order to desegregate all public transportation

6. A president is most likely to advance his proposal in Congress in which of the following ways?
   (A) Denounce on national television members of Congress who oppose the proposal
   (B) Promise a key committee seat to supporters
   (C) Withdraw PAC funding from members of Congress who oppose the proposal
   (D) Solicit support from party members to build a coalition
   (E) Run advertisements to win public opinion of the proposal

7. Compared to Democrats, Republicans are more likely to
   (A) favor social spending
   (B) pursue union votes
   (C) attract the votes of women
   (D) hold conservative views
   (E) raise taxes

8. Presidents exercise their influence over the ideology of federal courts by
   (A) appointing only judges who agree with their ideology and political views
   (B) requesting that Congress impeach judges who are too liberal or too conservative
   (C) demoting judges to lower courts
   (D) allowing them to hear only those cases on which judges are likely to agree with the president's point of view
   (E) meeting with members of the Senate Judiciary Committee when they are performing oversight

9. Which of the following statements accurately describe voting tendencies among groups of the electorate?
   I. Women are more likely to vote for Republicans.
   II. Jewish voters overwhelmingly vote for Democratic candidates.
   III. Minority groups tend to vote for Democrats.
   IV. Rural voters usually endorse liberal Democrats.
   (A) I only
   (B) III only
   (C) II and III only
   (D) I and IV only
   (E) I, II, and III only

10. Which of the following groups is most likely to vote in elections?
    (A) People under the age of 21
    (B) Senior citizens
    (C) People without a college degree
    (D) Union members
    (E) Men with low-income jobs

11. The Supreme Court asserted which of the following principles in *Marbury* v. *Madison?*
    (A) The Fourteenth Amendment guarantees all individual freedoms under state laws.
    (B) Freedom of religion is guaranteed, but some religious practices may violate the establishment clause.
    (C) Under the Tenth Amendment, the federal government can regulate commerce among states.
    (D) The exclusionary rule must be upheld in all state court trials.
    (E) The Supreme Court has the power to declare laws passed by Congress unconstitutional.

12. In the process of political socialization, citizens
    (A) form their political beliefs
    (B) participate in a direct democracy
    (C) decide how they feel about an issue
    (D) evaluate and select their representatives
    (E) engage in political protest against a law

13. The failure of the Articles of Confederation and necessity for a new Constitution were made evident by the
    (A) success of the American Revolution
    (B) legislature's inability to select a president
    (C) need for a bicameral legislature
    (D) government's inability to subdue Shays' Rebellion
    (E) excess of centralized power in the national government

14. Voter turnout in the United States is low in part because
    (A) minority groups still struggle for the right to vote in southern states
    (B) registering to vote has become more difficult
    (C) voters see little difference between the platforms of the two parties' candidates
    (D) many low-income people are not able to pass the literacy test in order to vote
    (E) candidates do little to win public opinion

15. Which of the following statements about the national debt is true?
    (A) The national debt has decreased by 50 percent over the past decade.
    (B) The national debt grew significantly as a result of tax cuts and defense spending in the 1980s.
    (C) The national debt is a direct result of the Social Security program.
    (D) The federal government earns enough in revenues to pay off its debt each year.
    (E) When revenues exceed expenditures, the national debt increases.

16. Congress performs legislative oversight over executive departments by
    (A) hiring and firing department heads
    (B) determining the federal budget
    (C) vetoing department proposals
    (D) issuing impoundment bills
    (E) coordinating department activities with the president

17. Members of Congress most often vote according to
    (A) their own policy preferences
    (B) the needs of their constituents
    (C) their relationship with the president
    (D) their party affiliation
    (E) the ideology of their geographic region

18. Which of the following is NOT specifically prohibited by the Constitution?
    (A) Gender bias in the workplace
    (B) Self-incrimination
    (C) Slavery
    (D) National religion
    (E) Cruel and unusual punishment

19. Regulatory agencies are most likely to turn to the industries they oversee when they
    (A) do not have enough money to meet their budgets
    (B) need to gain the president's support
    (C) are not sure how to execute an ambiguous policy
    (D) are making budget proposals to Congress
    (E) are trying to win public approval

20. The largest federal expenditure is
    (A) national defense
    (B) public education
    (C) Social Security
    (D) grants to the states
    (E) political campaigns

OUTLAYS BY MAJOR SPENDING CATEGORY, 1970–2002			
(in billions of dollars)			
Year	Discretionary Spending	Entitlements and Other Mandatory Spending	Net Interest	Total Outlays
1970	120.3	72.5	14.4	195.6
1975	158.0	169.4	23.2	332.3
1980	276.3	291.2	52.5	590.9
1985	415.8	448.2	129.5	946.4
1990	500.6	626.9	184.3	1,253.2
1995	544.9	818.5	232.1	1,515.8
2000	614.8	1,029.8	223.0	1,788.8
SOURCE: Congressional Budget Office.				

21. Which of the following are true of the data in the table above?
   I. Entitlements and mandatory spending are the fastest-growing federal expenditures.
   II. Total expenditures increased the most between 1980 and 1985.
   III. The federal government spends about one-third of its revenues on entitlements and mandatory spending.
   IV. Payments made toward interest on the national debt typically double every five years.
   (A) III only
   (B) I and II only
   (C) II and III only
   (D) III and IV only
   (E) I and IV only

22. The two main responsibilities of congressional committees are
   (A) making and implementing policies
   (B) determining the budget and confirming the appointment of federal judges
   (C) writing guidelines for federal programs and educating the public
   (D) making policy recommendations and performing legislative oversight
   (E) suggesting candidates for cabinet positions and writing tax codes

23. All of the following are recent trends in presidential nominations and campaigns EXCEPT
   (A) declining party identification among voters
   (B) increasing costs of campaigning
   (C) decreasing importance of national conventions
   (D) increasing reliance on PACs to sustain campaigns
   (E) infrequency of presidential primaries among states

24. Single-issue groups represent people in the electorate who
   (A) have little political access and influence
   (B) donate money to political campaigns
   (C) pressure candidates to be less ambiguous about their ideology
   (D) feel strongly about a certain cause
   (E) advocate campaign finance reform

25. Presidents have sought to expand their power by
   (A) trying to take control of the federal budget
   (B) appointing party leaders to committee chairs in Congress
   (C) requesting the use of the line-item veto
   (D) appealing to Supreme Court justices
   (E) overseeing federal departments more strictly

26. When a president vetoes a bill,
   (A) Congress rarely overrides it
   (B) it will not become a law
   (C) the Supreme Court must approve the veto
   (D) Congress usually overrides it
   (E) his public opinion rating usually drops

GO ON TO THE NEXT PAGE

27. During the budgetary process, Congress does not normally revise spending for
    (A) national security
    (B) aid for public schools
    (C) highways and roads
    (D) agricultural subsidies
    (E) Social Security

28. The Supreme Court has upheld which of the following in its interpretation of the freedom of speech?
    (A) All forms of speech, including obscenity, are protected under the First Amendment.
    (B) The government cannot under any circumstances censor information.
    (C) Protests against the government are not protected under the First Amendment.
    (D) Forms of symbolic speech are protected under the First Amendment.
    (E) The freedom of speech is guaranteed by federal law, but it does not have to be upheld by the states.

29. The rise of the primary election system has led to
    (A) the increasing role of political parties in presidential elections
    (B) the public's more direct involvement in the election of the president
    (C) a decline in media coverage of presidential campaigns
    (D) a shift in power from national to state party organizations
    (E) fewer candidates seeking each party's nomination

30. Congress did the most to check the military power of presidents by
    (A) refusing to confirm their appointments for defense secretary
    (B) amending Article II of the Constitution
    (C) taking away their control over the defense budget
    (D) agreeing always to vote not to declare war
    (E) passing the War Powers Resolution

31. Unlike members of the House of Representatives, senators can influence policy debates by
    (A) relying on partisan support
    (B) calling for a vote
    (C) using a filibuster
    (D) forming a presidential coalition
    (E) running televised ads

32. The federal bureaucracy is the least democratic government institution in that
    (A) its members are not elected by the public
    (B) it does not take the needs of the public into account
    (C) Congress and the president closely oversee all of its actions
    (D) is not obligated to report on its activities to the public
    (E) its regulatory powers go unchecked by the other branches of government

33. The Constitution specifies which of the following about the appointment of federal judges?
    (A) A balance of liberal and conservative judges must be maintained.
    (B) Congress is responsible for filling judgeships.
    (C) There may be only nine Supreme Court justices.
    (D) They may serve terms of life if they maintain good conduct.
    (E) The appointments of lower federal judges do not need to be confirmed by Congress.

34. A president can be removed from office in which of the following ways?
    (A) The Supreme Court rules that he is incompetent or has violated the law.
    (B) In a recall, citizens can vote to remove the president from office.
    (C) The House votes to impeach him, and the Senate tries and convicts him.
    (D) The Senate votes to impeach him, and the Supreme Court tries the president.
    (E) Both houses of Congress vote to remove the president by a simple majority.

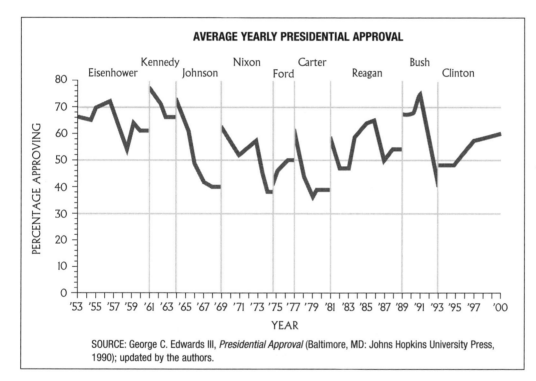

AVERAGE YEARLY PRESIDENTIAL APPROVAL

SOURCE: George C. Edwards III, *Presidential Approval* (Baltimore, MD: Johns Hopkins University Press, 1990); updated by the authors.

35. All of the following statements accurately describe the data in the graph EXCEPT
    (A) only two presidents did not experience a drop in public approval ratings
    (B) presidents Bush and Johnson lost the most public approval during their presidencies
    (C) three presidents experienced both significant increases and decreases in their approval ratings
    (D) on average, most presidents have approval ratings of just over 50 percent
    (E) Democratic presidents usually have higher public approval ratings

GO ON TO THE NEXT PAGE

36. Which of the following allowed southern states to sidestep the right to vote guaranteed under the Fifteenth Amendment?
    (A) Supremacy clause
    (B) Grandfather clause
    (C) Necessary and proper clause
    (D) Establishment clause
    (E) Equal protection clause

37. The government institution responsible for the drawing of congressional district lines is the
    (A) state's governor
    (B) Senate Committee on Governmental Affairs
    (C) state's legislature
    (D) House Rules Committee
    (E) Department of the Interior

38. Political parties help promote democracy in which of the following ways?
    (A) They allow a wide variety of political views to be represented in government.
    (B) They select presidential nominees through the use of closed primaries.
    (C) They help concentrate the government's authority over the electorate.
    (D) They serve as an outlet through which citizens have access to the government.
    (E) Both parties represent a good variety of groups in the electorate.

39. The media has the most influence over which of the following aspects of a presidential election?
    (A) The way electoral votes are distributed
    (B) The outcome of the popular election
    (C) Who decides to run for office
    (D) The outcome of primary elections
    (E) The party's national convention

40. The framers' distrust of the public when writing the Constitution is best illustrated by the
    (A) Electoral College
    (B) Bill of Rights
    (C) process of electing federal judges
    (D) creation of a bicameral legislature
    (E) ability to amend the Constitution

41. Congress increased the power of the federal government to enforce regulations in employment by passing the
    (A) Fourteenth Amendment
    (B) Civil Rights Act
    (C) Fifteenth Amendment
    (D) Equal Rights Amendment
    (E) Voting Rights Act

42. Which of the following best explains the expansion of the bureaucracy?
    (A) The growth of the military-industrial complex
    (B) Concentration of power in the executive branch
    (C) The failure of Congress to effectively oversee policy implementation
    (D) Budget surpluses allowing for more government spending
    (E) The public's desire for more government programs and services

43. In *Miranda* v. *Arizona*, the Supreme Court ruled that persons accused of a crime
    (A) cannot be denied bail
    (B) have the right to a fair trial
    (C) have rights during police questioning
    (D) have equal protection under the law
    (E) cannot be searched illegally

44. The principle that the Constitution gives states all powers neither granted to the federal government nor denied the states refers to
(A) states' rights
(B) reserved powers
(C) federal supremacy
(D) concurrent powers
(E) federalism

45. Critical elections tend to occur under which of the following circumstances?
(A) When a third-party candidate wins some electoral votes
(B) After a presidential scandal has been exposed in the media
(C) When the United States engages in a military operation
(D) After a serious domestic crisis alters the political agenda
(E) When one of the parties suffers a major defeat in a congressional election

46. Voters learn little about presidential candidates' platforms by watching the news because
(A) the news media pay more attention to congressional campaigns
(B) campaign reform laws prevent the news from discussing presidential platforms
(C) news coverage of presidential campaigns is often biased and misleading
(D) the news focuses mostly on the candidates' daily campaigning activities
(E) the news media report mostly about the candidate's political experience and personal history

47. Which of the following statements are true of political parties?
  I. The United States has a multiparty system.
 II. The electorate is becoming increasingly independent of political parties.
III. The use of television advertising allows candidates more independence from their political parties.
 IV. The two major political parties are neither too liberal nor too conservative.
(A) II only
(B) III only
(C) II and III only
(D) I, III, and IV only
(E) II, III, and IV only

48. State legislators often become career politicians because
(A) there is little opportunity to move on to Congress
(B) they win their seats through the patronage system
(C) statewide campaigns are much cheaper to run
(D) the Constitution prohibits them from taking on any other political office
(E) most states do not set term limits for state legislators

49. Which of the following is an example of how an agency might regulate an industry?
(A) Consumers must send in all of their receipts to an agency.
(B) An agency approves all applicants for employment in power plants.
(C) An energy company files paperwork proving compliance with pollution standards.
(D) State welfare programs register their guidelines with an agency.
(E) An agency reports on the effects of a decline in the cattle market to a legislative committee.

GO ON TO THE NEXT PAGE

50. The Rehnquist court has been characterized by its
    (A) conservative leaning
    (B) racial diversity among the justices
    (C) advocacy of abortion
    (D) civil rights decisions
    (E) independence from the president

51. Which of the following is true of relationships between the president and Congress?
    (A) Presidents usually have little success in forming presidential coalitions in Congress.
    (B) Presidents work most with minority party leaders to win minority support.
    (C) Policy gridlock results when the president's party is not the majority in Congress.
    (D) Members of Congress almost always vote in favor of presidential initiatives.
    (E) Presidents usually have closer relationships with members of the House than they do with senators.

52. The speaker of the House is an important political figure because he or she
    (A) is unanimously chosen to lead the House
    (B) acts as the key liaison between the houses of Congress
    (C) serves as Congress's spokesperson to the public
    (D) is second in line to assume the presidency
    (E) is the only member of Congress with diplomatic responsibilities

53. Which of the following statements accurately describes iron triangles?
    (A) Iron triangles are composed of members of the military-industrial complex, Congress, and the Defense Department.
    (B) Iron triangles are formed in specific policy areas to advance policies among groups that benefit each other mutually.
    (C) Iron triangles are formed to generate support for presidential proposals in Congress.
    (D) Iron triangles help coordinate policy among the executive, legislative, and judicial branches.
    (E) Iron triangles help perform policy implementation among the local, state, and federal levels of government.

54. The federal bureaucracy exercises its authority over policy by
    (A) requesting department budgets from Congress
    (B) performing legislative oversight
    (C) influencing the president's policy agenda
    (D) establishing guidelines and administering all federal programs
    (E) making policy recommendations to committees through iron triangles

55. The establishment clause, as interpreted by the Supreme Court, prevents
    (A) states from passing laws that conflict with federal laws
    (B) the government from violating the rights of individuals
    (C) Congress from exercising any powers beyond those necessary to execute the law
    (D) gender discrimination in the workplace
    (E) the incorporation of religion into policy

56. *Regents of the University of California* v. *Bakke* and *Adarand Constructors* v. *Pena* are Supreme Court cases that addressed
   (A) affirmative action
   (B) prayer in school
   (C) the rights of the accused
   (D) the right of privacy
   (E) desegregation through busing

57. One of a president's most powerful tools for gaining support of his proposals is
   (A) his financial resources
   (B) executive privilege
   (C) public opinion
   (D) senatorial courtesy
   (E) his cabinet

58. Republican presidents tend to favor
   (A) tax expenditures
   (B) tax increases
   (C) tax reductions
   (D) tax loopholes
   (E) tax exemptions

59. Members of Congress are more likely to vote according to their personal ideology when
   (A) the issue is not well known by their constituents
   (B) they are up for re-election
   (C) the piece of legislation was introduced by the president
   (D) they are on the committee responsible for the piece of legislation
   (E) interest groups have been actively involved with the piece of legislation

60. In the era of globalization, which of the following presidential powers is becoming important?
   (A) Diplomatic recognition
   (B) Negotiating economic agreements
   (C) Declaring war
   (D) Authorizing the use of weapons of mass destruction
   (E) Appointment of ambassadors

END OF SECTION I.

IF YOU FINISH BEFORE TIME IS CALLED, YOU MAY CHECK YOUR WORK ON THIS SECTION.

DO NOT GO ON TO SECTION II UNTIL YOU ARE TOLD TO DO SO.

United States Government & Politics Section II

Time: 100 minutes

Directions: You have 100 minutes to answer all four of the following questions. It is suggested that you take a few minutes to plan and outline each answer. *Spend approximately one-fourth of your time (25 minutes) on each question.* Illustrate your essay with substantive examples where appropriate. Make certain to number each of your answers as the question is numbered below.

1. One major function of the Constitution, according to its main architect, James Madison, is to "secure the public good, and private rights, against the danger of . . . a faction, and at the same time to preserve the spirit and the form of popular government." Has the Constitution fulfilled Madison's promise?

Address BOTH of the following institutions in your response.
   - Interest groups
   - Third parties

2. Television has had a major impact on politics in the United States. It has changed the way Americans perceive their elected officials and the government as a whole. The new role of television has had both positive and negative consequences.

Select TWO of the following aspects of government.
   - Campaigns and elections
   - The president's relationship with Congress
   - Military actions and public opinion

For each of the topics you selected, do BOTH of the following.
   a. Explain how this aspect of government was altered by television.
   b. Identify ONE advantage and ONE disadvantage of television in relation to this aspect of government.

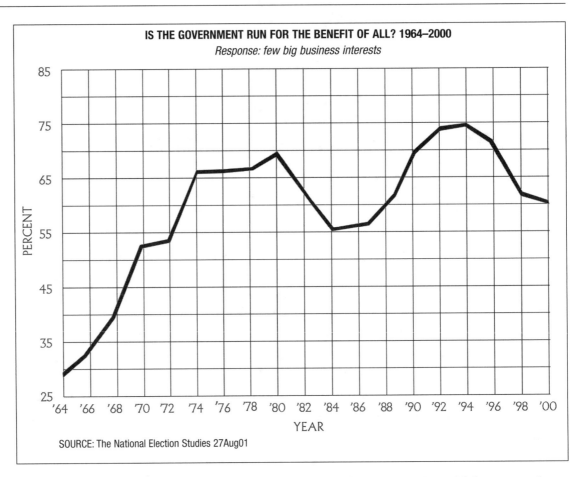

IS THE GOVERNMENT RUN FOR THE BENEFIT OF ALL? 1964–2000

Response: few big business interests

SOURCE: The National Election Studies 27Aug01

3. The above graph shows the results of a survey in which respondents answered whether they perceive the government as being run for the benefit of a few big interests rather than for the benefit of the public. Using this information and your knowledge of U.S. politics, do each of the following.
   a. Briefly describe what the graph shows about people's changing beliefs about the government over time.
   b. Identify two factors that may have encouraged people to view government as the servant of big business interests.
   c. Explain how each of these factors has involved big business interests in politics and what consequences have arisen as a result.

4. The Tenth Amendment reserves for the states all powers neither denied nor designated to the federal government in the Constitution. For decades, this afforded states a good deal of freedom in writing their state laws. However, the ratification of the Fourteenth Amendment allowed the Supreme Court to exercise its authority over the states in an attempt to advance the civil liberties of all Americans.

How did the Fourteenth Amendment help advance civil liberties? Cite TWO Supreme Court cases in your discussion.

Practice Test 1

Section I

❚ **1. (B) is correct.** Political action committees were created by the Federal Election Campaign Act of 1974 to regulate how much business, labor, and other groups could contribute to a candidate's election. Through them, the federal government can better regulate campaign financing, because all PACs must register with the Federal Election Commission and report all of their spending activities to the government and the public.

❚ **2. (E) is correct.** The Constitution establishes the system of checks and balances to maintain equal power among the three branches of government. The president checks Congress by being able to veto legislation, and Congress confirms presidential appointments and may impeach the president. However, it is Congress that controls the budget as a means of overseeing the activities of the executive branch.

❚ **3. (A) is correct.** According to the data in the chart, the number of nonconnected PACs nearly tripled between 1980 and 1985 alone, increasing from 374 to 1,003. Although this number did not change much in the next few decades and even declined a bit, in 2001 nonconnected PACs were the third most predominant type with 1,026.

❚ **4. (B) is correct.** Although the Supreme Court does have original jurisdiction, the majority of its cases are appealed from lower federal courts. Most cases submitted to the Supreme Court are refused by the justices, who screen them and select only about 2 percent to place on the docket.

❚ **5. (C) is correct.** The Supreme Court's 1954 landmark decision in *Brown* v. *Board of Education* was the first civil rights achievement in decades. The decision required that the federal government oversee the desegregation of public schools. Throughout the 1950s and 1960s, both the Court and Congress continued to pursue civil rights.

❚ **6. (D) is correct.** Presidents often rely on party support to advance their agendas in Congress. Together with party leaders, the president approaches members of the party to win their support. He may promise to back a congressperson's piece of legislation in return, or he may even grant presidential favors such as his endorsement during re-election in exchange for cooperation.

❚ **7. (D) is correct.** Generally, Republicans hold more conservative views than Democrats. They also tend to oppose too much social spending, pursue business votes, favor lower taxes, and, recently, not receive many votes from women.

❚ **8. (A) is correct.** Presidents work hard to seek and appoint judges who agree with their own political ideology. Not only would the judges be more likely to favor the president's agenda, but also (because they have no term limit) they would continue to influence policy long after the president's term has ended. The appointment of Supreme Court justices is a golden opportunity for presidents, but it is also one that is highly scrutinized by Congress.

9. (C) is correct. Jewish voters are highly likely to choose Democratic candidates. In the 2000 election, 90 percent of Jewish voters cast their ballots for Democrat Al Gore. Today's Democratic coalition, which began during the Great Depression, also includes most minority groups. Gore was preferred by 89 percent of African-American voters and 57 percent of Hispanic-American voters.

10. (B) is correct. Senior citizens have the highest voter turnout rate. They tend to be the most active and informed group in the electorate, especially because Social Security and health care have become major political issues. People with college degrees or union affiliations also vote in higher percentages, but young people and people of low-income do not.

11. (E) is correct. In the 1803 case of *Marbury* v. *Madison,* the Supreme Court under Chief Justice John Marshall first asserted its power of judicial review. Judicial review allows the Supreme Court, whose responsibility is to interpret the Constitution through the eyes of the law, to declare laws unconstitutional. This power helped solidify the system of checks and balances among the three branches of government.

12. (A) is correct. Political socialization is the process through which citizens learn about government and form their political beliefs. Family, school, the media, and religion play major parts in influencing how people see the government and with which party they identify themselves.

13. (D) is correct. Shays' Rebellion occurred when a group of Massachusetts farmers raided several courthouses in protest of the government's foreclosure of their farms. Under the Articles of Confederation, the national government was not able to raise a militia to stop the group, and so the rebellion was an embarrassing failure for the new government. It served as the final proof that the government established by the Articles lacked centralized power and legitimacy.

14. (C) is correct. People who have not voted often cite the generally indistinguishable ideologies of the two parties' candidates as one major reason for their inaction. This perception may be partly the result of the media's focus on the campaign game rather than on the two candidates' platforms, but it is also due to the fact that, because there are only two major parties in the United States, each one must remain near the center of the political spectrum in order to win elections.

15. (B) is correct. The national debt had consistently been less than $1 trillion until Congress enacted President Reagan's major tax cut proposals in 1982 (and at the same time significantly increased defense spending). In just four years, the national debt doubled. After Reagan's two terms, the debt continued to rise steadily, and today the national debt is more than $5 trillion.

16. (B) is correct. One of the ways Congress oversees the activities of the departments in the executive branch is by determining their budgets. Each department submits its budget proposal to the president, who in turn coordinates them and submits his proposal to Congress. Congress makes the final decision, however, about how much each department can spend on its programs and activities.

17. (D) is correct. Members of Congress do sometimes vote according to their own ideology. However, they most often vote according to their party affiliation. In doing so, they may presume that the constituents who elected them as a Democrat or Republican probably agree with that party's political ideology. By voting along the party line, they are also voting according to their constituency's preferences.

18. (A) is correct. Gender discrimination is not specifically addressed in the Constitution or its amendments. However, it is prohibited under the Fourteenth Amendment as a form of civil rights discrimination.

19. (D) is correct. Regulatory agencies and industries are most likely to work together when Congress is appropriating funds during the budgetary process. Industries therefore increase their lobbying pressure during the budgetary process to convince the relevant committees of their need for the money they have requested.

20. (C) is correct. In the past few decades, Social Security has become the largest federal expenditure. It alone accounts for nearly a quarter of all expenditures. There is a good deal of concern that in another few decades it will become too costly for the federal government to maintain.

21. (B) is correct. Statement I is correct—by 2000 expenditures for entitlements and other forms of mandatory spending grew to 14 times the amount in 1970. According to the table, these are now the biggest federal expenditures by far; no other expenditures grew nearly that much. Statement II is also correct. Total expenditures increased the most between 1980 and 1985, when they rose by $356 billion.

22. (D) is correct. Congressional committees play an important role in the legislative process. They review and assess bills for their feasibility and consequences, and they either revise or kill them. If they pass a bill on to the floor, they make a recommendation for it, and many other congresspeople are likely to vote according to the recommendation. The other major function of a committee is to perform oversight of all the federal departments and agencies under its jurisdiction. Committees do this by setting agencies' budgets and by assessing their performance and activities in committee hearings.

23. (E) is correct. The use of presidential primaries has been increasing, not decreasing. Almost every state now holds a primary election. These have, in turn, led to a much longer campaign season and have added significantly to the cost of campaigning. However, they do make the nomination of presidential candidates a more democratic process that involves voters directly.

24. (D) is correct. Single-issue groups attract people who feel very strongly about one particular issue. These issues, such as abortion or gun control, often incite emotional responses. Single-issue groups pressure senators and representatives to vote according to that one issue, and members themselves often vote for political officials based solely on their stand on the issue.

25. (C) is correct. Only governors have the authority to use the line-item veto. It allows them to reject any part of an appropriations bill without vetoing the whole thing; in a sense, they have the power to customize every piece of budget legislation. Presidents have sought the power to use it as well, and in the budget crisis of 1996 Congress tried to give this power to the president. Since it didn't have the votes for a constitutional amendment, Congress passed a law that used a convoluted process to try to skirt the Constitution and give the president the power to rescind portions of spending bills. In 1998 the Supreme Court voided the law after finding it unconstitutional.

26. (A) is correct. Congress rarely overrides a presidential veto. This is partly because overriding a veto requires a two-thirds majority vote in both houses, which is usually hard to achieve. Most of the time, the president has the final say on a piece of legislation.

27. (E) is correct. Social Security is a form of mandatory spending because it is an entitlement program. Once Congress has set the eligibility requirements for the program, the government must pay everyone who qualifies for the fixed amount. The only way to change federal spending for Social Security would be to amend the eligibility requirements.

28. (D) is correct. In the 1989 case of *Texas* v. *Johnson,* the Supreme Court determined that flag burning, a form of symbolic speech, is protected under the First Amendment. Symbolic speech is that which communicates nonverbally; participating in parades or protests is another form of symbolic speech.

29. (B) is correct. Primary elections give voters the opportunity to participate more directly in the presidential election process. In their state's primary election, people can nominate either a candidate or delegates pledged to that candidate. This process circumvents the traditional role of political parties in the nomination process, especially when a blanket primary is used.

30. (E) is correct. In an attempt to reassert its own authority to declare war, Congress limited the power of the president by passing the War Powers Resolution. This law allows presidents to send troops into military situations for a maximum of 60 days; if Congress does not declare war during that time, the troops must be withdrawn.

31. (C) is correct. Only senators have the ability to use a filibuster to hold up debate on a bill. The Senate imposes no restrictions on the length of time for debate over a piece of legislation, so senators are free to talk as long as it takes for their colleagues to lose interest and choose not to vote on the bill. Southern senators made effective use of the filibuster during debates over civil rights legislation.

32. (A) is correct. Civil servants in the federal bureaucracy are the only federal officials who are not elected by citizens. They are either appointed by the president or hired through an extensive process based on the merit system. This makes the bureaucracy a less democratic institution.

33. (D) is correct. The Constitution establishes only the Supreme Court. Instead of establishing the whole system of federal courts, it delegates this power to Congress. It specifies, however, that judges and justices may hold their seats on the bench for life as long as they maintain good conduct. This was done to protect them from any outside political influence that might accompany their election or appointment.

34. (C) is correct. The Constitution sets forth the process of removing a president from office. First, the House votes to impeach the president. Then the Senate tries the president, with the chief justice of the Supreme Court presiding. The Senate must reach a two-thirds vote in order to remove the president from office. Only two presidents have been impeached, but neither was removed from office through this process.

▌ **35. (E) is correct.** John Kennedy and George Bush achieved the highest approval ratings in the graph. Bush was a Republican, so it is not true that Democratic presidents have the highest ratings. Eisenhower, another Republican, also maintained fairly high approval ratings. In fact, overall, Democrats have achieved the lowest approval ratings.

▌ **36. (B) is correct.** Southern states used the grandfather clause to prevent African Americans from voting. This clause allowed only those men whose grandfathers had been able to vote before 1860 to participate in elections. It effectively prevented ex-slaves and the descendants of slaves from voting.

▌ **37. (C) is correct.** State legislatures have the task of drawing congressional district lines for their state. Every ten years, the population count of the national census determines how many House seats each state receives. If seats must be reapportioned, the state legislature redraws district lines accordingly.

▌ **38. (D) is correct.** Political parties allow citizens to participate in government by representing the views of party members throughout all government institutions. A member of the Democratic Party, for example, will be represented by a Democratic president and Democratic legislators. Parties therefore help link people and politicians with common political views.

▌ **39. (D) is correct.** One of the major criticisms held against the primary system is that it allows the media too much influence over election results, particularly in the early primaries. Media attention skews the results by branding winners and losers so early in the campaign process that losers have little chance to score victories in later primaries.

▌ **40. (A) is correct.** The authors of the Constitution were a group of elite intellectuals who distrusted leaving government too much in the hands of the uneducated masses. Therefore they arranged for the president to be chosen by the Electoral College, a group of chosen electors, rather than by the public at large. Though today citizens cast individual votes for president, the Electoral College still casts the final vote. In fact, Al Gore won the popular vote in the 2000 election but lost the presidency because of the distribution of electoral votes.

▌ **41. (B) is correct.** By passing the Civil Rights Act of 1964, Congress outlawed discrimination in the workplace. Consequently, the Justice Department was granted authority to enforce equality in employment and to pursue violators of the Civil Rights Act.

▌ **42. (E) is correct.** In the past few decades, social issues have become increasingly important on the political agenda and in the federal budget. The public's demand for more federal programs in welfare, education, and health care has created a need for more bureaucratic departments and offices. The bureaucracy has grown more at the state level than at the federal level, however, as implementation of many federal programs has been designated to the states.

43. (C) is correct. The Supreme Court enhanced the rights of the accused in its decision in *Miranda* v. *Arizona.* This decision required that all people arrested for a crime be informed of their rights before questioning.

44. (B) is correct. The Tenth Amendment articulates the reserved powers of the states. All powers not denied by the Constitution or specifically designated to the federal government are held by the states. Many states have used this principle of reserved powers to their advantage, particularly in the case of civil rights. Many Supreme Court cases of the twentieth century focused on limiting the power of states to make laws that conflict with federal law.

45. (D) is correct. Most critical elections follow a serious domestic problem that significantly alters the political landscape. The Great Depression is one such crisis that generated a critical election. Republicans lost power to a new coalition of Democrats that included workers, minority groups, and southerners.

46. (D) is correct. The news actually conveys little information about candidates' political platforms. Most news media outlets report on the daily campaigning activities of each candidate and on the campaign game. This is one reason why Americans are politically ill-informed—though many people watch the news, they are not able to learn much about the politics of candidates or of government in general.

47. (C) is correct. Political parties are losing power because both candidates and voters have come to rely less on them. Because candidates can address voters directly through television, the public does not have to fall back on party identification in order to choose candidates. At the same time, candidates who use television do not need their party to help attract voters as much as in the past.

48. (E) is correct. Only a few states have set term limits for their state legislators. In fact, many state laws that set term limits for members of Congress have been found unconstitutional by the Supreme Court. As a result, once state politicians reach the legislature, especially given the advantages of incumbents in elections, they tend to stay there.

49. (C) is correct. Agencies employ a number of measures to regulate industries. Not only do they write the regulations that industries must follow, but they also send inspectors to investigate industry compliance and issue licenses to monitor who performs which function in the industry.

50. (A) is correct. The Rehnquist court has been shaped largely by appointments made by Republican presidents. It is therefore particularly conservative in its ideology. Though it has not overturned any decisions made by more liberal justices, it has restricted some of them, particularly on the issue of affirmative action.

51. (C) is correct. The relationship between the president and Congress tends to be strained when the president's party is not the majority party in Congress. The two often have conflicting policy goals and work together less often than do a president and Congress of the same political party. Policy gridlock occurs more frequently today because this kind of divided government happens more often.

52. (D) is correct. The speaker of the House has more political clout than most politicians because, after the vice president, he or she is next in line for the presidency. In fact, this political office is one of the few that are specifically designated in the Constitution.

53. (B) is correct. Iron triangles are unofficial political entities composed of interest groups, agencies, and legislative committees that are all concerned with the same policy area. Each group helps the others to help itself in the policy arena. For example, interest groups lobby committee members for larger agency budgets so that the interest groups will benefit from the agency's money.

54. (D) is correct. Federal agencies have a great deal of leeway in establishing and administering federal programs. Often Congress passes general laws and leaves the details to the agencies to iron out as they implement policies. These generalizations allow agencies the freedom to shape the programs they are responsible for administering.

55. (E) is correct. The establishment clause, located in the First Amendment of the Constitution, establishes the separation of church and state in all levels of government. Religious qualifications cannot be imposed on public officials, and the government cannot regulate, restrict, or endorse religious worship.

56. (A) is correct. Both cases dealt with the constitutionality of affirmative action. In *Bakke,* the Supreme Court upheld the principle of affirmative action but shot down the use of quotas to establish racial diversity. In *Adarand,* the Rehnquist court weakened affirmative action by declaring any federal contracts reserved specifically for minority firms to be unconstitutional.

57. (C) is correct. A president relies heavily on the power of public opinion, because, with the backing of the public, members of Congress have little recourse but to support him as well. This power has grown in recent decades as presidents have been able to communicate directly with the public through television.

58. (C) is correct. Republicans usually have a more conservative agenda that favors tax reductions. Republicans ideologically oppose big government and therefore favor cutting government spending and reducing taxes. Moreover, they rely heavily on support from businesses, so they often attempt to cut corporate taxes.

59. (A) is correct. Because their constituents usually are familiar with only the most publicized issues, members of Congress have many opportunities to vote according to their own ideology on smaller, less publicized issues. In theory, because they were elected by people who share their ideology, representatives and senators would still be voting according to the wishes of their constituents.

60. (B) is correct. In the recent era of globalization, foreign policy is shifting toward economic concerns. The president, as chief diplomat, has both increasing power and responsibility as the nation's negotiator of treaties and executive agreements. Many of today's agreements focus on expanding free trade among nations around the world.

1. *One major function of the Constitution, according to its main architect, James Madison, is to "secure the public good, and private rights, against the danger of . . . a faction, and at the same time to preserve the spirit and the form of popular government." Has the Constitution fulfilled Madison's promise?*

Address BOTH of the following institutions in your response.
- *Interest groups*
- *Third parties*

Madison seems to be asking the impossible by endorsing a popular government without factions. Such groups are necessary in a country of nearly 300 million people, even if they do sometimes cause political conflict. In some ways, factions advance a more popular form of government by representing groups of people, but in others, they distort the idea of a "public good" by representing only some groups of people. The Constitution, therefore, has not fully maintained the delicate balance that Madison set forth.

Interest groups are exactly the sort of faction that Madison warned against. They claim to represent people in the electorate, yet they use money and politicking to influence policymaking. Each has its own agenda, and often groups conflict with each other, no matter how legitimate their concerns are. For example, the energy demand in a state may necessitate the building of power plants, endorsed by one industry group, while an environmental group might lobby against the building of plants because they pollute the nearby neighborhoods. The government must weigh both sides, and, in the end, it may be the more persuasive group that determines the policy outcome. Some theorists argue that this leads to hyperpluralism—the government, overwhelmed by so many interest groups working for the "public good," tries to appease them all and ends up creating confused or diluted policies. Furthermore, these factions may seem to represent a diversity of opinions among the public, but, as elite theorists argue, only those groups with money will be heard by the government. The more money a group has, the more power it has to bend the will of congresspeople. This imbalance of plurality, then, indicates that a popular government has not been wholly achieved, even with the existence of factions.

Political parties are other kinds of factions that might, in a multiparty system, work toward the public good by representing a diversity of public opinion in government. However, because the United States evolved into a two-party system, again the government falls short of Madison's delicate balance. Whereas too many interest groups distorts the public good with the power of money, the shortage of political parties may actually inhibit the advancement of the public good in politics. Third-party candidates offer an alternative to the staid platforms of the two major parties. Many people who choose not to vote claim that they see little difference between the two parties, which, for the most part, remain fairly centrist. Third-party candidates offer voters a distinct alternative, and often, as in the case of Ralph Nader, actively pursue the needs, wants, and security of citizens rather than playing the political game as insiders. However, third-party candidates have few advantages in the political system. They often do not receive federal funding for campaigns and therefore have fewer opportunities to reach the public. The media too does its share to maintain the two-party system by overlooking third-party candidates. Third-party candidates, in fact, face so many disadvantages that they have rarely succeeded in winning office. The plurality of views and advancement of the public good that they might have achieved are denied in election after election.

The impossibility of Madison's claim is twofold: Interest groups show that factions may inhibit the public good and a healthy popular government. They are exactly the competing factions that Madison warned against. On the other hand, the failure of third parties to achieve any prominence in the political system indicates exactly the opposite: Having too few factions also inhibits a popular form of government. Either way, Madison's "delicate balance" has, for the most part, not been realized by the government as it has evolved.

This essay makes a strong argument that Madison's "delicate balance" has not been maintained in today's political system. The student cites two theories of interest groups, hyperpluralism and elitism, to prove that interest groups do not fairly represent the public good in a popular form of government. Second, the student offers good evidence that third parties might be factions that actually endorse a more popular government, but that they have not had much success in the American two-party system. The essay is full of substantive examples that demonstrate the student's understanding both of the theoretical underpinnings of government and of the realities on which the government operates.

2. *Television has had a major impact on politics in the United States. It has changed the way Americans perceive their elected officials and the government as a whole. The new role of television has had both positive and negative consequences.*

Select TWO of the following aspects of government.
- *Campaigns and elections*
- *The president's relationship with Congress*
- *Military actions and public opinion*

For each of the topics you selected, do BOTH of the following.
- *a. Explain how this aspect of government was altered by television.*
- *b. Identify ONE advantage and ONE disadvantage of television in relation to this aspect of government.*

Television has had a profound impact on the relationship between government and the public. With the advent of television, for the first time Americans could put faces on public officials and could begin to judge them by their personalities. For several decades now television has not only increased the visibility of government, but also it has provided firsthand and nearly instant information about the government's activities.

Television has revolutionized the process of campaigning in the United States. Through television, candidates can appeal directly to the public when they are campaigning. This allows them to relay their political agenda personally, so that voters can make up their minds as much by the candidate's attitude and persona as by his or her words. However, one major disadvantage of television in campaigning is that it is extremely expensive to buy air time, and air time has become essential to the success of a campaign. Campaigns, as a result, have become very costly. This, in turn, has other negative consequences—candidates must rely heavily on money from political action committees in order to finance their campaigns, and many people who want to run for office cannot afford to do so. Ultimately television helps to make the election of political officials—especially the president—more democratic, because people can be more intimate with the government, but this closer relationship comes with a hefty price tag.

Through the news, television has also allowed the public to see the results of political actions, especially in military situations. The Vietnam War gave Americans their first shocking glimpses at the harsh realities of combat. Footage was largely uncensored and was broadcast in a much more timely manner than ever before. This in part resulted in the sometimes violent backlash of war protestors. Today, television offers such instantaneous communication of information that even presidents watch the news to learn the latest results of a military action. Again, television allows the public greater access to the government and provides more opportunities for people to hold the government accountable for its actions. In fact, during the Vietnam War, this helped lead to the decline in popularity of President Johnson—although he promised that the war was ending, Americans could see on television that it was far from over and that it was largely unsuccessful. As a result, their confidence in the government was shaken. Another disadvantage of television reports of military actions is that public opinion and the public agenda may be influenced by what footage is shown and what is not shown. The government maintained support for the Gulf War, for example, by censoring what was shown on television. Viewers, in turn, are likely to take what they see on television, however it is packaged, as truth.

Television can be a powerful political tool. It has all the persuasiveness of "seeing is believing," and yet its content can be cut and shaped to any number of ends. Furthermore, the expense of television has added significantly to the burden of entering the political sphere. At the same time, however, television has the ability to draw all people, voters and politicians alike, together as common consumers of real-life, firsthand information.

This writer clearly and explicitly conveys the revolutionary impact of television on government and politics. The student offers both advantages and disadvantages of television and draws them from different aspects of politics, such as public opinion, campaigning, and the influence of the news media. The student's discussion of the impact of television during the Vietnam War is particularly thorough and insightful.

3. *The above graph shows the results of a survey in which respondents answered whether they perceive the government as being run for the benefit of a few big interests rather than for the benefit of the public. Using this information and your knowledge of U.S. politics, do each of the following.*
   a. *Briefly describe what the graph shows about people's changing beliefs about the government over time.*
   b. *Identify two factors that may have encouraged people to view government as the servant of big business interests.*
   c. *Explain how each of these factors has involved big business interests in politics and what consequences have arisen as a result.*

Americans' opinion of the government has not been entirely favorable in the past few decades. As the graph indicates, people have increasingly felt that government is no longer of and by the people, but that it serves the interests of big business and influential interest groups. In 1964, just 25 percent of people polled expressed their suspicions about the government, but by 2000, that number had reached nearly 60 percent. In fact, since 1970, at least half of all Americans have shared this distrust of the government.

One major change in national politics that may have affected public opinion is the dramatic rise in the number of interest groups. In the past few decades, thousands of groups have sprung up and sent lobbyists to Washington to represent hundreds of causes. Americans tend to view lobbyists with great distrust for their methods of exercising or achieving their influence; if elite theorists are correct, then it is only the wealthiest groups that succeed in influencing policy. Business interest groups are the most common type of interest group and also the ones with the most money. Even smaller interest groups, however, have infiltrated the political arena and succeeded in forming iron triangles with committees and agencies sympathetic to their needs. Interest groups have made themselves known to the public by running television advertisements endorsing their cause or refuting the claims of opposing interests, so Americans are well aware of their increasing presence in government. Finally, as mergers dominate the headlines and multinational corporations expand around the globe, it is evident that business interests are consolidating with great economic and political power.

Another factor that offers evidence to the public that government is dominated by big business interests is the rise of political action committees. These are funding vehicles established by interest groups to channel money into presidential and congressional campaigns. They were created by campaign finance reforms in the early 1970s as a means of making the business of campaign financing more open. According to the graph, at about the same time that people began to be aware of the role big business interests play in political campaigns, their distrustful opinion reached the 50 percent mark and has not gone below it since. Political action committees, in effect, represent a direct link between interest groups and politicians; moreover, this relationship is clearly based on the exchange of money. Therefore, it is no coincidence that many of the issues on the political agenda are those which are taken up by interest groups. For example, health care is a major issue, and the AARP is the largest interest group in the country. Both interest groups and their PACs give the public reason to believe that policies benefit big business interests more than they do all Americans.

This essay offers a succinct and accurate description of the data in the graph. Moreover, the student analyzes two factors that may have influenced the public opinion detailed in the graph: interest groups and PACs. The student shows how both of these entities have become important players in modern politics—how they have achieved their power and how they wield it. Finally, the student includes pertinent examples that show a knowledge of trends in U.S. politics.

4. *The Tenth Amendment reserves for the states all powers neither denied nor designated to the federal government in the Constitution. For decades, this afforded states a good deal of freedom in writing their state laws. However, the ratification of the Fourteenth Amendment allowed the Supreme Court to exercise its authority over the states in an attempt to advance the civil liberties of all Americans.*

How did the Fourteenth Amendment help advance civil liberties? Cite TWO Supreme Court cases in your discussion.

The Fourteenth Amendment was the first time the word *equal* appeared in the Constitution. Passed at the end of the Civil War, the amendment extended freedom to slaves by granting them "equal protection of the laws." For the Supreme Court, this one clause also opened the door to protecting individual freedoms and rights under state laws, despite the freedom given to states under the Tenth Amendment. In the cases of *Gideon* v. *Wainwright* and *Miranda* v. *Arizona,* the Supreme Court cited the Fourteenth Amendment as a means of extending the authority of federal law over state law.

In *Gideon,* the issue was whether states should be required to supply legal counsel for poor defendants. They were not required to do so unless the defendant was accused of a capital offense. Florida refused legal aid to Clarence Gideon, who appealed his conviction directly to the Supreme Court. The state of Florida encouraged other states to support its side of the case, arguing that taxpayers would have to pay for legal counsel and that convictions would be harder to get. Many states, however, filed briefs supporting Gideon's right to counsel as guaranteed by the Sixth Amendment. The Court agreed, arguing that Gideon had been denied due process of the law, a major premise of the Fourteenth Amendment. The case set a precedent requiring states to provide defense attorneys in all state criminal trials.

The Court took an even more radical step a few years later in *Miranda.* Ernesto Miranda had been arrested and interrogated, had confessed, and had been convicted and sentenced to prison. The case was appealed because Miranda had not known that the Constitution protected him from having to incriminate himself, and that he possessed the right to have an attorney present during questioning. Against a great deal of criticism, the Court narrowly found in favor of Miranda. It cited the Fourteenth Amendment's claim of "equal protection of the laws" as a means of extending the protection of the Fifth Amendment to all citizens. The decision supported the earlier *Gideon* decision, and states were again angry that their responsibility to provide counsel and to obtain evidence fairly was being enforced. As a result of the case, police officers are required to read "Miranda rights" to anyone whom they arrest. These inform the person that he or she does not have to answer police questions without an attorney present, and that a lawyer may be appointed if he or she cannot afford to pay for one.

The Fourteenth Amendment has been a powerful tool for the Supreme Court and the public. Though the Tenth Amendment had given states some freedom to bypass other amendments, such as those that protect the rights of the accused, the Fourteenth Amendment finally allowed the federal government to exert its supremacy for the benefit of all citizens' civil liberties.

This essay offers an in-depth analysis of two cases that demonstrate the Supreme Court's use of the Fourteenth Amendment to curb states' abuses of civil liberties. The student is familiar with the facts and context of both Gideon v. Wainwright *and* Miranda v. Arizona. *Moreover, he or she analyzes the consequences of the cases for states, the federal government, and the public. Lastly, the student shows a clear understanding of the role of the Supreme Court and of one of the methods the Supreme Court uses to interpret the Constitution and apply the law.*

United States Government & Politics AP Exam Practice Test 2

United States Government & Politics Section I

Time: 45 minutes
60 Questions

> ***Directions***: Each of the questions or incomplete statements below is followed by five suggested answers or completions. Select the one that is best in each case and then fill in the corresponding oval on the answer sheet.

1. In which of the following elections are voters allowed to choose candidates from either party for different offices?
   (A) Open primary
   (B) Critical election
   (C) Gubernatorial election
   (D) Blanket primary
   (E) Recall election

2. Which of the following would play the main role in an impeachment trial of the president?
   (A) Judicial committee
   (B) Federal commission
   (C) Subgovernment
   (D) Executive advisory committee
   (E) Select committee

3. Popular elections are held for all of the following governmental offices EXCEPT
   (A) senator
   (B) president
   (C) federal judge
   (D) member of the House of Representatives
   (E) governor

4. Generally, the Democratic coalition consists of which of the following groups in the electorate?
   (A) Wealthy businessmen, southerners, and Midwesterners
   (B) Rural voters, African Americans, and women
   (C) Jewish voters, urban voters, and wealthy businessmen
   (D) Women, Hispanic Americans, and people in the highest income bracket
   (E) Minorities, southerners, and urban voters

GO ON TO THE NEXT PAGE

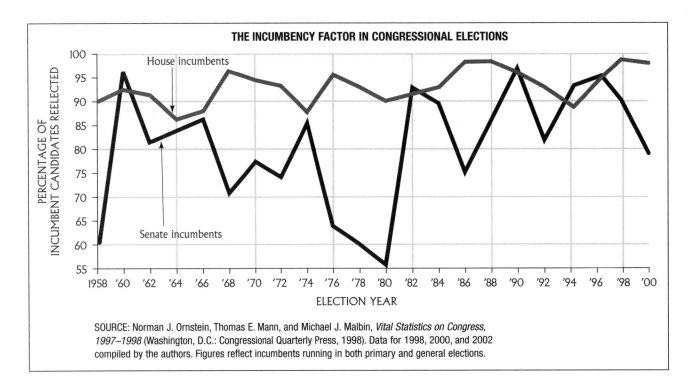

THE INCUMBENCY FACTOR IN CONGRESSIONAL ELECTIONS

PERCENTAGE OF INCUMBENT CANDIDATES REELECTED

House incumbents

Senate incumbents

ELECTION YEAR

SOURCE: Norman J. Ornstein, Thomas E. Mann, and Michael J. Malbin, *Vital Statistics on Congress, 1997–1998* (Washington, D.C.: Congressional Quarterly Press, 1998). Data for 1998, 2000, and 2002 compiled by the authors. Figures reflect incumbents running in both primary and general elections.

5. Which of the following conclusions may be drawn about incumbents based on the data in the graph above?
   (A) In the past 40 years, at least half of incumbents consistently have won re-election.
   (B) Senate incumbents are reelected at a greater rate than House incumbents.
   (C) The most congressional incumbents were reelected in 1960.
   (D) Almost no senatorial incumbents won re-election in 1980.
   (E) House incumbents tend to win elections more often than senatorial incumbents because their elections are less publicized.

6. The elastic clause grants Congress the authority to
   (A) amend the president's budget proposal as it sees fit
   (B) make any laws that enable it to carry out its assigned responsibilities
   (C) expand the federal bureaucracy by creating new executive departments
   (D) create any number of legislative committees and subcommittees
   (E) reapportion seats based on the nation's changing population

7. Most citizens express their political views by
   (A) participating in political protests when they disagree with the government's decisions
   (B) writing letters to the editor of a local newspaper
   (C) voting for candidates who seem to share their political ideology
   (D) writing letters or trying to contact their representative in person
   (E) joining an interest group and lobbying members of Congress

8. The Constitution authorizes Supreme Court justices to be appointed for life for which of the following reasons?
   (A) To shield judges from political influence and pressure
   (B) To reward judges for their distinguished careers
   (C) To create a strong relationship between the court and Congress
   (D) To allow politicians to use the patronage system
   (E) To limit the power of presidents to appoint judges too frequently

9. One common criticism of the media's participation in politics is
   (A) its bias in favor of one party over the other
   (B) the way it has redefined the president's relationship with the public
   (C) its live and uncensored coverage of committee hearings
   (D) its exploitation of political scandals to earn ratings
   (E) its failure to shape the public agenda through its news coverage

10. Which of the following groups in the electorate has the lowest voter turnout rate?
    (A) The elderly
    (B) High school graduates
    (C) Women
    (D) Protestants
    (E) Young people

11. Which of the following statements about the budgetary process is true?
    (A) The president submits a budget proposal to Congress, which ultimately decides how to allocate money.
    (B) The president assigns a spending minimum and maximum to each agency in the executive branch.
    (C) Interest groups have little influence over this aspect of policymaking.
    (D) The Office of Management and Budget handles the entire budgetary process.
    (E) Committees submit their internal budget requests to the Congressional Budget Office.

12. According to the Supreme Court's interpretation of the law, which of the following is true about the freedom of religion?
    (A) The government cannot interfere with the ways people practice their religious beliefs.
    (B) State governments may base their politics on religion, but the federal government cannot.
    (C) Prayer in school violates the separation of church and state.
    (D) The establishment clause applies only to non-Christian religions.
    (E) Religious schools are not allowed to receive any federal funds.

GO ON TO THE
NEXT PAGE

13. Which of the following powers are granted to Congress by the Constitution?
    I. Appropriate money
    II. Confirm justices
    III. Send troops into war
    IV. Enforce laws
    V. Regulate commerce
    (A) I and IV only
    (B) II and III only
    (C) III and V only
    (D) I, II, and V only
    (E) III, IV, and V only

14. Which of the following authorized the Justice Department to send federal officials to oversee state elections?
    (A) Fifteenth Amendment
    (B) Voting Rights Act
    (C) Motor Voter Act
    (D) Thirteenth Amendment
    (E) Civil Rights Act

15. In which of the following cases is a congressional candidate most likely to be elected?
    (A) If he or she has a good television presence
    (B) When a state has just gained seats due to reapportionment
    (C) If he or she is new to politics
    (D) After a critical election for the presidency
    (E) If he or she is an incumbent

16. Which of the following is true of iron triangles?
    (A) An iron triangle is composed of the president, the speaker of the House, and the chief justice.
    (B) Iron triangles inhibit the policy process by interfering with the debate over a piece of legislation.
    (C) Iron triangles help unify the three branches of government in pursuit of a single, clear policy agenda.
    (D) Iron triangles help advance legislation and implementation in a particular policy area.
    (E) Iron triangles rarely form in government at the federal level because they lack sufficient resources for sustainability.

17. An environmental lobby would be LEAST likely to exert its influence by meeting with a
    (A) federal judge hearing a case on the constitutionality of an environmental regulation
    (B) member of the House committee that authorizes money for the building of power plants
    (C) staff member of the Environmental Protection Agency
    (D) newspaper in the town where environmental laws are being violated
    (E) staff member of the White House who is known to be sympathetic to environmental concerns

18. The election of which of the following public officials is funded in part by public money?
    (A) State legislator
    (B) President
    (C) Senator
    (D) Governor
    (E) State attorney general

19. Many Supreme Court cases of the 1960s involved issues of
    (A) gender discrimination
    (B) states' rights
    (C) constitutional powers of the president
    (D) rights of the accused
    (E) campaign finance reform

20. If the Supreme Court rules that a newly passed law is unconstitutional, Congress can
    (A) ask the president to appoint new justices
    (B) change the Constitution to redirect the Supreme Court's interpretation
    (C) appeal the Court's decision to the Senate Judiciary Committee
    (D) issue a referendum to allow the public to vote on the Supreme Court's decision
    (E) vote to override the Supreme Court's decision

21. Which of the following factors influence citizens' political socialization?
    I. Religion
    II. Education
    III. Income
    IV. The media
    V. Race
    (A) II only
    (B) I and III only
    (C) II and IV only
    (D) I, II, and IV only
    (E) II, IV, and V only

22. If the House and Senate pass two different versions of a bill,
    (A) the Senate version has seniority and is sent to the president
    (B) the Supreme Court chooses the better version
    (C) the two versions are sent to a conference committee to work out a compromise bill
    (D) the president has the authority to choose which version he will sign into law
    (E) each house must amend its bill and take another vote

23. One tool that allows the president to sidestep congressional approval of his diplomatic duties is the
    (A) power to negotiate treaties
    (B) authority to enter into executive agreements
    (C) ability to send troops into war
    (D) freedom to appoint ambassadors
    (E) privilege of receiving foreign diplomats

24. Which of the following is an accurate statement about the caseload of the Supreme Court?
    (A) Only a small portion of cases seeking review are heard by the Supreme Court.
    (B) The Senate Judiciary Committee selects which cases will be placed on the docket.
    (C) Most cases that reach the Supreme Court are appealed from state courts.
    (D) The solicitor general is responsible for assigning cases to the Supreme Court.
    (E) The Supreme Court attempts to hear every case appealed to it.

GO ON TO THE NEXT PAGE

25. The Supreme Court has extended federal supremacy over state laws through its interpretation of the
    (A) Tenth Amendment
    (B) supremacy clause
    (C) First Amendment
    (D) Fourteenth Amendment
    (E) establishment clause

26. Which of the following is an incumbent's greatest advantage during an election?
    (A) Automatic endorsement from the president
    (B) A clean political record
    (C) Prior service to the constituency
    (D) More campaign resources and funding
    (E) A large number of undecided voters in the constituency

27. Television has had which of the following effects on political parties?
    (A) It has helped lower the cost of campaigning, thereby saving the parties money.
    (B) It has forced candidates to rely more heavily on their parties.
    (C) It has caused a decrease in party identification among the electorate.
    (D) It has led to the declining importance of national conventions.
    (E) It has caused party realignment because parties can appeal to new groups in the electorate.

35. In *Texas* v. *Johnson,* the Supreme Court determined that
    (A) the drawing of unreasonable school district lines cannot be used as a means of integrating schools
    (B) symbolic speech is protected under the First Amendment
    (C) affirmative action quotas are unconstitutional
    (D) the death penalty is not a form of cruel and unusual punishment
    (E) obscenity is not protected by the First Amendment

36. Which of the following is usually a result of a critical election?
    (A) Party dealignment
    (B) Divided government
    (C) Policy implementation
    (D) Party realignment
    (E) Policy gridlock

37. The greatest weakness of the Articles of Confederation was that they established a government that was unable to
    (A) raise a militia
    (B) be recognized by foreign governments
    (C) pay off its war debts
    (D) centralize its powers
    (E) make decisions through a legislative process

38. The Federal Reserve Board oversees which of the following policy areas?
    (A) Social welfare policy
    (B) Foreign policy
    (C) Monetary policy
    (D) Health care policy
    (E) Domestic policy

39. Which of the following is a major difference between the Democratic and Republican parties?
    (A) The Democratic Party campaigns fairly, but the Republican Party does not.
    (B) A wider variety of groups in the electorate vote for Republican candidates.
    (C) The Republican Party is much older than the Democratic Party.
    (D) The Republican Party endorses raising taxes, whereas the Democratic Party favors cutting taxes.
    (E) The Democratic Party has a more liberal ideology, whereas the Republican Party has a more conservative ideology.

GO ON TO THE NEXT PAGE

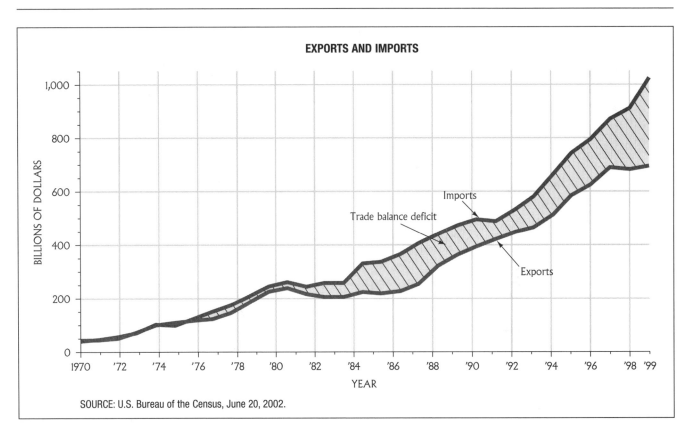

EXPORTS AND IMPORTS

BILLIONS OF DOLLARS

Imports

Trade balance deficit

Exports

YEAR

SOURCE: U.S. Bureau of the Census, June 20, 2002.

40. The shaded area of the graph indicates that
   (A) there is a growing balance-of-trade deficit
   (B) the national debt is growing
   (C) free trade agreements are damaging the U.S. economy
   (D) lowering tariffs has resulted in decreased exports
   (E) interdependency is becoming common in a new global economy

41. Federalism is a system of government in which
   (A) an executive, legislative, and judicial branch share equal powers
   (B) political officials are elected by the public in a popular election
   (C) legislative committees and federal agencies work together to make and implement policy
   (D) more than one level of government oversees a body of people
   (E) the president is chosen by an electoral college rather than by popular election

42. The rise of the Social Security system has had which of the following effects on the federal budget?
   (A) It has led to cutbacks in defense spending and the building of new weapons.
   (B) It has become the largest federal expenditure.
   (C) It has increased Americans' trust in a government that provides for all Americans.
   (D) It has caused income tax rates to double since its initiation.
   (E) It has discouraged senior citizens from participating in politics.

43. One way federal agencies regulate an industry is by
   (A) hiring corporate leaders in the industry
   (B) issuing bonds to the industry
   (C) fixing stock prices in the industry
   (D) limiting its ability to trade internationally
   (E) sending inspectors to investigate an industry's regular activity

44. Members of Congress are most likely to endorse a president's proposal when
   (A) one party holds the majority in Congress by only a slim margin
   (B) the congressional session is nearing its end
   (C) the president has a high public approval rating
   (D) the issue at hand is not well publicized
   (E) it involves amending the federal tax codes

45. Which of the following is a basic weakness inherent in the presidency?
   (A) Except in military affairs, presidents must rely on the support of other people in order to influence policy decisions.
   (B) Because they are limited to only two terms, presidents rarely have enough time to achieve any of their policy goals.
   (C) Media attention focuses heavily on the president, which leads the public to hold him accountable and, in turn, deprives him of power.
   (D) The president is commander in chief, yet he cannot act in military situations without congressional approval.
   (E) Because the Electoral College officially elects the president, presidents usually lack legitimacy among the electorate.

46. Despite their influence over the political agenda, interest groups may be seen as democratic institutions in that they
   (A) help voters decide how to cast their ballots in an election
   (B) fund campaigns through political action committees
   (C) run advertisements to generate public support for a presidential proposal
   (D) promote equal representation of citizens' political beliefs
   (E) represent the concerns of groups in the electorate in the political arena

47. The power of the president has expanded for which of the following reasons?
   I. Increasing importance of foreign relations
   II. The shift toward candidate-centered politics as a result of television
   III. The use of primaries in presidential elections
   IV. The easing of tensions among social groups as a result of the civil rights movement
   (A) II only
   (B) IV only
   (C) I and II only
   (D) III and IV only
   (E) I, II, and III only

48. Which of the following represents a shift in recent foreign policy?
   (A) Defense spending has become the largest federal expenditure.
   (B) The arms race has picked up speed since the end of the cold war.
   (C) The president has had to limit his increasing power by following Congress's lead in foreign policy.
   (D) Presidents have negotiated treaties to reduce the number of weapons of mass destruction.
   (E) States have assumed greater foreign policy responsibilities through increasing global trade.

GO ON TO THE NEXT PAGE

49. The House of Representatives differs from the Senate in all of the following ways EXCEPT
    (A) House seats are distributed according to each state's population
    (B) House debates are scheduled, whereas the Senate allows unlimited debate
    (C) representatives tend to act more independently, whereas senators usually vote according to party lines
    (D) power is distributed more hierarchically in the House than it is in the Senate
    (E) senators have the ability to filibuster, but representatives do not

50. An American citizen's approval of the president depends most heavily on
    (A) the president's ability to stand up to Congress
    (B) whether the president is of the same party with which the citizen identifies himself or herself
    (C) whether the president has balanced his attention to foreign and domestic policy
    (D) how accessible the president is to members of the public
    (E) the media's bias in favor of or against the president

51. One way the federal government may attempt to influence the outcome of a Supreme Court case is by
    (A) filing an *amicus curiae* brief
    (B) appointing which justices will hear the case
    (C) having the solicitor general preside over the justices
    (D) requesting the chief justice to meet with the president
    (E) issuing an opinion on the case

52. The president may exercise authority over the federal bureaucracy in all of the following ways EXCEPT by
    (A) advising cabinet members and agency heads on department activities
    (B) proposing budgets for each department to Congress
    (C) appointing department secretaries who share his political goals
    (D) creating or dismantling agencies and departments
    (E) conducting oversight of the departments' activities and performance

53. In some states, citizens can participate directly in lawmaking by
    (A) appointing legislators to committees
    (B) presenting a budget proposal in the state legislature
    (C) approving legislation through referenda
    (D) writing letters to the governor
    (E) setting the requirements for who can run for office

54. Which of the following is a true statement about the presidential election of 2000?
    (A) It resulted in a strongly divided government.
    (B) The Democratic candidate won the popular vote but lost the electoral vote.
    (C) It was the first election in which campaign finance reforms noticeably reduced the cost of campaigning.
    (D) The Republican candidate won the popular vote by a large margin.
    (E) One candidate's reputation was damaged during the campaign by a political scandal.

55. In a state that has 6 electoral votes, the Republican candidate wins the popular vote by 54 to 46 percent. The electoral votes would most likely be allocated in which of the following ways?
(A) The Republican and Democrat would each get 3 electoral votes.
(B) The Republican would get 5 electoral votes, and the 1 electoral vote reserved for a third-party candidate would go unused.
(C) The Republican would get 4 electoral votes, and the Democrat would get 2.
(D) The Republican would get 6 electoral votes.
(E) The Republican would get 5 electoral votes, and the Democrat would get 1.

56. Senators are often more willing to allow a filibuster than they are to vote for cloture because
(A) voting for cloture looks bad on the senator's congressional record
(B) they want to ensure that their colleagues will not vote for cloture when they choose to filibuster
(C) voting for cloture does little to stop a filibuster
(D) they fear losing public approval by refusing to hear the full debate
(E) filibusters often generate well-developed, successful policies

57. The president exercises influence over policy-making most by
(A) vetoing legislation passed by Congress
(B) setting the congressional agenda
(C) introducing legislation for debate
(D) participating in committee hearings
(E) appointing party leaders in both houses of Congress

58. Which of the following states have become more populous, and, as a result, have gained both electoral votes and House seats?
(A) Virginia, New York, and Massachusetts
(B) Alabama, Wyoming, and Maryland
(C) California, Florida, and Texas
(D) Oklahoma, Nebraska, and New Mexico
(E) Oregon, North Carolina, and Pennsylvania

59. The use of blanket primaries has led in part to policy gridlock because they
(A) decrease the importance of and need for political parties
(B) allow for ticket-splitting, which in turn leads to divided government
(C) bring only one party into power in government, so that party must shoulder a great deal of responsibility
(D) encourage voters to rely too heavily on party identification, rather than on forming a clear public agenda
(E) introduce a number of third-party politicians who disagree with the major parties into the political arena

60. For which of the following legislative tasks are subcommittees primarily responsible?
(A) Enacting policy recommendations
(B) Passing legislation on to the floor or killing it
(C) Conducting research on the feasibility of the proposal
(D) Setting the length of debate for the bill
(E) Deciding whether or not the bill may be amended during debate

END OF SECTION I.

IF YOU FINISH BEFORE TIME IS CALLED, YOU MAY CHECK YOUR WORK ON THIS SECTION.

DO NOT GO ON TO SECTION II UNTIL YOU ARE TOLD TO DO SO.

United States
Government & Politics
Section II

Time: 100 minutes

Directions: You have 100 minutes to answer all four of the following questions. It is suggested that you take a few minutes to plan and outline each answer. *Spend approximately one-fourth of your time (25 minutes) on each question.* Illustrate your essay with substantive examples where appropriate. Make certain to number each of your answers as the question is numbered below.

1. Since its founding, the United States has generally become a more democratic nation. The writers of the Constitution favored the ideals of democracy, yet they feared putting too much power in the hands of the people.

   ▪ Explain TWO ways the American government has become more democratic AND analyze the impact that these changes have had on politics in the United States.

2. A divided government is one in which neither political party dominates both the legislative and the executive branches. This has become an increasingly common political phenomenon in recent decades.

   a. Identify and explain TWO factors that create a divided government.
   b. Identify and explain TWO consequences of divided government.

GO ON TO THE
NEXT PAGE

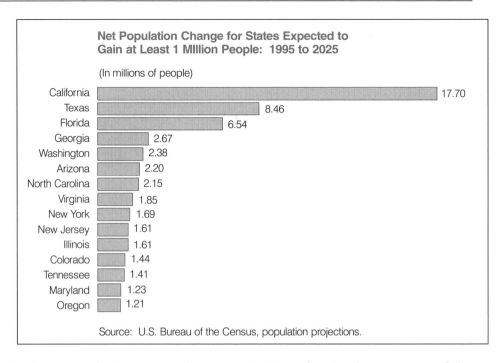

Net Population Change for States Expected to Gain at Least 1 Million People: 1995 to 2025

(In millions of people)

California	17.70
Texas	8.46
Florida	6.54
Georgia	2.67
Washington	2.38
Arizona	2.20
North Carolina	2.15
Virginia	1.85
New York	1.69
New Jersey	1.61
Illinois	1.61
Colorado	1.44
Tennessee	1.41
Maryland	1.23
Oregon	1.21

Source: U.S. Bureau of the Census, population projections.

3. The above graph shows population projections for the first quarter of the twenty-first century. All of the states listed are expected to gain at least a million people in the next few decades.

Using the data above and your knowledge of U.S. government and politics, identify and explain THREE ways that these shifting populations will have an impact on government.

4. During the budgetary process, Congress weighs revenues and expenditures to determine how to allocate money within the federal government. Social spending has become a major component of the federal budget in recent decades, but in some cases Congress is not able to adjust spending for it.

  ▪ Identify TWO social programs whose funding is not usually amended during the budgetary process. For each one, explain why spending is not cut AND discuss the implications of this inflexibility of the budget.

END OF EXAMINATION

Practice Test 2

Section I

▌ **1. (D) is correct.** In a blanket primary, candidates of all parties are listed on the ballot. A voter may choose a candidate from one party for one office and a candidate from another party for a different office. This is called ticket-splitting, and it is on the rise because more states are using blanket primaries. Two consequences of ticket-splitting are a decline in the power of political parties and an increase in divided government.

▌ **2. (E) is correct.** An impeachment trial is an unusual case that requires the formation of a special committee called a select committee. Select committees are composed of members of both houses, and they are formed to handle only specific situations, such as the investigation into a political scandal or the impeachment trial of a president.

▌ **3. (C) is correct.** Federal judges are not elected by the public—they are appointed by the president and confirmed by the Senate. This process is intended to insulate them from the political pressures of campaigning so that, in office, they are free to make unbiased decisions without having to return favors or worry about re-election.

▌ **4. (E) is correct.** The Democratic coalition includes many different groups in the electorate, including minority groups, southerners, and urban voters. These voters, who seem to have little in common, came together during the party realignment that took place as a result of the Great Depression when they all supported Franklin Roosevelt and his New Deal.

▌ **5. (A) is correct.** In 1960, senatorial incumbency was at 60 percent and House incumbency at 90 percent. In 2000, the numbers were still high, at close to 80 percent and 100 percent respectively. Even when incumbency dropped to its lowest point—senatorial incumbency in 1980—incumbents were still elected at a rate of about 55 percent. This graph clearly shows how advantageous incumbency can be in congressional elections.

▌ **6. (B) is correct.** Located in Article I of the Constitution, the elastic cause enumerates the implied powers of Congress. It gives the legislature full authority to make any laws "necessary and proper" to carry out those responsibilities assigned to it by the Constitution.

▌ **7. (C) is correct.** Voting is the most common way people express their political views. By participating in an election, voters choose those candidates whom they feel agree with their political beliefs, and these candidates therefore act on their behalf in government.

▌ **8. (A) is correct.** Supreme Court justices are granted life terms on the condition that they remain in good conduct. This allows them to make judicial decisions objectively without the pressures of political influence. They do not have to appeal to the public or represent any one interest if they are guaranteed their position of authority.

9. (D) is correct. The media often focus heavily on political scandals for the sake of achieving high ratings. However, this may distort the public's perception both of the politician (whose career otherwise may have been highly successful) and of the situation (which may be much less consequential than it has been portrayed in the media).

10. (E) is correct. Young people are the least likely group in the electorate to vote. This is partially because young people have not yet formed their political beliefs or determined their needs from government. As people age and bear more responsibilities, they tend to participate more actively in politics.

11. (A) is correct. In the budgetary process, federal agencies and departments in the executive branch submit their budget proposals to the president and the OMB, which amend and combine them into a single proposal. Then the president sends this proposal to Congress, which, through its committees, ultimately decides how much money each department or agency gets to spend in the coming year.

12. (C) is correct. Most notably in *Engel* v. *Vitale* and in *School District of Abington Township, Pennsylvania* v. *Schempp*, the Supreme Court ruled that prayer in public schools violates the establishment clause. This clause of the Constitution ensures the separation of church and state, and, because public schools are state- and federally funded, any exercise of religion in them is a breach of the separation of church and state. Don't be fooled by answer *A*: You can't break the law in the name of religion. For example, polygamy is a crime.

13. (D) is correct. Some of Congress's enumerated powers are to appropriate money, confirm the appointment of justices, and regulate commerce. Congress also has the power to declare war, but it cannot send troops into war. It can make laws, but it cannot enforce them. These two responsibilities instead belong to the president, who is both commander in chief and head of the executive branch.

14. (B) is correct. The Voting Rights Act was passed to enable the government to enforce African Americans' right to vote as guaranteed by the Fifteenth Amendment. Southern states had employed a variety of means, including intimidation, to prevent African Americans from voting. As a result of its new power to enforce the law, the Justice Department sent in federal officials to oversee elections in southern states.

15. (E) is correct. Incumbents have enormous advantages in congressional elections. They have better exposure, a political record with the constituency, and more campaign money with which to eliminate any chance of their challengers' success. As a result of these advantages, usually more than 50 percent of congressional incumbents are reelected.

16. (D) is correct. Iron triangles, or subgovernments, often work like well-oiled machines to produce and implement policies in a specific policy area. Interest groups may suggest policies or lobby Congress to pass legislation, and then federal agencies and interest groups work together to implement the policy.

17. (A) is correct. Lobbyists have the least influence over judges, because they have no leverage with which to influence judges who hold their offices for life.

However, interest groups can file *amicus curiae* briefs to try to influence a judge's decision.

■ **18. (B) is correct.** Campaign finance reforms established a public fund for presidential campaigns. This fund is meant to help free presidents from the influence of interest groups, but the fund has been losing money. It is composed partly of voluntary contributions, but people have been making fewer contributions in recent years.

■ **19. (D) is correct.** Many important and controversial Supreme Court cases in the 1960s addressed the rights of the accused. *Miranda* v. *Arizona* is one well-known case in which the Fifth Amendment right of protection from self-incrimination was enforced by the Court. Other cases also extended the right of counsel to the poor and confirmed the exclusionary rule, preventing the use of evidence gained through unreasonable search and seizure from being used in trials.

■ **20. (B) is correct.** The Supreme Court is the interpreter of the Constitution, but Congress is the keeper of it. If the Supreme Court finds a law unconstitutional, Congress has the authority to amend the Constitution to suit the law. Then the Supreme Court would have no choice but to interpret the law in light of the amendment to the Constitution.

■ **21. (D) is correct.** Political socialization is the process through which people learn about government and form their political beliefs. Several factors help shape their political ideologies. For instance, religion, education, and the media all influence Americans' feelings about political issues and government in general.

■ **22. (C) is correct.** A bill may be amended or altered during debate in either the House or the Senate. It is often the case that the two houses pass different versions of the same bill. When this happens, the bill is sent to a conference committee composed of members of both houses. The committee works to develop a compromise between the bill's two versions. If the compromise is accepted by a majority of each house, the final piece of legislation is sent to the president for his signature.

■ **23. (B) is correct.** The president has the power to negotiate executive agreements as well as treaties. Treaties are more formal and tend to address major issues; these require the approval of Congress. Executive agreements, however, deal with smaller matters, so it is often easier for the president to handle them independently.

■ **24. (A) is correct.** Thousands of cases are appealed to the Supreme Court each year, but only a few are actually placed on the docket. The justices meet regularly to review appeals and, as a group, choose to hear only those cases they feel are most deserving of appeal or may have the greatest impact on the interpretation of the law. Answer C is true, but it does not answer the question.

■ **25. (D) is correct.** The Tenth Amendment reserves many unwritten powers for the states, so states have made their own laws, which (especially in the case of civil liberties) have at times conflicted with federal law. The passing of the Fourteenth Amendment, however, offered the Supreme Court the opportunity to assert federal supremacy over such state laws. This amendment grants all people equal protection under the law and the right to due process of the law. The Court has cited the Fourteenth Amendment in numerous civil liberties and civil rights cases.

26. (D) is correct. Although incumbents do often benefit from a record of good service to their constituency or a clean political record, their *greatest* advantage in an election is their abundance of campaign resources. Incumbents receive as many as three times the number of contributions that their challengers do, in part because incumbents have already established relationships in their constituency. With the easy ability to outspend challengers, congressional incumbents, especially in the House, almost always win.

27. (C) is correct. Television allows viewers to see and judge political candidates without the structure of a political party. Candidates too can address the public directly without having to channel their campaigns through the party machine. As a result, both candidates and the electorate have become more independent from political parties. While most people still vote according to their party identification, they are more frequently considering themselves political independents.

28. (B) is correct. Receipts and disbursements for open seats in the Senate in the 2000 election were unusually high. Candidates received and spent twice as much as they had in 1996—and nearly six times as much as they had in 1998. This is a good indication that there were many competitive races for open seats in 2000.

29. (E) is correct. Spending in House campaigns in 1998 was lower than it had been in the 1996 campaigns by about $25 million. However, the 2000 campaigns were more expensive than the 1998 campaigns by about $120 million.

30. (E) is correct. More people are considering themselves independents rather than Democrats or Republicans. This is a result of the decline in party identification as parties have slowly been losing their hold over political campaigns. However, most people still vote according to their party identification because there are usually only two parties represented on the ballot.

31. (B) is correct. Presidents do have a significant amount of influence over the federal budget, because they compile the budget proposal for all of the departments in the executive branch. However, they cannot be said to oversee the budget, because Congress plays an equal, if not greater, role in allocating money and passing the final budget legislation.

32. (C) is correct. The Civil Rights Act officially prohibited discrimination in any public facilities and in employment. It also authorized the Justice Department to enforce the act by investigating and suing any company that violated civil rights as outlined by the law.

33. (A) is correct. The Rules Committee is very influential on legislation, because it determines the length of debate for each piece of legislation. It also has the authority to declare whether or not a bill may be amended during debate. The less flexibility it affords a piece of legislation, the greater the likelihood that the bill will not be passed easily.

■ **34. (E) is correct.** Committees oversee agencies, both by holding hearings and by setting their budgets. These are two ways the legislative branch checks the power of the executive branch. However, both committees and agencies are lobbied regularly by interest groups that hope to influence either policymaking or policy implementation.

■ **35. (B) is correct.** *Texas* v. *Johnson* brought the issue of flag burning to the Supreme Court. The Court ruled that flag burning is protected under the First Amendment as a form of speech. The case therefore set a precedent that symbolic speech is considered "free speech" in the eyes of the law.

■ **36. (D) is correct.** Party realignment often accompanies a critical election. Such elections are noteworthy because they initiate a new party era: They shift politics toward one party's platform and away from the platform of a party that has been in power for a while. Such major changes often are a result of new party affiliations among the electorate.

■ **37. (D) is correct.** The Articles did prevent the new United States from raising militias and paying its war debts. However, these were consequences of the fact that the government simply was too weak—it did not have enough centralized power to give it legitimacy and, ultimately, to allow it to function.

■ **38. (C) is correct.** The Federal Reserve Board oversees monetary policy. It is an executive institution that regulates the economy by controlling the flow of currency. For example, it has the authority to determine how much money banks have at their disposal and how much credit is available to the public.

■ **39. (E) is correct.** One basic difference that defines the two parties against each other is their contrasting ideologies. Democrats tend to favor liberal policies such as social spending, whereas Republicans usually endorse more conservative policies, such as those that limit the role of the federal government.

■ **40. (A) is correct.** A balance of trade occurs when a country's imports equal its exports. The shaded area of the graph shows that U.S. imports are exceeding exports. This is known as a balance-of-trade deficit. It is partially the result of lower tariffs and increasing free trade among nations around the world.

■ **41. (D) is correct.** Federalism imposes a tiered structure on government. More than one level shares authority over the people. In the United States, people are subject to the laws of both state and federal governments, and they also may elect their leaders in both the state and federal governments.

■ **42. (B) is correct.** Social Security has replaced national defense as the government's biggest expenditure, at about 23 percent. To pay for Social Security, social insurance taxes have risen somewhat comparably, but it is highly likely that the Social Security system will go bankrupt in the next few decades.

■ **43. (E) is correct.** Regulatory agencies set industry standards to ensure both the quality of products and the safety of industrial workers. In order to oversee industries, agencies often send inspectors to determine whether specific companies are complying with industry standards. For example, the Food and Drug Administration send inspectors to test the quality of meat at meatpacking plants.

44. (C) is correct. Public approval can be a powerful tool for the president. If public opinion is high, Congress is more likely to endorse his proposals. To go against a president who is well liked by voters might hurt a representative or senator's own chances for re-election.

45. (A) is correct. Presidents are not legislators. They may propose policies indirectly or try to influence the policy process, but they cannot actually participate directly in policymaking. This means that they must rely heavily on the support of other people to help them pursue their political agenda.

46. (E) is correct. Interest groups play a role in democratizing government by serving as linkage institutions between politicians and the public. Interest groups represent the needs of different groups of people to lawmakers, so these groups help the constituency to be heard. Although not all groups may be heard equally, they at least have the opportunity to try to affect policymaking for the benefit of some citizens.

47. (C) is correct. The new global economy and frequent military crises have increased the president's power and prominence as chief diplomat. The president has also become more powerful because he may act more independently than ever before. Television allows presidential candidates to reach the public directly without having to rely on political parties, and it also provides presidents with a means to address the public directly and to gain its support.

48. (D) is correct. The arms race has slowed since the policy of détente was initiated in the 1980s and the cold war came to an end. Since then, presidents have worked with other nations to cut back on weapons building and even to reduce weapons stores by destroying thousands of stockpiled missiles.

49. (C) is correct. Senators actually act more independently of their party. This is partially due to the fact that they have longer terms than representatives do. Party affiliations and party leadership are also much stronger in the House, so representatives tend to vote along party lines.

50. (B) is correct. Party identification plays a large role in the public's perception of the president. An American citizen is more likely to approve of a president who is of the same party. By virtue of being of the same party, it is assumed that the president is advancing political views with which the citizen agrees.

51. (A) is correct. Once justices have been appointed to the bench, there is little that the government can do to directly influence their decisions. It may, however, through the solicitor general, submit briefs stating the official position of the federal government on the issue at hand. State governments, interest groups, and members of the public are also allowed to file *amicus curiae* briefs to endorse their views.

52. (E) is correct. Congress, not the president, is responsible for conducting oversight of federal agencies. The president and agencies together make up the executive branch, and in this case it is the legislative branch that maintains the system of checks and balances.

53. (C) is correct. Some states allow citizens to participate directly in policymaking at the state level. A bill is listed on the ballot, and voters can either choose to approve or kill it. If they approve it by a simple majority, the bill bypasses the state legislature and becomes law—or in some states, it goes directly to the governor for his or her signature or veto.

■ **54. (B) is correct.** The 2000 presidential election was a landmark political event in that a candidate won the popular vote but lost the electoral vote and, hence, the presidency. This has happened only a few times in American history, and for some it calls into question the fairness of—and need for—the Electoral College. Many people see this as an antiquated institution that no longer serves any useful purpose, but states with a large number of electoral votes are unlikely to endorse reforms.

■ **55. (D) is correct.** It is an unwritten tradition that the winner of a state's popular election receives all of that states electoral votes. This makes the more populous states powerful, because they have more electoral votes to wield. In this case, the Republican would receive all 6 of the electoral votes.

■ **56. (B) is correct.** Senators like to reserve the power of filibustering, so they are unlikely to do anything to encourage their colleagues from trying to prevent them from using it. If a senator were to move for cloture, the next time he or she attempted to filibuster, the same might be done to him or her.

■ **57. (A) is correct.** The veto is one of the president's strongest legislative tools. Most of the time, it allows him the final say on every piece of legislation. The veto also encourages legislators to shape policy in such a way that the president will not choose to reject it, so it gives the president some say in policy formation.

■ **58. (C) is correct.** The population has generally shifted away from the Northeast to other coastal areas of the country. States that were once influential, such as New York, are beginning to lose seats in the process of reapportionment. Politically, Florida, Texas, and California have benefited the most from increasing populations.

■ **59. (B) is correct.** Because blanket primaries list candidates from all parties, voters are free to choose different candidates from different parties. This method of ticket-splitting has often led to a divided government in which the president and the majority party in Congress are not the same. Policy gridlock arises because they often do not have the same political agenda or political views.

■ **60. (C) is correct.** Subcommittees are the first legislative bodies to review policy proposals. They perform research and analysis to assess the piece of legislation, then report their findings to the main committee. The committee reviews this information, may revise the bill, and either decides to kill it or to pass it on to the House for debate.

1. *Since its founding, the United States has generally become a more democratic nation. The writers of the Constitution favored the ideals of democracy, yet they feared putting too much power in the hands of the people.*

   ■ *Explain TWO ways the American government has become more democratic AND analyze the impact that these changes have had on politics in the United States.*

The writers of the Constitution were a group of well-educated, wealthy men who wanted to create a democratic form of government but feared that it could be corrupted or abused in the hands of the uneducated public in the young United States. In some ways, the Constitution provides such a minimal structure that informal institutions have sprung up to link the people with the government. In other cases, however, the Constitution has been amended in order to bring about greater democracy in the United States.

Although James Madison warned against factions, they were not expressly prohibited by the Constitution. Therefore, over the course of time, many different groups have formed to represent the public within the sphere of politics. Some of the earliest groups were political parties. These parties united people of like political beliefs in an organized body that aimed to influence government through elections. Even today, political parties help democratize government by involving people in the political process. Parties run candidates with specific political platforms for office; voters choose the candidate who shares their beliefs; and that candidate then represents those voters in office. Moreover, parties function as networks that unite people with similar political beliefs, so that a voter has something in common with many different public officials. Parties therefore advance the will of party members in the electorate. Interest groups are a similar but more recent type of linkage institution. They also represent groups in the electorate, but they try to promote a more specific policy agenda in government. Interest groups receive a good deal of criticism for their methods of influencing policymakers but, ultimately, they are lobbying for the sake of people who have no political voice during nonelection years. Both political parties and interest groups have helped draw the people into the government.

In the case of civil rights, however, it has not been so easy to democratize the United States. A representative democracy is based on the principle of citizens electing people to represent them in government. When the Constitution was written, however, only white males had the power to vote, so only their voices were heard in government. It took a war, three amendments to the Constitution, and further legislation such as the Voting Rights Act to fully extend suffrage to African Americans. Women, furthermore, did not gain the right to vote until the Nineteenth Amendment was passed in 1920. Only then could all adult Americans vote in elections and, in turn, participate in a truly democratic government. Since then, women and members of minority groups have themselves been elected to represent the people in government. In recent years, for example, several women have been elected as governors. Moreover, with these representatives speaking for groups in the electorate who previously had little political power, the political agenda has become more democratic. Today, issues such as discrimination in the workplace, pregnancy leave, and family assistance have become important fixtures in political debate. The right of all citizens to vote, therefore, has also helped unite the people and the government in a more traditional form of democracy.

The student identifies two means by which the public and the government have moved closer together. Linkage institutions like political parties and interest groups help represent the needs of the people in the political arena. The student defines the role each of these types of groups plays in politics—such as that political parties are involved primarily in the election process—and explains how these groups can be democratizing institutions. Secondly, the student identifies the expansion of suffrage as a way of making the government more democratic. The student identifies the laws and amendments through which voting rights have been granted to different groups and explicitly identifies some consequences of this change, such as the democratization of the political agenda.

2. *A divided government is one in which neither political party dominates both the legislative and the executive branches. This has become an increasingly common political phenomenon in recent decades.*

   a. Identify and explain TWO factors that create a divided government.
   b. Identify and explain TWO consequences of divided government.

In a divided government, the president is not of the same party as the majority party in Congress. For most of American history, one party has dominated both political institutions. This has helped to make the policy process easier, because both Congress and the president have shared similar political views and goals. Today, however, divided government is becoming more common. The shift has happened for several reasons and has had some important consequences for the functioning of the federal government.

The introduction of the blanket primary has contributed to divided government. In a blanket primary, candidates from all parties are listed on one ballot, so voters are free to choose whomever they want, regardless of party affiliation. They might choose a Democratic president and Republican senators, for example. This is called ticket-splitting. As more states have begun holding blanket primaries, ticket-splitting has become more common. The result is a divided government in which one party dominates the legislative branch while the other party controls the executive office.

Another cause of divided government is the lesser role political parties are beginning to play in the campaign process. Candidates as well as voters feel less devotion to parties. This is largely a consequence of the increasing reliance on television in campaigns. Television allows candidates to appeal directly to voters without having to stick so closely to their party's political agenda. It also allows voters to judge candidates more independently, because voters are able to see candidates and hear them speak for themselves. In fact, more people today are labeling themselves independents. Therefore they are less likely to vote for a candidate strictly based on party identification, but instead they may pick and choose candidates regardless of their party affiliations.

Divided government can have serious consequences for policymaking. A president and Congress of different parties are likely to disagree often on policy and are likely to have trouble working together. For example, the president may veto more legislation from Congress if that legislation has been shaped largely by his opposition party. Congress too is likely to become frustrated at having to compromise legislation in order to have it signed by the president. Ultimately, the government wastes time and money debating policies when the two main political instruments are constantly and fundamentally in disagreement.

One specific example of the frustration divided government can cause is the appointment and confirmation of federal judges, justices, cabinet secretaries, and other executive officials. Congress grants the president power to appoint people to these posts, and he is going to choose people who will support his policy agenda. The most obvious choices, then, are people of his party. However, Congress has the authority to confirm, or not to confirm, the president's choices. If the majority party is different, it may be more reluctant to offer its confirmation. Again, time and money are wasted in political battles over executive appointments. Divided government therefore is not really a welcome phenomenon in recent politics.

The student clearly identifies two causes of divided government (the rise of blanket primaries and decreasing party identification) and two consequences of this political trend (difficulty in making policy and in making presidential appointments). The student explains each of these causes and consequences. Moreover, the student understands different facets of U.S. government and politics and synthesizes causal relationships between voting patterns and government responsibilities.

3. *The above graph shows population projections for the first quarter of the twenty-first century. All of the states listed are expected to gain at least a million people in the next few decades.*

> ■ *Using the data above and your knowledge of U.S. government and politics, identify and explain THREE ways that these shifting populations will have an impact on government.*

The size of a state's population determines both how many seats it receives in the House of Representatives and how many electoral votes it has in presidential elections. The greater a state's population, the more power it has.

The graph clearly indicates that Florida, Texas, and especially California are expected to see the largest increase in population in the next 20 to 25 years. California may gain an enormous 17 million people, and even Texas and Florida will gain double or triple the amount of people that other states may gain. Moreover, at the same time that these states are expected to become more populous, other states are expected to lose people. Some of the most populous and therefore powerful states have been in the Northeast, but people are moving to jobs in the Sun Belt and on the West Coast. States like New York actually lost seats in the House in the most recent reapportionment.

California, Texas, and Florida will therefore experience a significant increase in political clout, as well. With more seats in the House, they will have more influence over national policy and may bring new issues that are pertinent to them to the federal agenda. Each of these states deals constantly with immigration, for example, so this could become a more prominent issue in politics. They will also wield more power in presidential elections because they will have more electoral votes. A state's number of electors is equal to the total of its representatives and senators, so if these states gain seats, they will also gain electoral votes. As a result, presidential candidates will focus their campaign efforts on these states. Again, their statewide issues could become national issues if a presidential hopeful wants to win the popular vote in those states. Political attention and, ultimately, political power, will therefore shift in the same trends that the population has.

The increasing power as a result of migration to these three states in particular may have other political consequences, because all three of these states have sizable populations of Hispanic Americans. This minority group, which is itself growing, may therefore win a greater voice in government. More Hispanic Americans may be elected to public office to represent largely Hispanic constituencies. They may also bring new social and economic issues particular to Hispanic Americans to the political agenda. The consequences of shifting populations in the United States are therefore both political and social, and ultimately they promise to create a different political agenda.

The student correctly interprets the data in the graph. He or she cites two major structural changes that will result from the shift in population: California, Texas, and Florida will gain seats in the House as well as electoral votes. By highlighting the political consequences of these changes (that these states will gain power), the student shows an understanding of some of the basic concepts of U.S. government. Lastly, the student identifies a social change relating to the population shift (that the percentage of Hispanic Americans is growing in these three states) and notes the political consequences of this change.

4. *During the budgetary process, Congress weighs revenues and expenditures to determine how to allocate money within the federal government. Social spending has become a major component of the federal budget in recent decades, but in some cases Congress is not able to adjust spending for it.*

 ■ *Identify TWO social programs whose funding is not usually amended during the budgetary process. For each one, explain why spending is not cut AND discuss the implications of this inflexibility of the budget.*

During the budgetary process, Congress cannot alter forms of mandatory spending, which include things like the interest payment on the national debt. One of the largest mandatory expenditures is entitlement programs. These are social programs that automatically pay benefits to anyone who meets the requirements of the program. Social Security and Medicare are two of the most extensive and costly entitlement programs.

The Social Security program issues benefits to all senior citizens because they no longer work to earn an income. The basic requirement of this program is that the beneficiary be retired, and the government must pay everyone who is entitled. The program, therefore, provides benefits for a large number of people in the United States. In fact, as life expectancies grow, more people will qualify to be recipients at any given time. Moreover, in a few decades the baby boom generation will begin to collect its benefits, and there is serious concern that the Social Security program will run out of money by the middle of the century. Thus far, the bulk of the program has been paid for by taxes specifically reserved for the Social Security fund. However, these taxes will have to keep rising in order to cover the cost of the expanding program, and it is quite possible that working people who pay those taxes today may not receive benefits when they come of age. The only way to cut this form of mandatory spending would be to amend the eligibility rules of the program. However, this is not likely because senior citizens are a fairly active group in the electorate. They have formed the largest interest group in the country, the AARP, to help protect their claim to Social Security benefits. They also vote in high numbers, so politicians seeking re-election are likely to act in the interest of Social Security recipients. Social Security therefore poses a serious threat to the federal budget.

Medicare, an entitlement program that helps pay for medical care for the elderly, poses an even more immediate threat. The number of recipients has grown steadily, and Medicare revenues cannot keep pace. This program may go bankrupt in the next decade. However, Congress is again powerless to amend it during the budgetary process. Senior citizens are very protective of their claim to health care benefits, especially because they are more likely to need health care and because it is so expensive in the United States. For fear of losing votes, members of Congress have not made any successful reforms to Medicare either. Their only recourse is to cut forms of discretionary spending, such as funding for national defense or public education. Otherwise, the national debt will continue to grow as a result of mandatory entitlement programs.

This student identifies the two major entitlement programs—Social Security and Medicare. This essay demonstrates a knowledge of the budgetary process, and it explains why these two programs cannot be cut and how these forms of mandatory spending are straining the government's resources. The student provides good details to illustrate an understanding of how these programs work, whom they benefit, and why politicians are unwilling to amend them in order to help ease the strain they place on the federal budget.